Katrina Blowers

tuning out

D1727765

First published in 2007 by Pier 9, an imprint of Murdoch Books Pty Limited

Murdoch Books Australia
Pier 8/9
23 Hickson Road
Millers Point NSW 2000
Phone: +61 (0)2 8220 2000
Fax: +61 (0)2 8220 2558
www.murdochbooks.com.au

Murdoch Books UK Limited
Erico House
6th Floor
93–99 Upper Richmond Road
Putney, London SW15 2TG
Phone: +44 (0) 20 8785 5995
Fax: +44 (0) 20 8785 5985

Chief Executive: Juliet Rogers
Publishing Director: Kay Scarlett

Project Manager: Jacqueline Blanchard
Editor: Mary Trewby
Concept and Design: Lauren Camilleri
Cover design: Ellie Exarchos
Production: Adele Troeger

Blowers, Katrina.
Tuning out : my quarter-life crisis.
ISBN 9781921208928 (pbk.)
1. Blowers, Katrina. 2. Blowers, Katrina - Travels. 3. Women broadcasters -
Australia - Biography. 4. Life change events. I. Title. 791.44092

Printed by i-Book Printing Ltd in 2007. PRINTED IN CHINA.

Katrina Blowers

tuning out

My quarter-life crisis

PIER
9

To Tom—

for going there with me.

contents

CHAPTER 1

Hello, demon. Who invited you?

YOU'RE MAKING THE BIGGEST MISTAKE OF YOUR CAREER, Katrina. Don't even think for a second that you're going to be able to stroll back into town and get a job anywhere near as good as this one.

I push my bag under the seat in front of me and try not to think about those words. The small black backpack bulges a little and I give it a gentle kick to wedge it further in. Every stick of furniture I own has been packed away in a storage facility. My last breakfast radio show has gone to air. My final pay cheque is in the bank. Even my voice has been lost in a smoky bar somewhere in Sydney after too many rowdy farewell parties. All the pieces of the life I've been living have been put away. The loose ends are firmly tied.

I am embarking on 'the trip of a lifetime', as lots of people keep telling me. Six months of travelling around the world. It's been planned for, saved for and talked about for years. I should be ecstatic.

Why not wait until later? These are your consolidating years, the most important ones of your entire career. Screw these up and you can kiss it all goodbye.

I feel overwhelmed and confused. Instead of focusing on the amazing places I am going, all I can think about is what I'm leaving behind. It's only for six months but right now it feels like an eternity. I'm scared everything will be different when I get back and my place in everyone's lives will have shifted. Most of all, I'm terrified my career achievements won't be worth anything, that I'll be forgotten and have to start again.

I try to focus on the sound of the engines starting. But those damn words echo on a loop, drowning everything else out. They've been going around like that ever since a manager at Nova, the radio station where I was a presenter until two days ago, said them to me: 'You're making the biggest mistake of your career.'

These words are feeding the demon inside my head, the one I've been trying to ignore for the last few months. Every time I throw him a bone of self-doubt, he whispers thoughts that stick like voodoo pins in my subconscious. His chatter keeps me awake in the middle of the night.

You're making a huge mistake. You're throwing away everything you've worked towards and dreamed about. Why are you going on this trip? And why now?

Well, Mr Demon, there are a few reasons.

I've got the travel bug for one. And I feel burned out after nine years of breakfast radio, of getting up at three or four in the morning. But the main reason is sitting next to me now. He's the tall one with dark hair—there in the window seat. My husband Tom.

Four years ago, when my career wasn't going nearly as well, Tom and I made plans to take this same trip. Back then, I had been at Nova for just under a year. It was the first FM station to launch in Sydney since the 1970s. I became the newsreader on the breakfast show hosted by the comedic duo Merrick and Rosso. I loved my new job but I'd been reading the news for years. The challenge had gone out of it. Tom and I told everyone we were leaving. I gave three months' notice and Tom did too, giving up his position as an environmental lawyer.

A month before we were due to fly out, the head of the radio network that owns Nova asked what it would take for me not to go. I'd never had anyone say anything like that to me before. I should have reeled off a list of sweeteners. Instead, I just shrugged my shoulders and squeaked a few times.

So he made me an offer. He said what the breakfast show was missing was a female voice to pull the larrikin personas of the boys into line. He was offering me the role of co-host. I hadn't expected that. It was a big opportunity. I couldn't say no.

When I told Tom, I could see the conflict written on his face. He was ecstatic for me but also devastated that it meant canning our trip. Even so, he put aside his disappointment, celebrated my promotion and went back to the partners at his firm to undo his resignation. I made a promise to him then that the trip wasn't cancelled, just postponed. We would definitely take it in two years' time.

Those two years turned into three, then four. There never seemed a 'right' time to go. The show went to number one in the ratings and stayed there. The perks rolled in. I was invited to parties and premieres. There were interviews with rock stars, actors and politicians. I no longer just read the news, I also had editorial control and the chance to cover major stories in more detail. I was realising a dream I'd had since I was seven years old.

Seriously. I can still picture the moment when I figured out what I wanted to do with my life. I was in the car with my mum. We were taking an interminable drive to dump something or other at the tip in Canberra, the city where I grew up. The backs of my legs were sticking to the vinyl in her new red Gemini, when suddenly a question popped into my mind.

'Mum, you know that lady who tells us the news on TV at night,' I said. 'What's the name of her job?'

'Well, she's a journalist.' She pursed her lips, thinking for a second. 'That's someone whose job it is to find out all the interesting things that are happening in the world and tell the rest of us about them. It's a very important thing to do.'

Wow, I thought. A journalist. Paid to be curious. I found the idea that such a job even existed intoxicating.

From that moment on, my heart was set on breaking into the media industry. I did work experience during my school holidays and wrote stories for the suburban newspapers. During my last year of uni, I got my first job reporting television news. I was sure this was my big break. I backcombed my hair into a sleek newsreader's bouffant, put on too much lipstick and wore jackets with enormous shoulder pads.

'Got a great yarn for you, kiddo,' said the news director one morning. 'I want you to take a crew down to the prime minister's joint.'

'You bet,' I said, breathless with excitement. A story involving the prime minister. It was bound to be important.

'Yeah,' my boss said. 'The PM's dog. It's disturbing the neighbours. Black lab or something. Probably bored shitless.' He stretched his legs out on the desk. 'Stake yourself out by the backyard for the day. We want to get some shots of him making some noise. You know, howling or whatever.'

In the story that went to air that night, I stood looking earnest in my red jacket with my helmet hair, doing my piece to camera in front of the fence as the dog barked up a frenzy.

Deciding I needed to be doing something with a bit more substance, I sent my résumé to newsrooms around the country and waited. When the opportunity to be a newsreader and reporter at a radio station came along, I jumped at it. That was around the time most people my age were going overseas for their gap year. As my twenties marched on, I was pulling the early morning shift on weekends. My friends were going out partying but I was in bed at 9 pm so I could be fresh for my 3 am start. I was convinced all my hard work would pay off. And it had.

Don't think for a second that you're going to be able to stroll back into town and get a job anywhere near as good as this one.

There go those words again. The more I think about them, the more it occurs to me they could be true. That's because, in my eyes, the job I'm leaving is a good one. In many ways it's my dream job. Over the past few months, I've been worrying more and more as the departure date has loomed. My fears have been compounded by other people's reactions when I tell them my plans. Some say they're jealous and they wish they had the guts or the means to do what I'm doing. But others ask point-blank if I've gone insane. Then, the other day as I was flicking through the morning newspaper, there it was in black and white. A columnist from the *Daily Telegraph* had written a piece about my departure, calling my job 'the best in Sydney radio'. Oh god. Maybe I really am crazy to be walking away?

I have to keep reminding myself that we will be visiting some amazing places—thirteen countries on five continents. We're going to spend time in big cities and tiny villages, eat our way through trattorias and street markets, chill out in the Mediterranean, see the Sahara Desert and climb a few mountains. I'd be mad not to want to go.

Tom taps me on the arm, bringing me back to the present. I've been staring into space, gripping the arms of my seat.

'Are you okay?' he asks, looking concerned.

I manage a weak smile. 'I think so.'

The plane taxis away from the terminal.

These are your consolidating years, the most important ones of your entire career.

Is there ever a right time to go? For the last four years, Tom and I have been living a bit in limbo. We've put off things like getting a dog and buying a house, knowing we need to be free of ties so we can take this trip. Over the last twelve months or so, the feeling of 'now or never' has taken hold. I've watched with envy as other people played with their dogs, wished we owned a house so we could paint a wall or tear up the garden and, as I've inched closer to thirty, the question of having children has also been on my mind. I couldn't delay us forever.

The plane picks up speed for take-off. I think back to a few nights ago, when I confided my misgivings to one of my oldest friends. 'Katrina,' she said, shaking her head, 'your career does not define you. Our jobs aren't who we are, they're just what we do.'

Nice theory, but who really believes that?

The nose of the plane lifts and I feel my shoulders press back into my seat. The people, friends and places I'm leaving run through my thoughts again. I try to force down the big lump in my throat.

This is ridiculous.

Tears sting my eyes and I concentrate on the exit sign, hoping Tom doesn't notice. Through the window I can see the marmalade glow of the setting sun tint the ribbon of cliffs between Bondi and Coogee below us.

Whirring sounds come from underneath as the wing flaps retract. I tighten my seatbelt.

This is it. I'm kissing it goodbye.

◆ ◆ ◆ ◆ ◆

It's been nearly thirty hours since we left Sydney and it's just gone lunchtime. At least, I think it has. My body is all addled. The plane we're on now—a short flight from Heathrow to Lyon—is only a quarter full. Tom and I stretch out in our own rows.

'Hey baby,' he calls out to me from across the aisle. 'We're leaving the British Isles.'

I sit up so I can see past the wing and the patchy clouds. Below us the English Channel is sparkling against a series of cliff faces so stark they appear to be gleaming. They must be the white cliffs of Dover. I'm finally going to Europe!

Tom, like many others my age, went on a big European expedition when he was eighteen during a year off between school and uni. I've always felt a little inadequate that I haven't been to this part of the world. Not that I can remember, anyway. My parents took me to England as a three-year-old but I can only recall two things: feeding the pigeons in Trafalgar Square and crying in terror at the guards in their bearskins outside Buckingham Palace.

The captain tells us we're about to fly over Paris. Tom squeezes next to me to get a better look. We peer down at the city, laid out in grids. It doesn't look like the chic capital I've seen in movies. More like a lumpy jigsaw with the steely Seine slashed through the middle.

'Hey!' Tom points at the glass. 'There's the Eiffel Tower. Can you see it?'

I laugh. 'It's so tiny, like something out of Legoland.' In three months we are coming back to Paris for my thirtieth birthday. Thirty. I shudder just thinking about it. How did that happen? It seems like yesterday I was eighteen.

'The thing that terrifies me is that when you reach thirty it's not about your potential anymore,' said my closest male friend, Paul, a few weeks ago. We were having dinner. As the night went on, talk had turned to how the big three-oh is sort of a life-stocktake time. 'You can't use "I'm finding myself" as an excuse any longer,' he continued. 'You are your potential. When you hit that magic number it's no longer about what you will be but who you are.'

I mull over what he said as I watch the outskirts of the city disappearing into countryside. Will those big questions be easier to deal with among the distractions of Paris?

The seat belt sign comes on as we start our descent. I pull out my journal from the seat pocket in front and flip through the pages. What will be written there by the time this trip's through? If I stay for the six months it will be full. But what will it say about me?

If I stay. I should explain that. While I was having the big on-air send-off, behind the scenes there was a plan to make it not 'goodbye forever', just 'goodbye for now'. In a vague rerun of the first time I quit my job, meetings were held to canvass the possibility of cutting my trip short and re-joining the station at the beginning of next year. It's left me feeling torn and Tom feeling betrayed.

I sought the advice of two friends, one a journalist and the other someone who had left his job recently to go travelling for a month.

'You're mad if you don't re-sign,' the journo said. 'It's a great gig. It's good for your profile—easy money.'

But the other friend snapped, 'Don't be ridiculous. That's not all you're capable of. If you sign up now you're sending a message that you're shit-scared. And, yeah, you probably are. But back yourself.' He looked at me pointedly. 'You've also made a commitment to Tom and it's important you see that through. You may feel completely different in six months. Travelling can change your mindset.'

I trusted he had the benefit of hindsight. So, full of false courage, I left without signing anything. I can't stop asking myself though, was it the right decision?

I can't imagine not wanting to go back to the radio show. Even though the hours are shocking, I enjoy it. It gives me a sense of identity. I don't want to go home to nothing. I'm also worried that without a steady career to define myself by, I won't have anything worthwhile to be proud of. I put my empty journal in my lap as we come in to land.

Here we go. The biggest mistake of my career.

CHAPTER 2

French women must get fat

MAURIZIO IS TO BECOME OUR CONSTANT COMPANION FOR the next three months. He will be our talking point with the locals, a porter of sorts, and his presence will make most people we come across think we are French. Now we are on the ground in Lyon our first priority is to meet him. Although, for the moment, we don't know his name. That's because he doesn't have one yet.

Lyon airport is a bit of a surprise. It's what life must have been like before terrorism became one of the most over-used words in the English language. We just mosey off the plane down to Immigration, where a man stamps my passport while his head is turned in another direction, and out the door. I clutch my passport, asking Tom, 'Didn't anyone want to look at my photo? I may not look like a shoe bomber, but how the hell do they know?' He shrugs and grunts something unintelligible by way of reply.

I don't take his disinterest personally because I know he's in organisation mode. He had pored over the websites of the different European car manufacturers, wooed at first by the Beemers, Audis and Saabs before admitting we had a restricted

budget. He eventually chose an economical but zippy Renault
hatchback. 'It'll be our ticket off the tourist trail,' Tom enthused,
happily imagining us motoring along the sleepy country roads
with no timetable to keep to but our own.

Now Tom walks purposefully to find the pick-up point for
the car. As usual, I dawdle behind taking in the surroundings,
which seem more like a quaint village than a functioning
airport. I can't help adopting the bug-eyed look of the new
tourist as I get excited over details that the locals rushing for
their flights would consider *très* mundane. But this is my first
taste of Europe—and I'm finding it magical.

Beside the main concourse are clusters of shops. I pass people
queuing for bread at a cheery *boulangerie* and sniff the fragrance
of lavender oil as it wafts from boutiques selling high-end
cosmetics. I also notice a stylish wine bar. Inside, customers in
tailored suits are sitting on high stools laughing and smoking
while waiters in starched white uniforms shuck oysters to order.
It's a far cry from the usual airport fast-food options.

Soon we're standing in the afternoon sunshine clutching a
printout of the email sent to us by the car lease company.

'We're looking for a yellow van. No, sorry,' Tom checks the
email, 'make that mustard.' I raise my eyebrows, surprised they
didn't make the distinction between Dijon and Hot English.
I leave Tom with our bags and wander to the kerb, turning back
to take a photo of him to mark this moment. All of a sudden,
my residual apprehension makes way for excitement.

'The beginning,' I cry, skipping back over to Tom, throwing
my arms around his neck and planting a kiss on his lips.

His face lights up. 'This is where it all starts, baby—we're
really here.'

After being collected by the *moutarde* van, we are driven to an
industrial area about fifteen minutes away. There's a mobile
office by a dirt car park and a couple of barking guard dogs
straining at their leashes behind a wire fence. Beside it, all alone
with the keys in the ignition, is our little Renault. He's a silver

box of a thing, looking more like a cockroach from the planet Zorkon than anything driveable. He has petal-shaped headlights, bright red French licence plates—which tell the trained eye that it's a tourist lease job—and is oozing with that universal new-car smell.

This is Maurizio—we name him a week later after the maintenance man at our Sardinian villa, the owner of which leaves us instructions that Maurizio is the go-to guy if anything goes wrong. 'Just ask the fabulous Maurizio for anything, anything at all,' she urges.

'Maurizio?' we ask. We imagine him to be part romance-novel bodice-ripper, part male gigolo. Tom and I never see the real Maurizio but others say he looks more likely to rip the top off a six-pack of Peroni and watch football than tear off someone's smalls. Still, our car looks so unmasculine, we think a name as swarthy as Maurizio might up its testosterone quota. And it sticks.

When handing over the car keys, the woman in the office, a stern young thing in her twenties with angular features, gives us instructions. 'Keep strictly to the right—espeshiahleey een, how you say? Round-ah-bouts. The other drivers, they get vereey vereey angreey eef you go een the left lane.' She breaks off to emphasise this point, wrinkling her nose and wagging her finger. 'Only the tourists who are vereey stupeed or vereey brave. Well,' she breathes in sharply through her nostrils, 'they are the only foreign people who drive there.'

So, sticking like jungle grip to the right shoulder of the road, we drive like French grandmas to our first stop: Graveson in Provence. We hear that it's supposed to be a typical Provençal village, a tiny place of a few thousand residents about 10 kilometres south of Saint Rémy de Provence, also known as Van Gogh territory. Sitting on the opposite sides of the car is as strange as being on the 'wrong' side of the road. I vow to let Tom do most of the driving for now, remembering how long it took to learn to drive a manual. We're also staying at the 130 kilometres-an-hour speed limit and that fact alone advertises in neon that we're from 'out of town'. A steady stream of Peugeots, BMWs, Citroëns and Saabs is tearing past us. Everyone else seems to think the speed signs are purely decorative. The countryside whizzes past and I stare out at it greedily, wanting to inhale every detail.

I've read my fair share of books by people who have come to live in the south of France and renovate villas. They all paint delicious scenes of country life—waddling geese, endless fields bursting with sunflowers, rustic farmhouses and swathes of lavender and wild thyme perfuming the air. But I'm shocked to find this is nothing like that. My first taste of the French countryside is one long homage to the Industrial Revolution. Sprawling grey factories litter the plains, nuclear reactors spew out mushroom clouds of steam and wind farms dot the hilltops like daggers.

'Don't worry,' Tom assures me. 'They have to put this kind of stuff somewhere. It'll get better once we get off the motorway. At least, I hope it will.'

Bored, after a while I get out my mobile phone and start punching out a text message.

'What are you doing?'

'Just letting people know we've arrived,' I say.

'They've probably put two and two together and worked out we're here.'

I let out an irritated sigh. Before we left, I had emailed everyone, giving them my mobile number, the number for the international SIM card I've bought and my three email addresses.

'Why on earth do you want to be so contactable?' Tom asks. 'Do you really need to take that with you everywhere?'

'It's my phone.' I throw it down on my lap. 'I'll take it if I want to. What's it got to do with you?'

'Most people go on holidays to switch off, take a break.'

'Well, this is longer than your average holiday. What if a news story happens in one of the countries we're in? I'd want to be able to cover it. I need my phone.'

'Baby.' He grips the steering wheel tightly then relaxes again. 'I don't know how to say this, but I need to know whether you can get on board.'

I force a laugh. 'I am on board right now. What are you talking about?'

'I'm serious.' He looks across at me. 'This trip is really important to me. I don't know if I'll be able to take a big chunk of time off to do something like this again. I really want to make the most of it. If you don't know whether or not you want to be here, well, that's going to detract from my experience.' He trails off and sighs. 'Look, I know this sounds really selfish and I'm sorry,' he goes on, 'but you need to decide. Otherwise you're going to ruin it for both of us.'

I think for a second and then switch my phone off.

'Okay,' I whisper.

After a couple of hours we see a turnoff marked Saint Rémy de Provence. Tom flicks on the indicator. 'Time to get off this awful motorway.'

Seconds later industrial France disappears and we're among the stuff Peter Mayle and his mates promised. I feel my spirits lift as I see narrow country roads embraced by rows of drooping trees, the plum and cinnamon hues of autumn. There are crumbling farmhouses with plump aproned women tending to the gardens, and vineyards, orchards and church steeples. A big archway marks the entrance to Graveson. Through it is a cobbled street where dozens of cats are sunning themselves on rooftops. It's all so charming, it feels like being in the theme park Provence World.

'Is this for real?' I ask. 'Are you sure they're not putting it on for the tourists? Do people actually live like this?'

Clearly, they do. As we search the back lanes for our guesthouse, we pass a group of men sitting at an outdoor café, wearing stripy tops with jumpers jauntily knotted around their shoulders. Then another bloke cycles past wearing a beret with a baguette tucked under his arm.

The weather is still warm and the days long but all the peak-season tourists have packed up and gone home. The only other people at the old post office we're staying in, a gorgeous labyrinth of a building with sandstone floors and tree-trunk ceiling beams, are French.

We flop on our bed exhausted, knowing there are loads of things waiting to be discovered, including priority one—dinner. We pore over the *Michelin Guide* and stop when we see a place called Les Glycines.

'Cheap and cheerful hearty food, made with local ingredients,' Tom reads from the review.

We're halfway out the door, when I remember my phone and rush back inside. I pretend to ignore Tom's rolled eyes as I put it in my handbag.

◆ ◆ ◆ ◆ ◆

As we drive towards the restaurant, I press on my stomach to stop it rumbling. It's so loud, it's practically trying to speak to me. If it could talk, I reckon it would sound like the plant out of *Little Shop of Horrors*: 'How good is this. I'm about to be fed in ways I've always dreamed about. Feed me! Feed me!'

But while my tummy is beside itself in anticipation of culinary delights, my brain is sending me different messages. 'Watch yourself,' it says, measuring my stomach folds between thumb and forefinger. 'You'll have to show some restraint. If you don't, you'll need to book two plane seats to get home.'

I'm torn. I'm a bit of a food tragic. I drool over photos in gourmet magazines and take cookbooks to bed to read before I fall asleep. It's a bit nerdy, but lately I've even been getting into food forums on the internet to research the best places to eat in Europe. And there are so many amazing things here to try. How am I going to sate my curiosity without super-sizing myself?

I've looked for the answer in that book *French Women Don't Get Fat*, but there was nothing all that groundbreaking in it.

Just the timeworn messages of restraint and chewing your *pain au chocolat* eleven hundred times. I figured it must be easier to stay slim in a country where the cuisine is served as teeny tiny works of art in the centre of big white plates. I put my hand on my stomach. Sssssh. We're about to find out how the French women really do it.

From the street, the restaurant looks empty. There's no one sitting at the set tables in the big room at the front. Feeling nervous about going somewhere so unpopular, we turn to walk away.

But then I hear a voice coming from the back. '*Madame, Monsieur!*' cries the chef, practically sprinting from the kitchen. He takes us by the arm, smiling and nodding—'*Bonsoir, bonsoir!*'—and leads us past empty chairs, down some stairs and out the back to a smaller room. It is full of locals chatting at wooden tables set with white cloths, wedged between pots of greenery. The air is filled with the smell of fresh bread and roasting meat. We are the only tourists here. A good sign.

The waitress appears to take our order. '*Parlez-vous anglais?*' I ask hopefully. She shakes her head. Damn, there goes one of the only French phrases in my repertoire. In such a famous area I thought my lack of language skills wouldn't be an issue—but, boy, am I wrong. Hardly anyone we've come across yet can speak English. I guess it's pretty arrogant to expect otherwise. I try to decipher the restaurant menu and order by pointing, while Tom's schoolboy French makes up for the rest.

'Check this out.' I point out the *menu à prix-fixe terroir*, the set menu of local specialties. 'I have no idea what any of the other dishes are, but I think that's *bouillabaisse* for first course.'

Provençal food—often called *la cuisine du soleil* or cuisine of the sun—is flavoured with the fragrant *herbes de Provence*, a mix of lavender, marjoram, savory, fennel seed, rosemary, sage and thyme. The local dishes star all the sun-loving fruits and vegies: peaches, plums, oranges, olives, tomatoes, zucchini and eggplant. *Bouillabaisse*, a hearty seafood soup, is one of the region's great creations. We won't be going to the port of

Marseille, which claims to be the home of the dish, but lots of restaurants in Provence feature it on their menus and I'm dying to try the real deal. We point to the set menu and the waitress nods and scribbles on her pad.

While we wait for our food, I steal a few glances at our fellow diners. Unfortunately, there aren't many women, except for our waitress, two grandmothers and a couple of kids. I'll have to conduct my research into the dining habits of the fairer sex some other time. But what I do see that gets me thinking are two men having dinner together at a table over in the corner. They hugged when they arrived, touch each other affectionately on the arm and stare into each other's eyes while they talk. They don't seem to be lovers, just good friends having a close conversation. I'm pleasantly surprised. The men I know wouldn't be caught dead having an intimate dinner for two with their mates. And blokey affection is uncommon—they might hug but they would be standing two feet away, thumping their palm against their friend's back as though they're burping a baby. Certainly no French-style kissing on the cheek.

The sound of knives and forks clatters around the room as entrées are finished. Then, as if on cue, everyone in the restaurant pulls out packets of cigarettes and lights up at their tables. They keep puffing away for the rest of the night. The room fills with so much smoke I can hardly see Tom. It's a surprise to see such a relaxed attitude to smoking after living in a country where it's been banned in restaurants for years.

Through the nicotine fog, I eventually see a plate piled with crispy croutons arranged around a pot of thick *rouille*, a hot red mayonnaise-like sauce, arriving at our table. Our waitress puts it by another dish, which contains two raw cloves of garlic.

'Do I do this?' I pick up a piece and rub the bread with it.

'*Oui.*' She looks relieved at not having to explain it.

'*Et …*' She points to the bread and makes a spreading motion with the pot of sauce. '*Puis …*' She pretends to put the croutons in the bowl, before making a mime of spooning broth on top.

'Aaaah,' we nod in understanding. The famed *bouillabaisse*. And now it's in front of me.

I build the creation as the waitress instructed, with croutons spread with a dollop of *rouille* going in first. The scent of tomato, fennel and orange zest wafts from the saffron-infused broth, which is the colour of a pretty sunset. I lift a spoonful flecked with thick flakes of white fish and it coats my tongue like liquid silk. The texture of the soup, the croutons and the salty paste is both crunchy and creamy. Tom tips his head back in mock ecstasy while I manage, in between mouthfuls, to get out a muffled 'it's amazing'.

Three courses later, we stagger out the door waving at the staff. Part of me is overjoyed at how delicious our first meal of the trip was. The other part is terrified. If they're all this good for the next six months I won't just need two seats on the return trip, I'm going to require my own row.

The next morning we go on a pre-breakfast walk to shake off the remaining jetlag cobwebs. We're just ambling along, watching the village stir into life for the day, when we turn a corner and stumble across a produce market. The local farmers have set up stalls in the town square. Under awnings striped yellow and black, robust men and women wearing aprons ply their wares. They arrange mounds of fresh fungi the colour of fudge on big wooden trestle tables. Crates spill over with sunny mushrooms shaped like sea sponges. Chickens stuffed with herbs and lemon are being roasted on rotisseries, their sweet-smelling fat sizzling into a tray below. Women stand over cast-iron pots which look like upturned medieval shields hefting dishes of snails and paella with wooden spoons.

Exercise is forgotten about for the moment. We are on holiday now, Tom reminds me. We can spend an entire day reclining under the shade of a tree with a picnic. Sounds brilliant to me. The olive vendor seduces us first. We pick out the garlic, chilli and rosemary combination and he digs into the container with a metal scoop. At the stall next door we buy a round of fresh chèvre, topped prettily with a lavender sprig and threatening to ooze out of its patty-cake wrapper. I select squishy peaches and cherry tomatoes strung together on their vine like jumbo marbles, which are placed carefully in brown paper bags. Then Tom heads for the deli van festooned with garlands of sausages while I join the queue at the bread seller. Everyone around me is chatting with neighbours and friends, wicker baskets filled with hunks of cheese balanced over their arms and long baguettes in paper bags. It's all so French. I'm thrilled to be part of this little window into village life.

Once I reach the head of the queue it's too hard to choose. There are sourdough rounds with criss-crosses on top, plaited *ficelles* freckled with olives and flat breads encrusted with sea salt. I eventually pick a *ficelle* by pointing at it and saying one of the only other French terms I know: '*S'il vous plaît.*' The woman behind the counter nods and says a price so quickly I can't catch it. I shyly hand over the biggest euro note I have in my hand and hope she isn't dudding me when she counts out my change.

An overexcited Tom joins me. He has bought half a pig's worth of ham off the bone.

'I asked for 300 grams,' he shrugs, 'and the man at the deli told me in no uncertain terms, "One does not order in grams. That is not how things are done in France. I will cut. You shall tell me when to stop".' We grin like kids. It beats shopping at the supermarket. A couple of Audrey Hepburn lookalikes brush past us with a bag of still-warm croissants and an apple tart. They munch on pastries as they walk. I shake my head. How do they eat like this and keep their figures?

I endeavour to learn more about this French paradox the next day when we lunch in Gigondas, a wine town in the Rhône Valley. The restaurant is in a charming two-storey building with terracotta roof tiles and green wooden shutters trimmed with cream. We take our seats in the formal dining room, feeling a touch underdressed in jeans and T-shirts.

'How good is this, just quietly,' Tom smiles, as I sip on a buttery white wine. 'If I were at work right now, I'd probably be eating a sandwich at my desk.'

Our plates come out covered with embellished silver lids. Ah, this must be how the French really dine. Pomp and ceremony with more delicate portions. But as our waiters simultaneously lift the lids, I am again astounded. Nouvelle cuisine seems to have gone the way of stegosaurus and the spiral perm.

I turn to scan the slender women in the restaurant, expecting to see them playing with their food, but do a double take when I see that all of them have cleaned their plates right down to the very last crumbs.

'It's delicious, but I'm full,' I tell the kindly looking waiter with a greying beard, who thankfully speaks excellent English. He strokes his belly, snug in a buttoned-up vest, and looks at my plate. It's holding an exceptionally yummy fish dish: crispy-skinned catfish on a bed of almond couscous. A tragedy to leave unfinished.

The waiter gives me a quizzical look. 'All right,' I pick my fork back up, thinking 'when in France'. 'Maybe just a few more bites.'

The waiter smiles and gives me a wink. '*Très bon, Madame, très bon.*'

◆ ◆ ◆ ◆ ◆

It's four o'clock the next morning. The only sound in our room is of the wind swishing in the pine tree outside our window. But inside my head it's noisy from a relentless babble of thoughts.

I turn over and sigh. I wonder how long it will take me to develop a new sleep pattern after all those years of having to wake up so early for work? An old breakfast radio hack once told me it takes at least three months for the body to readjust to normal. 'It's excellent training for breastfeeding,' she said, referring to the military-style self-discipline you need to wrench yourself out of bed as soon as the alarm goes off. I would normally stagger to the shower and let the water wash over me while my eyes were still shut. Minutes later I had to be creative, bright and bubbly while most people were snuggling with their doonas.

After all those years of conditioning, the second I stir awake in the morning my brain whirs like a wind-up toy. It's impossible to go back to sleep. On the days when I don't have to go to work, it's these hours between my brain switching on and the sun coming up that I think my darkest thoughts. Krill-sized worries inflate to blue whale proportions.

I get up now to check my mobile phone. No new messages. Tiptoeing back to the bed, I lie down again, making out the raked wooden ceiling in the dark. I allow myself to soak in self pity. No one even misses me. Maybe they're wondering what the hell I'm doing texting them when I should be having the time of my life. I put my hands over my eyes, cringing as I imagine their response. I know I shouldn't care about being out of touch seeing that I'm the one who's made the decision to go.

Tom is peaceful next to me. I turn and hear him breathing gently. He's such an even keel compared with me. So rational and rarely filled with anxiety. I envy him his black and whiteness while I just feel a million shades of grey. We're as different physically as we are emotionally. I'm a fair-skinned blonde, petite and 158 centimetres. Tom seems even taller than his 181 centimetres. He's got thick dark hair, broad shoulders and eyes that look like big black stones fringed with the longest lashes I've ever seen.

We used to be able to talk about everything. But I can't share any of this with him. He'll just think I'm putting me ahead of us. Again.

Tom can't understand why I'm feeling this way. We've been arguing a lot about it lately. I'm worried about the distance between us. The different hours Tom and I have been keeping mean that we have developed separate social circles and separate interests. I guess that was inevitable. Some weeks the only times we saw each other was when one of us was asleep. Ships passing in the night, we joked. Only it's not really that funny.

To be honest, this trip is an act of faith that we can reconnect. We're about to have more time alone together than ever before. A chance to rediscover the ties that bind us. I hope we can find them.

◆ ◆ ◆ ◆ ◆

Knowing almost no French beyond the basic *bonjour* and *au revoir*, it is with some nervousness that I've been making contact with the locals over the last few days. That's because, growing up with an English father, talk of the French was never positive.

'Bloody Frogs,' he'd fume whenever the French-Australian celebrity chef Gabriel Gaté came on television. 'They're just so bloody arrogant.' Whenever I'd ask why, he'd state knowingly: 'Because that's the way they are.'

This viewpoint has been reinforced by people telling me tales of the French refusing to speak English to you even if they can, ignoring you in shops or brushing snootily past you in the street. But from what I've discovered so far, the French are victims of a character assassination campaign. Everyone I've met has been falling over themselves to be charming.

It's our second last day in Provence and we've been wine-tasting all day. The idea of picking up a dinner of bread and cheese has been thrown around and we decide our best bet at this late hour is to visit Saint Rémy de Provence, one of the bigger towns in the area. A gorgeous place with rows of stone terraces, boutiques and streets lined with plane trees, it is where Van Gogh painted *The Starry Night* and *Irises*. We pull over and park in a small back lane. Unbeknown to us, we are about to be ambushed, yet again, by a charisma offensive.

Wandering around in the dimming light, we spy a sign for a *fromagerie*, only to see the shutters already closed.

'Damn,' I curse, peering through the door. But then it opens. Standing in front of us is a tall man in a long white coat.

'*Bonjour*,' he says in that sing-song way the French have.

Monsieur Fromager motions us into his delightful little shop as if we're old friends. He encourages us to taste his cheeses and actually apologises because he can't speak very good English. I look at him dumbfounded. Here I am in his country completely ignorant of his language and he's saying sorry to me?

Afterwards Tom and I stand on the street wondering where we'll find a *boulangerie* open at this time. A voice startles us.

'Excuse me.' It belongs to a man who has slowed his car down and is leaning out the window smiling. 'I just heard you talking in English and I thought I would help. I think you'll find a very good *boulangerie* just around the corner. Good luck.' He motors off while we stare dumbly after him. Are the French conspiring to become known as the friendliest nation on earth?

One of the other gripes Dad used to have was that the French 'have no sense of humour'. All evidence to the contrary when I buy a can of mineral water in a tobacco store. The owner, a middle-aged man with dark movie star looks, watches me as he leans on the counter.

'Wot er you lewking fer?'

'A straw,' I reply.

'Wot eez that?'

'Ummmm, ah, er ...' Unfortunately I fail to come up with any other word that explains what I mean so end up repeating helplessly, 'Ah, um, a straw?'

Tom offers to step in. He sometimes fancies himself as a bit of a knight in shining armour. Especially when it comes to speaking French. For the last few days he's been revelling in his position of authority, which is based on knowing how to speak a little of this language. Frankly, I am starting to get the shits with his corrections and snickering laughter at my pronunciation.

I sigh. 'All right, honey. Be my guest.'

Tom presses his lips together, searching his vocabulary for the French word. After a few moments he comes up blank and decides to choose a different tack—the art of mime. And so begins a questionable charade that involves making sucking noises and phallic shapes with his hands.

The shopkeeper cocks his head to one side. He lets him continue for a good thirty seconds or so.

'*Ah, oui*,' he laughs finally, signalling the penny has dropped. He nods and pulls a container full of straws from behind the counter.

'See,' Tom turns to me, looking all puffed up. 'Sometimes when all else fails you just have to get creative.'

The Frenchman gives me a wink and with a cheeky smile says to Tom, 'Oh, I understood wot you were sayeeng all along. I just thought you were amusing.'

◆ ◆ ◆ ◆ ◆

On our last day in Provence I get lost in translation again. But this time, miming my way through is completely out of the question. That's because the item I'm scouring the local super-market for is tampons.

I'm kicking myself for not bringing any with me, in a bid to pack light. Anyone who has been on an extended holiday knows the stress always begins when you pack your bags and realise a convoy of caravans is required to carry all your shoes, clothes and beauty products. I have had to fit my entire life for the next six months into a medium-sized backpack. This is quite a challenge when you bear in mind we are travelling from sticky Mediterranean summers to European and American winters. Then there's the fact I can be a little on the vain side and a bit of a girly-girl. So it was a painful moment indeed when I learned I would have to live without my department store's supply of toiletry products.

I set to work putting everything I wanted into a pile. Moisturiser, fake tan, tampon supply, cleanser, cotton buds, cotton tips, bandaids, perfume, hair bands, hairdryer, hand cream, shampoo and conditioner, face mask, hair treatments, make-up, etcetera. Just the essentials. I called Tom over to survey my leaning tower of cosmetology. We looked at each other. We looked back at the pile. We looked at each other again. It was clear I'd have more success trying to coax an elephant into an esky.

'You've no choice. You're going to have to cut it in half—at least.' Tom shook his head.

'No.' I collapsed on the ground like a two-year-old. 'You don't understand. I need these things.'

'What exactly do you have here?' He pulled out my A4-size zip-lock bag of tampons. 'Surely you don't need to take six months' supply,' he said, laughing. 'Oh baby, they do sell tampons in Europe you know. And what about this?' He held up my bottle of fake tan. 'What do you need this for?'

'We're going to a beach house in Sardinia the week after we arrive,' I replied, indignant. ' I don't want to look pasty in my bikini.'

Still laughing, Tom said, 'I bet you can buy fake tan there too. We're not going to the moon, you know.'

He let out one last snigger.

Right, I thought eventually, I'm going to have to be brutal. I took out the tampons and fake tan first. Tom's got a point, I reasoned. How silly of me to think you wouldn't be able to buy those things over there. After all, our first stop is France. Buying cosmetics should be a cinch.

Now, here I am in this supermarket, futiley searching for the 'feminine hygiene' aisle. I can see beauty products, shower gels, all the lotions and potions you can imagine for mother and baby. But tampons and pads are nowhere to be seen. There must be some mistake. It must be in a different section. Stalking the aisles one by one, I make a complete tour of the store, becoming more confused. After twenty minutes, still no tampons. I give up.

Tomorrow we drive across the border to Italy, catch the car ferry to Sardinia and meet up with our Australian friends Greg and Wil. I worry there won't be as many supermarkets and chemists there, so on our way out of Provence we drop into a larger town called Avignon. Reasoning that French women must go to pharmacies to get their supplies, I lob up to a swanky-looking chemist.

'I need two things,' I direct Tom. 'Fake tan and tampons. If you can look for the tan, I'll get the other stuff.'

A groomed attendant in a crisp white uniform approaches me, asking in French if I need any help.

'*Oui*,' I say, frantically. 'Product for period?' I try in English. She looks at me blankly. 'Women's products.' I'm thinking in double time now and finally throw in, 'Uh, menstruation?'

'Oh.' Recognition registers in her eyes and she pulls me out of earshot of the other customers.

'Madame,' her voice is hushed. 'We do not sell'—her eyes dart around the store, then she whispers—'products for the lady here. There is another store in Avignon that you can go to.'

She gives me directions involving turning corners and travelling along back lanes. I can't believe the embarrassment my request has generated. It's very weird. First no tampons in the supermarket and now this reaction, like I'd asked where I could find a leather gimp mask. Do French women not have periods? Maybe that's why French women don't get fat. Because … they're not human!

Tom returns, triumphantly brandishing a bottle. 'I found the fake tan.'

'That is a very good brand,' declares the attendant, brightening now that the filthy subject of 'products for the lady' has been changed. We buy the bottle and I walk out of the store bewildered.

On board the ferry the next day, I look at my legs, which are the colour of driven snow, and decide to give my new fake tan a whirl. Searching through the box, I discover there are instructions in German, Dutch and even Arabic but none in

English. How hard can this be? I think smugly. Surely you just put it on and wait.

I spray myself liberally with the clear sticky liquid. Unfortunately, you can't tell where you've put it. Being a fake-tan veteran, though, I am confident I've done a good job. Later that night, as we sip espresso in the ship's airy lounge, I inspect the progress of my tan. Nothing. Another couple of hours pass and my legs still look as pale as they did before. We go to sleep in bunk beds, gently rocked by the motion of the ferry motoring its way across the sea.

In the morning the first thing I see is Tom's face, a picture of surprise as he looks down at me from the top bunk.

'Good morning,' I say sleepily.

'My god.' He flicks on the overhead light. 'You're so, ummm, brown.'

I shuck off my blanket and look at my legs and arms. I have emerged from my albino chrysalis and metamorphosed into Donatella Versace. The colour is brownish, but tinged with a distinct orange hue. I shriek in horror while Tom clutches his stomach laughing.

'You match the woodwork on the bunk bed.'

'I look like a walking Jaffa ball,' I wail. This in itself wouldn't be such a problem if it were an even all-over Jaffa experience— after all, Donatella's made that her trademark look for years. But I've missed a spot. A few spots, as it happens. I rush towards the mirror and see that the underside of my right arm has a long white patch in the middle, the cracks between my toes contrast so my feet look like top-deck chocolate and I have swirls on my thighs and hips.

I try rubbing at a patch, but it won't budge. 'It's a French fake-tan disaster,' I moan. As Tom titters at my expense, I feel like someone upstairs is teaching me a lesson. I'm not only paying the ultimate price for vanity, but as I yearn for the fake tan and tampons I left behind I'm reminded again of how you don't know what you've got 'til it's gone.

CHAPTER 3

Say formaggio!

SARDINIA IS THE WORST PLACE IN THE WORLD FOR car-sickness sufferers. Constant corners are my natural enemy and this island is littered with hairpin bends. They squiggle around sandy beaches then snap up into the granite-flecked landscape of the interior. I hang my head out Maurizio's open window like a dog, focusing on the horizon and trying to gulp in fresh air. It's only been about sixty minutes since our ferry arrived, but it will take us another two hours to twist our way to Cagliari, the capital. There we pick up our friends who are flying in to meet us for a ten-day holiday.

I've been desperate to go to Italy since primary school when my imagination was captured by a project I did on Pompeii. I've dreamed of eating meals in rustic trattorias run by several generations of the one family and stumbling upon tiny villages rich with tradition. But now that I'm finally here Italy's making me want to spew. 'Can we pull over for a break?' I croak. 'I need a few minutes out of this car.'

We see a sign for a service station and pull into the car park. I barrel through the swinging wooden doors to the toilets and spend the next few minutes hunched over the sink, taking deep breaths and splashing cold water over my face. When I emerge, I find Tom in the attached restaurant, propped up at the counter watching an Italian game show blaring on the television. A young couple move like lightning, serving customers. I look at the menu and it becomes clear this is no Australian truck stop with soggy meat pies and cartons of chocolate milk. We are in the middle of nowhere, yet we have found our first Italian espresso bar.

Tom goes to order us each a *macchiato*, but the woman behind the counter shakes her head. She points to another woman sitting at a cash register down the other end. We are confused.

'First, give money,' she instructs. So we pay the cashier for our coffees and she gives us a receipt. Then we return to the counter, hand over our docket and place our order again. This is the process everywhere in Italy. There's no point even thinking about ordering without paying the cashier first. Nothing will guarantee a barista will spit in your milk more. Well, apart from ordering a cappuccino after midday.

Now that we've followed the correct procedure, the woman grinds the beans. Then the big stainless steel machine dispenses a trickle of chocolate-coloured liquid, tiger-striped with *crema*, into tiny glasses. A dollop of silky foam finishes them off. She plonks the cups unceremoniously on the counter in front of us with two sparkling mineral waters. They're perfect.

We stand and sip, trying to act like we do this all the time. Carried away in the moment, we have two more each and then spend the next hour with caffeine jitters. But while we're getting pepped up, the locals are taking the edge off. The liquor laws in Italy are so relaxed that bars are allowed at petrol stations. We watch in alarm as people pull over, down a shot and speed off. *Mamma mia!* What about drink-driving laws? Thankfully there aren't too many high-performance cars here—everyone seems to drive tiny Fiat Panda hatchbacks. Nonetheless, we again stay in the safety of the vacant right-hand lane, just in case.

We reach Cagliari after a few unscheduled stops where I try and look glamorous while retching into a bag. There's a bit of time to kill before Greg and Wil's plane arrives, so we do what you do during your free time in Italy. Eat something, of course. Unfortunately, a shopping centre food hall is to be the scene of our first Italian meal. Not exactly the family-run *cucina* I had in mind.

The vast room with its fluorescent lights and fake pot plants has the usual suspects—a McDonald's, a takeaway pizza shop and an espresso-cum-sandwich bar. We stop there and order a ham and cheese *panini*, the Italian equivalent of the toasted sanger. We're not expecting anything fancy. Silly us. When it comes to the serious business of food, Italians do it better. Out comes a crisp roll stuffed with slices of prosciutto and provolone. Yum. We eat, and watch as a teenage girl takes her cup of McDonald's soft-serve ice cream to the coffee shop and asks for a shot of espresso to be poured over the top. It's a *McAffagato*. Genius. The marketing people at the golden arches should get on to that one.

When Greg and Wil arrive at the airport fresh from a week in Florence, they're both sporting leather-market souvenirs of shiny shoes and weekender bags. These two are not hard to miss. They each have hair that enters a room before they do. Wil—short for Wilhelmina—has long honey-coloured medusa curls. Greg, who sports a blonde version of Hugh Grant's do from his *Four Weddings and a Funeral* period, has a habit of flicking it back off his face with a jerk of his neck. They spot us across the arrivals hall and their faces light up. Greg and Tom embrace first in a clumsy man-hug. They went through high school together and then uni, where Tom introduced Greg to Wil. When I came on to the scene we clicked instantly and now they feel like extended family.

Maurizio's crammed with luggage, conversation and laughter as we drive east to our beach villa at a place called San Ruxi. Greg and Wil recount their trip so far, describing each and every gelato they ate, a great food and wine fair and how most Italian men are wearing bright red pants and all the fashionable Florentine girls are baring their midriffs.

We're about halfway there when we decide to pull into a supermarket to stock up on provisions. 'What's the kitchen supposed to be like in this place?' Wil asks as we walk through the carpark. Greg shrugs. Our accommodation for the next two weeks is free, thanks to a family connection of his. Like Tom and me, Wil's a keen cook—she will whip up something fabulous like ricotta hotcakes for breakfast at the drop of a hat.

Wil goes off in search of buffalo mozzarella. At the meat section I become entranced by the abundance of packaged offal and fat pork chops. When I see a tray holding a dark red steak the size of a dinner plate, I stop, perplexed. I peer at the label: *carne di cavallo*. Hmmm. What could it be? It's lean and glossy. *Cavallo*. I rack my brains trying to match the word with the scant Italian I've taught myself.

Suddenly I figure it out. It can't be true. I drop the tray in horror and take a few steps back, covering my mouth. It's, it's … Phar Lap!

A woman with a basket scoots in front of me. She picks up the tray and gives me a look of surprise. '*Molto deliciozo,*' she tells me, tapping the top of the plastic. I nod, unconvinced, remembering how an Italian friend told me her family considered horse meat to be quite the delicacy. They were devastated when they came to Australia and found it was illegal. Australia is not the only country where horse meat is taboo. It's not on any menus in Britain or America either. It's also forbidden by the Jewish faith and some Christian denominations. Pope Gregory III tried to ban what he felt was a pagan practice back in the eighth century. But if there's any residual Catholic guilt in this supermarket, it is well hidden. In the few minutes I stand by the fridge the horse meat is literally, well, galloping off the shelf. Thanks to mad cow disease, horse meat sales are fifty per cent higher now than they were five years ago. It's supposed to taste like a cross between beef and venison. I walk away from the cabinet. That is just a little more adventure than my tastebuds can handle.

As we drive under the boom gate marking the entrance to where we are staying, we gasp at our good fortune. Our villa is in a swanky complex of terracotta-roofed holiday homes complete with tennis courts and a swimming pool. We follow the driveway up a gravel road and see the deep red stuccoed walls of the house. Wasps buzz around honeysuckle and frangipani in the front garden. And best of all, it's about a gnocchi's fling from the beach.

'I reckon we should unpack this stuff,' Greg says. I notice his face has gone pink in the heat. 'And then we can go straight down for a dip.'

I marvel at Greg's outfit: a navy suit jacket over chinos. No wonder he feels uncomfortable—it's about thirty degrees in the shade. As usual, he looks as if he's stepped out of the pages of *GQ*.

Greg has spent the last two years serving as an Australian diplomat in Washington and has developed a sartorial affinity with preppy American labels. Wilhelmina, on the other hand, appears to be itching to get into a sarong. The child of dyed-in-the-wool hippies, she works as a senior project manager at a multinational consultancy firm. The only outward sign of her heritage is her summer wardrobe of batik sarongs and Birkenstocks, which she changes into now.

Down at the beach we race each other into water that is as flat as a swimming pool. Just like Provence, peak tourist season has finished and our Anglo faces stand out among the remaining holidaymakers, who are mostly Italian. They sit under straw umbrellas chain-smoking or prowl the beaches. Their deep caramel tans are accessorised with heavy gold jewellery.

Tom and I bob in the water for a while. I look over at Greg and Wil, who are swimming out to try and catch a rare wave, and think how happy it makes me to spend time with them. Even though I've only been away from Sydney for a week, the sense of isolation is intense. It's great to hear other Australian accents and be able to laugh with people who have the same cultural reference points as I do. Their company provides a connection with home. And having the faces of friends around means home doesn't seem quite so far away.

Dinner that night is at one of the open-air restaurants in the nearby resort town of Villasimius. We fold triangles of paper-thin pizza in half to capture the tomato sauce, but every now and then we get a splodge or two dripping down our chins. The waitress brings over a jug of chilled red.

Greg looks up at her. 'How do you say "cheers" in Italian?' he asks.

She shrugs shyly, 'Ummm, sorry. What do you say?'

'Uh, you know,' Greg pauses, thinks and repeats the word again. 'Cheers.'

She stops and bites her lip. 'Ah,' she says after a time. 'That's easy. In Italy we say "*formaggio*".'

We all look at each other, uncertain, but raise our glasses anyway. '*Formaggio!*' we cry.

I take a sip and then put down my glass. 'Hang on a second.' I start to giggle. '*Formaggio*'s not cheers, it's cheese. Greg, she thought you asked her how to say cheese in Italian.'

Wil snorts with laughter. 'Oh, no. They must be wondering what the hell those crazy Aussies are doing raising their glasses and yelling out the name of a food!'

After dinner we go back to our villa and pick our way down to the beach in the dark. We sit on the soft sand, commenting on how bright the stars look, and pour champagne into chunky water glasses we found in the kitchen cupboard. The waves brush the shore with a gentle swoosh and I feel the anxiety I've been carrying around with me begin to ease. This is more like a holiday.

Next to me, Greg, Wil and Tom crack up at a joke someone's made. Before I ask them what they're laughing about, I pause. I want to savour this moment. This feels good. I want to keep this up, try and let go a little more. Be more in the moment. Here's to that.

I quietly tilt my glass to the sky. '*Formaggio!*'

◆ ◆ ◆ ◆ ◆

A few days later, I go back into Villasimius to send some postcards. That's when I discover you could die waiting in line at an

Italian post office. Regimes could change, slugs could rise up and take over the earth, half a century's worth of New Year's Eves could be celebrated and you could still be waiting to buy one measly stamp.

I have been standing here second in line for twenty minutes. I fidget with the postcards I'm holding and aim a death stare at the back of the man who's holding us up. He has hair on his arms so thick you could weave wigs from them. Around his neck and wrists are chunky gold chains. Peeking from his T-shirt like the tips of tattoo icebergs are what I can only imagine are jungle cats. And he is about 195 centimetres tall. The guy is huge.

The reason this hirsute giant is taking so long is that he's filling out paperwork to send three enormous boxes to god only knows where. Each time he signs the bottom with a flourish I hold my breath, thinking he must be done. But the man behind the counter only stamps it officiously before going out the back and getting yet another form.

I check behind me. There are about twenty people in the queue and just two people behind the counter. I shift my filthy look to the other person serving, a woman under a sign saying 'Banca'. She's sitting there customer-less examining her cuticles. I feel like screaming at her, 'For god's sake, woman, it might not be your department but pick up the slack! All you have to do is shove thirty centimetres over to your right, open the drawer and hand over three stamps. I'm begging you.' But I stay silent, tapping my foot and looking at my watch.

Another five minutes go by. I should leave. But I've invested too much time to walk away. Italy's postal system with all its bureaucratic red tape has thrown down the gauntlet. To walk away now would be admitting weakness. It's a matter of pride.

Joining me in this Bermuda triangle of postal services are several elderly people. Some lean on canes. A few look like they are not coping well with the heat and wilt on a bench, fanning themselves. I wonder nervously if anyone knows CPR. They should have corpse cupboards in here like they do on jumbo jets. That way, should someone meet their maker before they meet the teller, they could just bundle them away and keep stamping those forms. Although the woman under the '*Banca*' sign would probably argue it's not her department.

'Can I help you? *Signora*, can I help you?'

I don't believe it. I am being served. As I walk out and check my watch, my jubilation quickly turns to infuriation. The transaction only took twenty seconds, but I've lost nearly an hour of my life.

The next morning, Greg wakes up with a severe dose of cabin fever. I'm impressed it has taken this long for the malady to strike. Normally he is like a caged lion itching to explore rather than read and sunbake. He and Wil tell us they have read about a small town called Jerzu, about a hundred kilometres inland. They say it's the main producer of *cannonau*, a wine that is one of Sardinia's most famous exports. Always enticed by a nice drop of red, we pile into Maurizio to take a look.

We wend our way up the coast. Groves of eucalypts, hibiscus and bougainvillea decorate the beaches. Turning inland, the terrain quickly becomes hilly with matted grass the colour of toffee. We peer down deep valleys where gnarled vines growing *cannonau* grapes patchwork up the sides. Vines have even been planted on the strip in the middle of the road. There are no tasting rooms and vineyards here, just working farms. You buy the local vino from the bottle shop.

The landscape is savage. Thousands of cone-shaped stone huts and fortresses dot the island, many dating back to around 2000 BC. The native animals add to the lost-in-time feel. Albino donkeys are supposed to live on one of the islands off the coast. There are also griffon vultures, miniature horses and monk seals.

Jerzu, perched on top of a cliff, is dusty and all but abandoned for the lunchtime siesta. I hadn't appreciated how serious the Italians are about their downtime until I found the shops all had their shutters down from midday to around four o'clock. The town is dead. We shrug, get back in the car and decide to take the long way home.

The next town has spooky old houses gutted like a movie set. With its bullet-pocked signs and derelict farmhouses, it feels like the Wild West; the town was probably attacked during the Second World War. The island has been invaded and re-invaded many times over the centuries—by Greeks, Romans and Spaniards. Yet the Sardinians insist they have never been conquered, they just moved up into the hills we are in now.

The road starts to twist up the top of the mountains. We stare at the strange fingers of shaly rock jutting out from their sides. The locals call these 'high heels' because of their resemblance to upside-down stilettos. Mist swirls around their points. Seconds later, we hear a clap of thunder. A curtain of rain draws down on us and all of a sudden we're driving in the clouds. I breathe in the smell of rain and pine needles. It is difficult to imagine that only twenty minutes ago it was sunny and barren.

We don't pass any other traffic for ages. People in the villages stop and stare as if someone's forgotten to tell them the car has been invented. I decide we must be the only tourists to venture this far away from the beaches in a long time. Then we are all silent, mesmerised by the scenery. I draw back, realising I'm fogging up my window from pressing my nose against it.

Tom turns down a village street and I see a father and son riding bareback using rope for reins. Clanking bells draw our attention to a stooped old man with a shepherd's crook who's herding billy goats uphill. It's thrilling to have found a pocket of Italy that matches my imagination. These tiny villages are seemingly untouched by modernity.

About half an hour later, we are in yet another small town. We ease down a street hemmed in by a row of sorbet-coloured houses.

'A guy I work with told me these lanes in small European villages have a habit of getting narrower and narrower,' Tom says, 'until, without warning, your car doesn't fit anymore.'

I notice there are just centimetres leeway either side of us—and Maurizio is not what you'd call a broad car.

Greg reaches out the window to fold in the side mirror. 'Uh, mate. This might be the street that bloke was talking to you about.'

Somehow we make it to the end. In front of us is a small piazza. This is where, in every Italian town, men of a certain age come together to gossip, chronicle and disapprove. The ones sitting here are all wearing fishermen's caps and leaning on walking sticks. As we drive towards them they look up at us as one, mouths agape.

Our next hurdle is finding a way out of the maze. We go around the piazza once. No way out. We go around again. Every small lane seems to lead back here. The men in the centre continue to watch, their mouths still open like sideshow clowns.

We come up for our third lap of the piazza. 'Take that left over there,' Wil points. 'It could be the way out.' We turn. I breathe in and will Maurizio to lose ten kilos.

Tom takes a hard left to make the angle. But there is no extra space. He pulls frantically on the wheel again, his left hand crossing over his right. Faster and faster. I see it and gasp. Tom jams on the brakes. But it's no use.

'Goddamnit!' Tom leaps out and slams the door. Greg follows and the two boys crouch down. I peek out the window. In front of us is a most inconsiderate step belonging to someone's house. And it has head-butted Maurizio bang between the eyes.

Wil nudges me and points at the old men on the bench. They are hunched over in hysterics.

'They'll probably be dining out on this story for years,' I say. Tom tries to rub out the tiny scratch across Maurizio's front panel. Perhaps that's why all the locals were marvelling at our car? Because only a fool or a tourist would be stupid enough to navigate these roads on anything but a horse.

◆ ◆ ◆ ◆ ◆

There are people in this world who are great at languages and people who aren't. I fall into the latter category. It's not for want of trying. Over the last four years I've enrolled in as many beginner Italian language courses at various community colleges and dropped out after the first week or two. That's because 'beginner' seems to be code for a whole bunch of middle-aged show-offs who've travelled to Italy seven times already and are able to converse semi-fluently with the teacher while I feel like a dunce.

About a month before we went away, I was bemoaning my lack of language skills to my friend Josh. 'I just want to be able to have a rough grasp of Italian,' I told him. 'Not because I want to get involved in intellectual debates with anyone. To be honest, my motivation is pure gluttony. Imagine if I stumble upon some out-of-the-way trattoria and don't know how to order anything delicious?'

Josh nods. 'You should do what I did. I got some Italian language CDs and played them in the car on my way to work. When I went to Italy last year, I was amazed by how much I'd picked up. It's Italian for lazy people.'

That concept suited me down to the ground. The next time I saw him, he handed over a chunky plastic box crammed with eight discs. 'Ignore the cover though,' he warned. 'It mightn't look it, but it's actually pretty good.'

I see the words 'Italian with Michel Thomas', then written underneath, 'Language Teacher to the Stars'. There is a picture of an elderly man wearing a suit and an obvious toupee. There are also gushing quotes from actress Emma Thompson about how Michel taught her everything she knows. 'Exactly how many actors need to learn Italian for their roles?' I ask Josh. 'Wouldn't you just need to pronounce your lines?' He shrugs.

Doubts aside, I downloaded all eight CDs on to my iPod. Then, as a lazy person does, I listened to about two of them.

Unlike other language instructors, Michel doesn't trifle with the basics. What some would call essentials—like, say, counting, days of the week, greetings and colours—Michel dismisses with a toss of his toupee. Instead, he jumps into conversation. So although I may not be able to count to ten, I can say stilted things like '*Quello è inaccettabile per me quel senso*' ('That is unacceptable for me that way') or '*Sto la casa stasera perché mi sono stanco*' ('I am staying home tonight because I am tired') and '*Volio la stessa cosa*' ('I would like the same thing').

Unfortunately, learning by rote doesn't take into account the variables you encounter in real life. I discover this when we go to the night markets in Villasimius. After feeling linguistically inept in France, I am now relishing being the one with the best Italian skills. I am probably showing off more than I should. We are walking past all the different stalls when Wil points to one selling loaves of nutty *torrone*, or nougat.

'Oooh, yummy!' Her eyes widen. 'Shall we get some of that?'

I seize the moment to flaunt my Italian skills. 'I'll order it,' I say, and swagger over.

A grandma-aged woman dressed in black is manning the stall. She seems to be exercising her psychopathic tendencies by smashing the nougat with a meat cleaver.

Grandma grunts mid-chop and looks up at me. '*Si?*'

I clear my throat. '*Volio la stessa cosa, per favore!*' I sing-song, giving the 'r's some solid vibrato. To make my point, I gesture to the woman whose order she is taking now. Wil looks impressed.

Grandma, however, stares at me curiously. She halts her chopping for a moment longer then shrugs, '*Si, si*', and resumes her work. I cross my arms, feeling *molto* multilingual.

A few minutes later, she calls me back over and hands me a bag that must weigh five kilos.

'But …' I protest, trying to figure out how to say 'too much'.

Grandma asks for fifteen euros.

'But …' I stammer again.

She points to the other woman, saying 'same, same'. This woman is happily patting her bag full of enough *torrone* to last until the next ice age.

'That's a lot of nougat,' Wil comments as she joins me. No shit. I realise I'm screwed. I did ask to be given the same thing and Grandma happily obliged.

I cough up the money, my cheeks burning. 'Damn you, Michel,' I mutter.

The next day I'm sitting on the beach near our villa, and it comes to pass that Michel works in mysterious ways. The others are at the house having an afternoon kip so I've come to catch the last of the sun and read a book. I hear someone trudging towards me across the sand and look up to see a man of about sixty wearing the ubiquitous red pants and no shirt. He's heading straight for my towel.

'*Buona sera, Signorina,*' he flashes a mouthful of pointy teeth. They remind me of a shark's.

'Uh, *Signora,*' I correct, pointing at my wedding finger. I curse myself for not wearing my ring. I had taken it off to go swimming. My Mediterranean predator is not deterred. Without asking, he crouches down next to me. I scoot away, trying to put some distance between us.

'I speaka no good English, uh?' He gives me a wink, his gold necklace glinting in the sun. 'But I-ah see so beautiful a lady as you sitting all alone and I say to myself, Angelo, you-ah must go and make-ah good friend.'

'Well, Angelo, that's very kind of you, but I must go. I have to meet'—I slow this down for emphasis—'my husband.'

'Aaah, but-ah you have no wedding ring on. Where-ah you from? Your skin, ah … *bellissimo.*' He puts his fingers to his mouth and kisses them. 'I think you are European, no? You're skin-ah, like German. But your nose and your mouth-ah, too delicate I think.' He smiles at me like a puppy with a ball, urging me to play his nationality game.

I look down at my book. 'I'm Australian,' I eventually say in a flat tone.

'Ha, ha! Kangaroo, eh? Koala bear, uh?'

I don't laugh. 'Yes.'

'How old you are? Angelo think you are this.' He leans forward, his wrinkly belly folding into rolls as he draws the number '19' on the sand.

I snigger in spite of myself. His attempts to woo me can't get much more pathetic. Unfortunately, he sees this as encouragement.

'No? What about-ah this?' he scrubs out the last number and draws a '23'.

I shake my head again. 'Angelo, it was nice talking to you but I really need to go and meet my husband now.'

He clicks the roof of his mouth with his tongue. Next he tips his head to the side and leans in.

'*Signorina*,' he whispers conspiratorially, 'Angelo know-ah there is no husband. Why he-ah leave a pretty girl like-ah you on the beach all alone, eh?' He gives a knowing chuckle. 'This is from me to you.'

I look on in horror as a love heart is drawn on the sand. Then, while giving me a look dripping with inappropriate meaning … he puts a withered hand on my knee.

I feel my blood pressure rise. I snap my book shut and leap to my feet, pulling my towel from under him. I stand tall, take a deep breath and yell in Italian that's loud enough for the whole beach to hear: '*Quello è inaccettabile per me quel senso!*'

Angelo is left slack-jawed on the sand as I stalk off feeling pretty damn rock 'n' roll. Sure, I may not be able to order nougat. But when it comes to dramatic scenes in the mother tongue, Emma Thompson, eat your heart out.

Tom's sister, Jess, joins us for the last four days in Sardinia, bringing the modern world with her. Armed with a Blackberry, mobile phone and work diary, she spends a great deal of time standing at the bottom of our driveway trying to get a signal. It's easy to see the family resemblance with her older brother.

She is tall, slender and has the same dark hair and eyes. Living in London for the past four years has given her an effortless stylishness. She turns Italian heads without realising in her hip-hugging jeans and high heels. Jess has a senior management job. Even though she had been frantically working to clear the decks to take time off, there is a spill-over of things left to be sorted out. Emails need checking, phone calls need making and decisions have to be approved. There is also a new-ish boyfriend who calls her practically every time he draws breath.

Greg has brought his mobile too and we have worked out you have to leave our complex to get reception. Whenever we roll out the door, Jess's phone goes off like an egg-timer and Greg busily checks his voicemail. Seeing them both preoccupied with work matters makes me feel better about still being consumed by mine. It takes the heat off me when I take my phone out too.

I give Tom a smug look. 'See, other people find it hard to just switch off too, you know.' He twists his face into a sour expression.

Like the rest of us, Jess has her scuba diving licence. So now that we have been on top of the island, we decide to see what lies beneath. We go out on a charter boat and have a dive. Afterwards, we're disappointed after only seeing a couple of ho-hum fish and a few rocks. That's when we figure it out: no one goes diving in Sardinia for the actual underwater stuff. Goodness, no. You go diving for the food.

As we wriggle out of our wetsuits, the boat's captain, Vincenzo, a nuggety fellow with white shoulder-length hair, comes staggering out of his tiny cab carrying a metre-long tray of *bruschetta*. He puts it down, grins warmly and rubs his brown belly, which is tied up like a present with belted jeans.

'Just a little something I prepare for you,' he declares, before re-emerging with two more plates stacked with olives, slabs of pecorino and a magnum of red wine. I look at it all in disbelief. Somewhere inside that two-by-four metre cabin

Vincenzo has chargrilled the ciabatta, rubbed it with garlic, crushed tomatoes and then topped the lot with olive oil and torn radicchio.

Back on shore, we return our gear and see Vincenzo holding court at a table on the front veranda. Spread out in front of him are two jugs of chilled white wine and a couple of bowls of roasted nuts. Looking jolly, or perhaps just plain drunk, he motions us over and pours us each a glass. 'It is all good vino here,' he says. 'In Sardinia, vino is just one euro a litre—cheaper than petrol.' I am realising this is the way things are done in Italy. Every activity is secondary to eating and drinking. And the cost of everything else is indexed to the basics: good wine, fresh bread and fabulous stinky cheese.

Vincenzo's attitude to the good life isn't unusual. Sardinians are fiercely proud of their local cuisine. Everywhere I turn there are signs enticing with '*Cucina tipica sarda*'. Delis are crowded with Italians from the mainland filling their arms with specialty groceries such as *fregola*, couscous as big as pearls, and *bottarga*, which is the dried tuna roe pressed into gelatinous rectangles that is grated over pasta. Two of the more unusual Sardinian specialties are *carto musica*, dinner-plate rounds of shepherd's bread, and *mirto* (pronounced 'meer-toe' with plenty of 'r' rolling), a truly disgusting liqueur made from the Sardinian myrtle berry. It's evocative of lavender, blueberry and strong naturopathic medicine. Much to Wil's and my dismay, Tom and Greg have caught *mirto* fever and have ended nearly every night chinking shot glasses and yelling '*mirrrrrrto!*' like a couple of drunken Russians. They then recite expressions like '*terramo mi dito*' ('pull my finger') from their Italian phrasebook and laugh hysterically. Not surprisingly, headaches are the order of most of their mornings.

But the one food that has really put Sardinia on the culinary map is *porcheddù*, or roast suckling pig. This dish, the stuff of folklore, proves to be elusive to pin down. The first time I heard about it was thanks to a tip-off from a Jewish friend. 'It's so good,' he told me, eyes flicking guiltily around the room, 'that I once had it three times in the space of a week.'

There are some strict rules about making *porcheddù*. The piglet must be only a few weeks old and must never have run around in the paddock, which causes the muscles to develop and toughens the meat. Sardinian chefs swaddle the deceased baby pig in sea salt, rub its flesh with olive oil and rosemary, then bake it over a fire. This produces a roast so tender, it's said, that you can cut it with a spoon.

We now have just three days to go before we leave and I have become unhealthily obsessed about finding a place where we can eat *porcheddù*. So much so that I decide to inflict my poor Italian language skills on the local shopkeepers again.

My unfortunate target this time is a woman at the butcher.

'*Buon giorno,*' I say. '*Dove è porcheddù, per favore? Mi mangiare la chena stassera.*'

I find out later that this roughly translates as 'Where is the roast pig? Me to eat the dinner tonight.' Not surprisingly, my question draws a blank. A few more failed attempts later and I find someone who speaks a little English. I pull out my map.

'*Si, porcheddù,*' she says. 'Here and here,' and circles two restaurants about a five-minute drive away.

Full of anticipation, Tom and I head out of town only to find the first restaurant shut. Undeterred, we consult the second option. This one's a bit further away and down a country road. The excitement reaches fever pitch when I pass a paddock of half a dozen plump pigs. We are in *porcheddù* territory. Pulling up outside the restaurant, I hear accordion music. In front of us is a courtyard with tables covered in stiff white cloths under a grapevine canopy. It's like something out of that Italian food movie *Big Night*.

'Can we make a reservation for dinner?' I ask, smiling at the burly owner.

'No, not tonight,' he waves his hand around at the set tables, 'private party'.

'Tomorrow night then?'

'Tomorrow night is Sunday. We close.' He states this impassively, as if I've asked him if the world is round. I feel like I am going to cry.

'But I need to eat *porcheddù*.' I can hear my voice becoming high-pitched and reedy. Tom gives me the kind of look you give someone who is mentally derailed and may snap at any moment. I pull myself together. 'Is there anywhere else please?'

The owner calls another guy from out the back. They consult in rapid Italian for a few minutes.

Finally he turns back to me. 'I think you go down the road to Ristorante Sa Bingia,' he orders. 'There is farm there and the food is good.'

We follow his directions and a few minutes later pull into a dirt car park. It faces a kitchen with big open windows. Inside, I can see a team of cooks arranging hunks of cheese on platters. We sniff the air and look at each other hopefully. I smell the rich scent of roasted meat An older woman in a peasant-style headscarf greets us at the door.

'*Porcheddù*?' I whisper.

'*Si,*' she nods. Eureka! We reserve a table.

When we arrive the next night, it is getting dark. About forty people, their faces glowing in an orange light, are gathered around a pit at the front of the restaurant. The perfume of wood smoke, roasting pork, myrtle leaves and sweet rosemary hangs in the air. Wil stays on the fringes. She is a vegetarian but has stoically agreed to keep us company after the assurance there'll be a salad option.

The rest of us walk over to join the crowd. They are mesmerised by three sizzling piglet halves skewered through the eye socket and out the tail over an open fire. As the meat turns in the leaping flames over a dirt pit, one of the cooks flings handfuls of salt at it as though he's feeding chooks. We stand watching in an awed reverent silence. All the other guests are Italian, but they are taking photos of this sight like foreign tourists. It's cinema for carnivores.

At 8 pm sharp we are ushered inside to a terracotta-tiled dining hall. The walls are decorated with rustic bakers' paddles, iron griddles and hand-painted bowls. The long tables are set with bottles of local olive oil and baskets full of rounds of coarse ciabatta for mopping up the oil. The deal is everyone has the same set menu for twenty-four euros a head—four courses including wines made on the property, *mirto* and *limoncello*. We have barely made contact with our seats when course number one arrives.

This gastronomic tribute to the pig begins with antipasti plates oinking with local sausage and tissue-thin prosciutto. White and red wines in carafes are poured into glasses. We are brought *bruschetta* topped with fruity olive oil and sweet tomatoes and *fegatini*, a warm doughy bread peppered with roasted capsicum. For our *primi* course we have fluffy gnocchi *napolitana* and ravioli with a rich roast lamb, pecorino and mint stuffing. It is so good I find myself closing my eyes when I chew. Normally I would devour the entire plateful, but as good as this is I remind myself it is not the reason I am here.

There is a gap in service while the star of the show is made ready. We are all in good spirits now, our glasses kept topped up, and there is a buzz in the air. Just when we feel like we can't wait any longer, the waiters swarm back in. Platter after platter is delivered to the tables, crammed high with every conceivable cut of roasted piglet. We get trotters, ribs, rump, ear and even, to Wil's disgust, a bit of the head with little piggy teeth.

The room erupts into a cacophony of crackling crunching, meat slurping and finger licking. The frenzied sounds are punctuated by the joyous staccato yelps of a pet dachshund at the next table whose owner is feeding it scraps. We join those around us diving in with our hands. We 'mmmm' enthusiastically, gnaw on the bones and wipe our greasy maws. Wil buries her head in her grilled haloumi, trying to think happy thoughts.

'It's a pork milkshake,' Greg declares mid-mouthful. As gross as that sounds, he's bang on the money. The meat is pinky off-white and oozes off the bones with a cutting look. By contrast, the crackling is as crisp as potato chips and rich with salt and herbs. It is easily one of the most delicious things I have tasted.

Sadly, though, it is so rich that after only a few pieces each we find ourselves unable to eat any more. I stare defeated at the leftovers as they're taken away. Our forks are poked unenthusiastically at dessert then I pass my *mirto* to the boys. The room is much quieter now. Even the dog is spent, lying under the table panting. I lean back in my chair, full to bursting, and feel rueful that after all this build-up the experience is over so quickly.

My phone beeps and I excuse myself to go to the bathroom to check it. Tom doesn't notice, thankfully. He's too busy chatting with Greg and drinking *mirto*. I look in my inbox. It's a text message from the guys at work. They have returned from holidays and are about to do their first breakfast show without me. I look at my watch and do the sums. If I were at home, right now I would be going to work with them.

'We miss you enormously,' it says. 'It won't be the same without you.'

I'm not sure whether it's the wine, the nostalgia or the late hour, but my emotions get the better of me.

I've really left. I hang my head while tears stream down my cheeks. The show is starting again, and I'm standing here on the other side of the world.

I blot my eyes with tissue, hoping they won't look red when I return to the table. Outside I can hear people laughing. I turn my phone off and lean against the door. The biggest mistake of my career. I wonder if I'm ever going to leave this nether world between home and here?

CHAPTER 4

War and peace

'WHERE THE HELL DID YOU PUT MY SUNGLASSES? I WISH you wouldn't put things where I can't find them.'

Greg, Wil and Jess grizzle and grumble around the villa, searching for the possessions we've managed to scatter everywhere. Bags eventually packed, we eat our last lunch together before heading to the airport in Cagliari. There is silence. Minds are already at their next destinations. Jess is thinking about her desk in London and all the work she has to do the next morning. Greg is silently rehearsing the conversation he will have with a colleague on foreign policy issues in Washington. Wil pushes her tomato around her plate, wondering whether their cat Snip has been eating while they have been away. The three of them are wearing the smart city clothes they arrived in and it's an odd sight after seeing them living in swimmers and sarongs over our holiday.

As the last suitcase is unloaded from Maurizio, Jess gives me a hug goodbye. 'See you when you come and visit me in London,' she says. 'You'll need your winter woollies by then. December is freezing.'

I laugh and turn and give Wil a kiss on the cheek. 'Do you think you can turn on a white Christmas for us when we come to Washington?' I ask.

'Be careful what you wish for,' she warns. 'Last year we had to dig the car out of the snow. You'll be with us for New Year's too, won't you?'

Tom nods. 'Yes. I reckon by then we'll be champing at the bit to take a load off and stay in the one country for a while.'

Wil grabs Greg by the arm, as he picks up their suitcase. 'You guys have got the rest of Europe to explore first. Please think of us slaving away in our offices, you lucky buggers.'

Tom and I are quiet as we get back into the car. Their holiday is over, but in a funny way it feels like the beginning for us.

I put my hand on Tom's arm. 'It's just the two of us now.'

He adjusts his sunglasses, wrinkling his nose at the reflection of the sun on the road. 'I know. I feel a little bit sad, but also really excited—like Sardinia and Provence were just the entrée and now we're on to the meaty stuff.'

I mull that over. Up until now, the sheer scale of our trip hasn't really hit home. I've been so busy thinking about what I was leaving and then looking forward to seeing our friends, I haven't thought much about the trip beyond Sardinia.

'I'm a little nervous, to be honest with you,' I say after a while. 'Really? Why?'

'We're not going to have anyone to share stuff with for the next few months. Who will we have a laugh with if everything goes to shit or no one can understand us?'

'Don't worry about it! We'll meet people,' Tom replies.

I fiddle with the radio, trying to find a station that plays something I recognise. 'We've left our youth hostel days behind us so I don't know what our chances are of making friends,' I continue.

'Look, it's a little nerve-wracking, but I find that exciting. We're taking a risk. How many people do you know who have gotten the chance to do what we're doing?'

'Yeah, I s'pose,' I say.

I start feeling guilty for being so negative. I look over at Tom concentrating on the road and pushing up his sunglasses, which keep sliding down his nose. As much as I try to pretend otherwise, I know he can sense my mood. The truth is, what is really worrying me about not having other people around is that I won't be able to hide behind the distraction of a crowd. My reticence will be easier to pick. I fear that will only cause more tension between us.

◆ ◆ ◆ ◆ ◆

After an uneventful ferry ride, we spend the next day gorging on seafood and gelati and exploring the beautiful cliffs of Positano. The day after that we are bowled over by the treasures of Pompeii, which is touristy but breathtaking. The following afternoon we reach the port town of Bari to catch the overnight ferry to Dubrovnik, Croatia's capital. We drive up the ramp into the ship. It looks like a Soviet version of the *Love Boat*. Dumping our bags in our closet-sized cabin, we decide a nightcap will help us sleep.

The bar takes up the entire top floor of the ferry. And judging by the decor, we really have travelled back in time. There's swirl-patterned electric blue carpet so gaudy it makes my eyes itch to look at it and the chrome tables have wraparound velour love seats. The only other two people in here are perching awkwardly at one of them. We sit down too and Tom makes a face as he tries the sickly maraschino cherry liqueur the barman recommends as his favourite. We flip open our guidebooks, which we've brought with us so we can work out where we're going for the next two weeks.

We're quite disorganised for the Croatian leg. We haven't even booked accommodation. All I know about the country are the scraps I picked up from TV news during the Yugoslav wars and from the Croatian friends I had in primary school. As a result I have an idea of Central Europe as a series of not very affluent countries where people speak with mouthfuls of consonants.

I push my book away and look at the red neon dance floor in front of us. There is even a white baby grand piano atop a small stage. 'That must be for grooving, ya?!' I ham it up for Tom with a mock accent.

'*Ne*,' he says distractedly, reading from our Croatian phrasebook. 'Let's see. *Hvala*—that's "thank you". *Ha-vaaaalah*. You say it kind of like "koala".' He continues mouthing words to himself for a while before tossing the book down in frustration. 'This is unbelievable! Every word seems to have a "z" in it. I can't even pronounce hello.'

The morning sun is just beginning to tickle the shores of Dubrovnik harbour as our ferry docks ten hours later. As we drive off the ramp, we have to slam on the brakes as dozens of yelling touts holding up signs saying '*penzion*' crowd around us. They knock on our windows, asking if we have a place to stay.

'Good god,' I say, stunned, shaking my head 'no, thank you' at them. 'This is like being in Thailand.' But as soon as we leave the port, the streets are quiet again. We agree to leave the accommodation search for later and explore.

The new part of town is modern with big white concrete homes, lots of new European cars, advertising billboards and swish-looking restaurants. It is sprawling, unplanned and soulless. I look at it in surprise. This doesn't feel much like an historical city to me. Then we get to the top of a steep hill. We pull over and look down the bottom. The sight makes me suck in my breath. Spread out before us against a backdrop of bright blue sky is the Dubrovnik of a thousand postcards. Built on a tiny piece of land, the old city juts out into the water, then twists back around on to itself like an apostrophe. Fat white walls, about twenty-five metres high, snake around the perimeter with medieval watchtowers on every corner.

Off to the left is a forested island where three big cruise ships are docked. I watch as the first of several dozen dinghies' worth of daytrippers motors across to the city walls. They ferry hundreds of people back and forth for tours of the ramparts all day long. Nearby, jet skis and speedboats trail waterskiers. Parasailers and inflatable doughnuts trail a white chop on the otherwise crystalline sea.

We drive further down, park the car and walk across the bridge separating the old and new cities. At the main gate is a plaque: 'City map of damages caused by the aggression on Dubrovnik by the Yugoslav army, Serbs and Montenegrins, 1991–1992.' The map shows the locations of burned buildings and the roofs that were damaged by grenades and gunfire. We walk through the gate and see stone steps which lead up, ladder-like, to a ledge above giant studded wooden doors over the end of a drawbridge. From up here, soldiers used to throw pots of boiling oil on invaders. We climb up for a bird's-eye view. The sun sparkles on the ocean and bounces off the walls of the buildings. It's a dazzling kaleidoscope of orange, white and blue.

Inside the walls we pass teenagers on their way to school, nearly all of them smoking and wearing the latest fashions. It's a stark contrast with the actors we see wearing twee medieval costumes. They dress as guards or prance as courting couples in tights and velvet gowns, putting on a show for the tourists. It's a bit naff and detracts somewhat from the historical setting. It must have been raining overnight, because I have to grab Tom's arm to steady myself as I slip on the white marble footpath of the main street, the Placa. Standing at one end, I can see where it runs straight as a ruler several hundred metres to the back wall of the town. Fancy outdoor cafés and clusters of pigeons line either side. As well as being wet, the footpath has been polished smooth from the thousands of feet that walk it every day.

'Can you believe how many people are here?' I say, marvelling at the crowds. 'It's just gone 9 am and it's already hard to move.'

Tom points up at the wall. 'Look up. You can see the shadows of people walking along the tops of the city walls.' The silhouetted figures moving along the edge appear as though they are on a travelator.

We stand to the side to let yet another tour group past, their leader holding up a pink umbrella so the rest of the group can see where she's going. It's a funny kind of irony. These city walls may have held back the Byzantines, the Venetians and the Ottomans over the last eleven centuries, but they can't withstand the invasion of camera-toting Brits, Germans and Americans. I lose my footing again as a fat middle-aged tourist wearing Bermuda shorts pushes into me then wanders off without apologising. Where's a pot of boiling oil when you need one?

That afternoon, we make our way to the place we have found to stay: a studio apartment on the top of a house where two generations of a family live. The woman who owns the place has just had a baby, so her mother—a pink-faced woman in her late sixties—shows us in. She has the plump figure and rounded cheeks of a fairytale grandmother. The stairs leading up to the studio are almost on a vertical incline and she stops every three or four steps to catch her breath and chat.

'Is this first time to Dubrovnik for you?' she manages to wheeze out.

Tom tells her yes. 'From what we've seen so far, you live in a very beautiful city.'

She leans her hand against the railing, continuing to breathe heavily. 'When I was girl, no shops here. We had to catch ferry to Bari twice a year to go shopping. Big excitement. Now, everything here you need. No have to go anywhere.'

'Have you always lived here?' I ask.

'I born here but then when I marry, my husband he go to America. I go there with him, but then come back here in 1989.' A cloud passes over her face. I assume she must be thinking about the siege. 'Those times, they very bad here. Many bombs, many gunfire. For three month we have no running water, we have to make clean in the sea.'

Our conversation leaves me wanting to find out more about what went on during that time, so the next day I go to a bookstore. Browsing through the history section, I discover that the same streets that Tom and I had been wandering around earlier had been among those pounded with shellfire in 1991. Seven out of ten of those buildings we admired from the lookout suffered direct hits. All up, 114 civilians lost their lives. I continue rifling through the books, remembering the teenagers we passed yesterday. Their older siblings probably had to dodge bullets on their way to school.

A voice with the slightest hint of an American accent interrupts me. 'No one really likes to talk about that anymore.'

I turn around to see a fair-haired guy who must be in his early thirties. He's been watching me from behind the cash register. He wanders over, handing me another book with more photographs showing the damage caused.

I thank him and open it. 'Why was the city attacked?' I ask. 'There aren't any military bases here, are there?'

'No, it doesn't have any military or logistical importance,' he replies. 'I think the attack was more a psychological one. Many people couldn't believe the Yugoslav army had struck at our spiritual heart. Croatians are so proud of this city—they call it the Pearl of the Adriatic, you know.' He pauses and narrows his pale blue eyes. 'Perhaps that's why they came, because they knew that ruining our most precious daughter would be the worst thing they could do to our people, our country. Now,' he gestures outside the door where a crowd has gathered to watch a string quartet, 'it's like nothing ever happened.'

I watch as he rearranges his angry expression into one of resignation. 'The repairs are almost done,' he continues, 'except for the monastery on the Placa. There's still scaffolding on that. That building dates back to the fourteenth century. It was such an important monument and used to have a library with thousands of books. I think about fifty shells fell on it. Anyway,' he shrugs, 'the tourists are back. Business is good.'

I nod, thinking about the eleven dollars I paid for an English newspaper earlier and the five-dollar cappuccino I had with it.

'We remember, but we do not talk much about it,' he says. 'We look to the future.'

I leave there feeling humbled. That guy, who's not much older than me, has seen far worse things in his life than I probably will. Yet he's able to put a positive spin on it all.

That night, Tom and I wander the riddled back streets of the old city searching for a place to have a drink. We squeeze to the side to let past people who are dragging suitcases on wheels across the cobblestones. Along the stone walls, flaming torches flicker off centuries-old wooden doors where peasants, Slavic nobility and Serbian soldiers have passed by. Today they mark the entrances to stylish restaurants and wine bars.

We are drawn towards the sound of music and turn a corner to find a pumping bar with a crowd of people sitting on wicker armchairs. They are watching a jazz trio. It's pretty entertaining. The bass player spends more time checking out the women in the crowd than concentrating on what he's doing. The young George Michael double at the piano is belting out jazzy versions of 'I Can't Get No Satisfaction', 'Your Song' and 'Girl from Ipanema' in appalling English. I look around. It's a stylish crowd. We could be in any modern city. The people are all extremely well dressed. The women are elegant with knock-out figures, the men strong and handsome with olive skin and sandy blonde hair.

But it's clear the Croats have a boombalada gene. It lies dormant in their youth like a ticking time bomb. Once they hit middle age … ker-blamo! The men explode into barrel shapes with bellies so round they could balance an entire tray of maraschino shots on top, while the slim-hipped women blow up into walking, talking babushka dolls. How the hell does this happen, especially in a place with this many stairs?

I wake on our final day in Dubrovnik and throw open the curtains. It's a stunning morning. We decide to make the most of it by going for a swim before breakfast. We climb down the hundred or so steps to the strip of restaurants along the shore. That's when I discover that the sand in Croatia is a lethal weapon.

'Goddamnit! Ouch, ouch, ouch!' I yelp, as I hobble barefoot across white pebbles that are so sharp they could julienne a carrot.

'Gotta love this European sand,' Tom yells over his shoulder. Being a boy, he is acting like the pebbles don't bother him.

I pause, rubbing one foot on top of the other, and watch as he wades into the clear water. He duck dives beneath the surface and freestyles out to a pontoon about twenty-five metres off shore. I go down to the water's edge, hanging back for a moment and then follow with a slow breaststroke. Eventually, I hoist myself on to the deck beside him.

He squints up at me, surprised. 'I didn't expect to see you come out so far.'

We laze around for a while, lying on our backs and letting the morning sun dry the salt on our skin. Back on shore, staff from the waterside bar are setting up for the day. They roll a red carpet out to the water's edge and put pillows on daybeds. I trail a toe in the water and giggle as striped fish swim up in the hope of food.

'A perfect holiday moment,' Tom says. He lies there for a few moments longer, then gets up and swan dives off the side. I go to the edge and stand there, feeling uneasy.

'Come on,' he says, encouraging me. 'It's beautiful in here.'

I am not a strong swimmer and usually don't like to come out to this depth. Tom treads water in front of me waiting. It looks like a long way down.

Then something clicks. I just get tired of it. Tired of feeling anxious. Tired of holding back. I take a deep breath.

Fuck it. It's time to start taking more risks. Slowly, I lift my arms over my head. One, two, three …

I bend my knees and launch off. As if in slow motion, I arc through the warm air. Beneath me, the sunlight shimmers like mercury on the top of the water. A split second later, I slice through it. The roar of cold white and aqua bubbles tickles my ears.

I break the surface and grin at Tom. He returns my smile, sharing the exhilaration at my small gesture of bravery. I flick some water at him and laugh. It feels good to let go.

◆ ◆ ◆ ◆ ◆

'Beautiful sniff,' declares the hotel manager theatrically. 'Just go pfffff, pfffff, pfffff—and they all dead.' I thank him and take the can of fly spray he's proffering. We have driven hundreds of kilometres inland to see another jewel in Croatia's tourism crown, the Plitvice Lakes. After leaving Dubrovnik, we spent a week exploring the island of Korcula, claimed to be the birthplace of Marco Polo. We had yet more days filled with swimming in clear blue water and lazing around in the sun. Now that we're inland, in the forest, the temperature has dropped from the coastal highs of thirty to less than ten degrees Celsius. Yet, for some strange reason the small cabin we're staying in is black with buzzing mosquitoes.

After fumigating our room with a sniff that's definitely not beautiful, we decide to head out for dinner. On the way to our car, I ask the manager-cum-exterminator to recommend a place that serves local food. He phones his brother to get the best answer. There is a lot of serious nodding into the receiver. 'Uh huh, uh huh, uh huh,' he eventually fires off like a machine gun and hangs up. He points us down the road. 'You'll like it there. Very cheap, but just like the food we cook at home.'

It's a dimly lit tavern with copper pots hanging from the ceiling. Looking at the menu, I see a day's worth of travel away from the ocean has brought about more than just a change in the landscape. The repetitive seaside fare of mussels *buzara* in breadcrumbs and cheese, bland risotto stained black with squid ink or seafood broth with *vegeta*, the secret Croat seasoning weapon that's really just MSG, is nowhere to be found. Inland Croatia is for those who like to rejoice, revel and gloat that humans are top of the food chain. Vegans and vegetarians best stay by the shore because the regional cuisine here is … animal carcass.

We order the simply described 'grilled meats for two' and a bottle of dry local red wine that tastes of sour cherries. Beside us, panting overweight men with ruddy complexions and bulbous red noses skewer hunks of flesh onto their forks between chain-smoking and inhaling shots of brandy. After a while, a giant silver tray is delivered to our table with an entire butcher's front window on it: fried pork chops the size of ping-pong paddles, an enormous crumbed schnitzel stuffed with ham and cheese, deep-fried battered steak (who thought that up? Elvis?) and a fat veal nut which the menu had promised was baked under a 'bell', whatever that means.

The sight of so much death brings one of the only other tourists, a fiftyish British man at the next table, to life. 'Platter for two,' he exclaims in astonishment after sitting silently with his wife throughout their meal, 'more like platter for a bleeding army.' I smile self-consciously, feeling like a barbarian and wishing we had a dog. I prod the carnage with serving tongs and find that underneath lies a mountain of chips strewn with brussel sprouts and corn, all with the absolute bejesus cooked out of them. There's also a mushroom sauce that tastes like licking a salt dish.

'This is a little worrying,' I say after a few mouthfuls. 'I can actually feel my arteries harden with every bite. The cardiac surgeons here must be multimillionaires.'

The next morning we try to walk off the coronary damage at the Plitvice Lakes. They are heavily promoted as one of Croatia's natural wonders but the sixteen interconnecting waterfalls are a touch disappointing. They seem on the weeny side to me. The most stunning aspect is the landscape of the national park that's named after the lakes. It is wild bear and deer country with a thick forest washed with the colours of autumn. The A-framed mountain lodges, lush woodland and aqua water of the lakes (something to do with a high level of calcium carbonate and other salts) make it look like the setting for a Milka chocolate ad.

Mmmmm, chocolate. I realise I'm hungry. I packed us a couple of peanut butter and honey sandwiches for breakfast, but we've been too busy looking at the view to sit down and eat them. Tom goes off to get a couple of coffees and I find a park bench near a school group of teenagers who I saw mucking around earlier on the wooden boardwalks, pretending to throw each other into the water. I fish the sandwiches out and curse when I see they've smooshed under the weight of my camera. Ah well, it all tastes the same.

Too hungry to wait for Tom, I decide to start without him. I'm lost in my own little world, looking at the birds in the trees and thinking random thoughts. I watch as a copper leaf spirals from a branch, drifting this way and that until eventually it settles on the grass. I take a deep breath and an even bigger mouthful of sandwich. I feel a fat globule of honey and peanut butter work its way down my chin. Absent-mindedly, I grope around in my bag looking for a napkin to clean myself up.

'Phew-wheew!'

What was that? It sounds like a wolf whistle.

'*Phew-wheeeeeeew!*' I jump in fright. That was louder and closer. I look around in surprise, my cheeks full to bursting with half-chewed sandwich. And that's when I see that I am being watched. By about ten teenage boys. And they're taking photos. Of me.

One of them whistles again and I feel my face burn several shades of crimson. My jaw drops open to yell at them, then I rapidly snap it shut after realising I've just exposed a mouthful of partially chomped crust. They've taken a photo of that too. The boys laugh riotously and continue snapping away like paparazzi. I smirk and give a little wave. Then I gather up my things and stalk off, face like a beetroot but head held high.

I find Tom inside the coffee shop and tell him all about it. He thinks it's hysterical.

'Those little ratbags,' I fume. 'I mean, to take photos while I was eating, for Christ's sake. What on earth would they even do with those photos? Who would want to keep pictures of a girl eating a bloody sandwich?'

Tom tips his head back and laughs some more. 'You've made it, honey. My wife, the Croatian pin-up girl.'

It was Tom's idea to go to the small fishing town on the Gulf of Venice called Rovinj, our final destination in Croatia. As it turns out he hardly gets to see any of it.

The night we arrive, after a long drive from the lakes, the landlady shows me around our apartment by the water, declaring it 'a place for lovers'. But Tom has to go straight to bed complaining of mysterious stomach cramps. The only thing that gets hot in here is his temperature. Tom sweats and shivers his way through the night while I anxiously stroke his forehead and look up the Croatian words for 'emergency' and 'organ transplant'. By the next morning, the fever has passed but he remains dizzy and nauseated. He barely has enough energy to get himself a glass of water. After propping him up with supplies, books and a DVD, I go sightseeing on my own.

I set out early feeling nervous about leaving him behind, but also enjoying the sense of freedom, of being able to do anything I want. I sit in an internet café for hours, emailing friends. Then I wander around the old town centre. Rovinj is on the northern coast of Croatia, up near the Italian border. I think it's more beautiful than Dubrovnik. The historical surroundings feel more authentic and far less touristy. Rovinj's old quarter is set around a small working harbour. There's a thriving fish market near the docks where the local fishermen bring their catches of squid, vongole and glittering fish each morning. By lunchtime most of the good stuff is gone and cats weave in and out of the stallholders' legs searching for scraps.

Rovinj has made its living from the sea for centuries and it seems to almost live in it too. Waves lap at the entrance of many of the dwellings that line the foreshore and small boats dock right outside some of the elaborate old wooden doors that swing open directly onto the harbour. I notice a strong Italian influence—there are pasta restaurants, gelato shops and a store selling Diesel jeans.

By the end of the third day, the novelty of being on my own has worn very thin. Tom is still not well enough to get out of bed and I've now walked every inch of the small cluster of marble and cobblestoned lanes. I've been to the church on the top of the hill and climbed the hundred or so steps up its tower. I've sat and read my book until I get pins and needles in my backside and I've searched the streets near our apartment for the source of a mysteriously strong smell of stewing prunes that permeates the air. Coming up empty, I notice a sign that says 'Zuzana Slezno: Pedicure' and decide to while away the afternoon by treating myself to a bit of girly pampering.

The sign is outside a white house with a heavy door encased in a metal grill. I press the intercom.

'*Bok*?' a male voice crackles in greeting through the speaker.

'Uh. Pedicure?' I ask.

'Eh?'

'Ped-i-cure' I spell out slowly, wondering if there is a Croatian consonant I haven't pronounced.

'*Da*!' The big door swings open. My eyes search up and up … to the face of a tall sinister man who looks like Uncle Fester from the Addams family. He is wearing a white coat and is rubbing his hands together as if he were a praying mantis. He looks like the kind of man you see on *America's Most Wanted*, the kind whose neighbours describe him as 'shy and quiet' but who actually has twenty-seven bodies stacked in his refrigerator.

'Hello?' he says again in English with a thick accent.

'Umm, I would like to book a pedicure please,' I say pointing at the sign. 'Is Zuzana here?'

He gestures behind him at a closed door down the corridor. '*Ne*. She is busy with customer.'

'Oh, well then. Can I make a booking for later?'

'Zuzana my mother. She give massage.' He pauses, looking me up and down, then slowly hisses air out of the corner of his mouth. 'I make pedicure.'

I inwardly freak. I can't imagine anything more repulsive than letting this creepy man touch my feet. I start to back away, but he takes a step toward me.

'Maybe you make booking for this afternoon?' he says.

'Uh, you know what?' I say quickly, 'I've just remembered I'm really busy today.'

'Tomorrow, okay. I can make then.'

'Oh, and tomorrow I'm busy too. Ha, ha, ha. Silly me. In fact, I'm not sure when I'll be able to do it. Thanks anyway. See you.' I turn and half-run around the corner, leaving him staring after me with one hand on the door.

I don't stop running until I find a bar next to where we're staying. I grab a chair in the garden overlooking the boat harbour and settle in with a gin and tonic. It's relaxing, listening to the boats clink against their anchors and watching the fishermen readying their nets for the following morning. I order another drink and sit for a while longer. The loneliness of the last few days begins to eat at me. Finishing my second drink I indicate to the barman that I'll have a third and lean my head against the back of the chair. This doing nothing and trying to fill my days is just a giant waste of time. I wish I had someone to talk to.

I look at my phone and think about calling my friend Kellie. She would definitely know how to make sense of all these thoughts that have been running through my head ever since I left Sydney.

Kel and I have been best friends since we were fourteen years old. She took pity on me because I was the only girl in my public high school whose parents forced her to wear the green and gold school uniform. We met in Mr Ezzy's science class and hit it off straight away, with a whole heap of common interests—boys, clothes and a world of private jokes. But six months into our friendship disaster struck.

I was sleeping over at her house one Saturday night. We shut ourselves in her bedroom drinking a bottle of port we'd nicked from Kellie's dad earlier in the day and hidden in one of her cowboy boots (she was very taken with Jon Bon Jovi's fashion sense back then). Then we got a phone call from Matt, a guy a year above us who I thought was particularly swoonalicious and so grown up for his, omigod, fifteen years. He was wondering, did we want to meet him and his friend down at the local park? We waited until Kellie's parents had gone to bed, took the flyscreen off the window and slithered outside.

I was on the front lawn waiting for Kellie to follow me when her mother opened the bedroom door. Her booming voice carried out the open window. 'What on earth are you girls doing?'

Quick as a flash, Kellie said, 'Oh nothing, Mum. Katrina and I were wondering how easy it would be for a burglar to break in, so she thought she'd go through the window and check.' Strangely, our parents didn't buy it. My mum and dad decided their sweet and innocent daughter had been corrupted and banned me from being friends with Kellie.

We were devastated. We were best friends. We decided to continue our friendship in secret. Six months later I was wagging school at the local shopping centre with Kellie and our friend Gabby, when we saw my mum.

'Shit!' I cried. 'We're so busted. I am going to be grounded for the rest of my life.'

We tried to make an exit but it was too late. She had spotted us and came over. 'Why aren't you at school?'

Gabby did all the talking. 'Oh, hello, Mrs Blowers,' she chirped. 'Our afternoon classes were cancelled at the last moment and we were just on our way over to see you in your office. By the way, have you met our friend Natalie?' She pointed at Kellie, who had recently changed the colour of her hair. My mum reached out and shook her hand. And that's how Kellie was re-birthed into my life.

For the next eleven years, whenever my parents were around, Kellie was Natalie. Other friends needed constant reminding to use her alias. The ruse only ended a couple of years ago. I told the story one morning on the radio. My co-hosts egged me on to finally confess everything and even got listeners to ring in. Every single one agreed that honesty was the best policy. That weekend I nervously went to visit Mum, poured her half a dozen glasses of wine and came clean. She thought it was hilarious. She said I'd get my karma back when I had a teenage daughter of my own.

Remembering that makes me smile. I look up at the sky and notice the sun is starting to go down. I rattle the ice in my empty glass. Reaching over to my handbag, I check my phone which is still set to Sydney time. It would be morning in Australia. I decide to give her a call.

'Kel, it's me.'

'Oh, my goodness! It's so good to hear from you. I miss you so much,' she says. 'Simon and I have been following your itinerary every day. Are you having the most amazing time?'

The combination of the familiar sound of her voice and the multiple G and Ts loosens my tongue. All my circling doubts come tumbling out. 'Honestly? Yes and no,' I reply. 'I mean, it's stupid—here I am in all these wonderful places and I'm seeing some incredible things—but I really miss my friends.' I hesitate. 'And believe it or not, I miss work.'

'Are you serious? What's to miss? It can't be the hours.'

'No,' I look out at the reflection of the setting sun on the water. 'I just … I'm finding it hard to get my head around having absolutely nothing to get up for or nowhere I really need to be.' I stop for a second and try to search for the right way to put it. 'I just don't feel like I'm achieving anything'.

Kel sighs. 'Ah, dear. Has it all been sightseeing? Or have you had a chance to relax too?'

'I've had the last few days on my own with Tom sick,' I tell her, 'but it's just given me too much time to think.'

'Oh, chicken, you'll get there,' she says. 'Leaving and going on this trip was the best thing you could have done. From what you've told me about the office politics of commercial radio, well, it sounded a bit like the cool kids' club at high school.'

'Hmm,' I reply.

'It's easy to wear rose-coloured glasses about these things too. I'd much rather be where you are than having to go to work every day.' She stops and her voice becomes more serious. 'It took a lot of guts to walk away, not when you were at the bottom—but when you were at the top. What you're feeling now is just part of the teething process. Give it a few weeks. I reckon you'll feel very differently.'

Tom is well enough to go for a walk the next day, which is our last before we drive back into Italy. We stroll along the waterfront toward a garden thick with pine trees planted centuries ago by a Slavic baron as a gift to his wife. My head is aching from my solo bar crawl the night before. I decide to open up to him about all the things I've been feeling. It's just the two of us now. I can't keep pretending forever.

When I finish, Tom is quiet for a few minutes.

'That's it,' he says eventually. 'I should have thought of this before.'

'What?'

'Well, it happened to me when I was eighteen. And I'd say it probably happens to everyone.'

'What are you talking about?'

'You're suffering from First Big Trip Syndrome,' he says, looking pleased.

'Huh?'

'Well, you've never been overseas on an extended trip like this. When I left for England to do my gap year, I remember feeling almost a kind of grief about the life I was leaving behind. I should have been lapping up the experience but instead I was pining for what I had back home,' he says.

We stop for a few moments and I watch a fishing boat return from its morning run, trailing a cluster of noisy seagulls. Tom shades his eyes from the sun. 'The reality is that things change. Life changes. Sure you can go home, cut the holiday short, but I think you'd regret it.'

We start walking again, more slowly this time.

Then he adds, 'I've always regretted going home early.'

'Really?' I'm surprised.

'Yeah, I missed my friends, but mostly I wanted to get back together with my ex-girlfriend. When I got home I discovered she'd met someone else while I was away. So I'd cut my trip short for nothing.' He puts his hands in his pockets and squints out at the horizon again. 'The truth is, that if you go home, it won't be the same as when you left. People will have moved on. They've moved on already. I know it's confronting, but the world turns whether you are in it or not, and things change without your permission.'

'Do you really think people will have moved on already?' I ask. I don't really like the thought of that.

Tom takes my hand and looks at me pointedly. 'Yes baby, I do. But the good part is *you* have forced that change. Not someone else. And the sooner you realise you're making the change happen, the sooner you'll be comfortable with it.'

Bloody hell, I think. This is all a little hard to take.

CHAPTER 5

One for the true believers

ALBERTO LEANS BACK IN HIS CHAIR AND STRETCHES HIS arms above his head. Tom and I do our best not to appear rolling drunk.

He turns towards me. 'You like-ah Italian food?'

His accented English has a syncopated rhythm like softly scatting jazz.

I go to reply, trying to enunciate my words clearly, but I'm aware that I'm slurring: 'Itshhh … my favourite.'

Alberto nods, unties his white chef's apron from around his slightly plump middle and gives me a lopsided grin. Then he continues chatting, either ignoring our condition or used to his customers ending up this way.

As soon as we crossed the border yesterday we cheered to be back in Italy. We were only in Croatia for three weeks, but how we missed the food and especially the espresso. During the next few hours of driving we made up for lost time, stopping at several autogrills beside the motorway for coffee so strong that I think it put hairs even on my chest.

We arrived late in Savigno, a town in Emilia-Romagna, the north-eastern part of central Italy. Many of the residents farm potatoes or pigs or work in sausage factories proclaimed to be the best in the country. Only a few thousand people live here. There is one place to stay, one small supermarket, one church and no internet café. Local life revolves around the large piazza used as a car park during the week and as an open-air market on weekends. There is a church up one end and two cafés facing each other. Early in the morning, as the church bells toll noisily (right outside our bedroom window), grey-haired men gather at the cafés' outdoor tables, dividing their loyalties between the two. They manufacture great clouds of cigarette smoke, sip espressos with grappa chasers and stare across the divide at their neighbours, like the Capulets and the Montagues. Savigno's women spend the morning shopping before the midday siesta. They bustle around the greengrocers and the *alimentari*s (food stores), suspiciously sniffing fruit and gossiping in line.

Savigno could be just another anonymous rural town. But it's not. The reason for its fame is displayed on a brightly coloured sign just past a narrow bridge leading to the piazza. 'City of the Truffle', it proudly announces to visitors. In truth it is not so much this delicacy but the best place in Savigno to eat them that brings people here. On weekends the main street is choked with gleaming Mercedes and Ferraris driven from nearby Modena and Bologna. Their owners have just one desire—a meal at Trattoria Da Amerigo. Its art deco sign hangs on a salmon-coloured building wedged between a deli and an apartment block, the same sign put up by Alberto's grandfather more than seventy years ago. Food reviewers from the international gourmet magazines have cottoned on and Michelin stars have followed. Savigno's secret is out.

Da Amerigo has the ubiquitous green and red Italian checkered table cloths. An original Faema E61—the king of espresso machines, made in 1961—gleams on the counter. A *dispensa* out front sells Alberto's *limoncello*, *zabaione* and cured meats. This is where we are sitting now, on our second night in town. We have just finished a meal of fresh pasta tossed with white truffles, garlic and olive oil, followed by local venison done three ways with polenta

(Alberto is a slow food enthusiast and says the deer-hunters are 'friends' who bring him whatever game they've caught every few days). For *dolce*, we had a flourless chocolate torte studded with crushed espresso beans. Just a typical Italian slap-up meal.

The reason we are speech-impaired is that our waiter matched each course with a local wine, leaving all the bottles on the table. I was hesitant at first. 'Do you think they mean for us to help ourselves?' But after a nod from the waiter we realise this is standard practice in this part of the world. They charge not by the bottle but by how much you've had from it. This means you can end the night with half a dozen bottles on your table, try a little from each and only pay the price of one. *Molto fantastico*!

Considering his Michelin-star status and popularity, Alberto is surprisingly laid back and softly spoken. There are no touches of the Gordon Ramsay about him. He is balding and his dark eyes are the kind the word 'twinkling' was invented for. It is after midnight on a busy Saturday and we are the only customers left. But although Alberto looks tired, he has gestured for us to come and sit with him.

'I love Italian food. It is the best-ah cuisine in the world. But I not eat it any other country than Italy.' He smiles paternally. 'I come to Australia two years ago. All very good food. I was invited to try-ah best Italian restaurant in Sydney but I say, "Why I eat Italian food in Australia, when I eat best Italian food all the time?"'

We nod our heads vigorously as if to indicate how crazy our compatriates are for even thinking we could compete.

Alberto stops now to take a sip from his small glass of *grappa*. 'The produce, the flavours, it could never be as good as it is here.'

We nod again.

'Where else are you eating while you are here?' he asks.

Tom is staring deeply into the bottom of his wine glass, so I shrug and say thickly, 'We only know about thish playsh.'

'Uh? Well I suggest-ah then,' I think he's winking at me now, but the room is spinning a bit so I can't be sure, 'maybe you go and visit a friend of mine.' And despite the late hour he picks up the phone and books us a table for the next night.

❖ ❖ ❖ ❖ ❖

'Can you see what he's written here?' It is the following evening, just after 7.30 pm. After a day spent drinking water and popping paracetemol to get over the effects of all those bottles, we're ready for another round. I'm using the dashboard lights to try and make out the map Alberto drew us showing the way to his friend's restaurant. Tom's driving.

'He did say this place was in an old abbey, didn't he?' I ask. 'I can't really remember much of what we talked about after dessert.'

Tom flicks the headlights to high beam and slows down as we begin to climb an extremely dark and narrow winding road. 'Yeah, he definitely said it was in an old abbey at the top of a mountain.'

We continue to twist our way upwards. After five minutes there's no indication we're heading in the right direction. There isn't a signpost or a street light anywhere. Mist begins to swirl around us. I start to feel nervous. 'Are you sure this is right?'

'Well, he said it was up the top of a mountain and that's definitely where we're going.'

'Yeah, but who'd put a restaurant out in the sticks like this? We haven't passed anyone else, there are no signs. We're kind of in the middle of nowhere.'

Our headlights are now barely piercing the thick mist. Suddenly a dark shape swoops in front of the car.

Tom slams on the brakes. 'Shit! What was that?'

I squint into the blackness. 'I think it was an owl.' I am reminded of those teen slasher flicks where the hapless characters are sent into an isolated forest then picked off, one by one, by a man with half a face and knives for fingers.

'Ummm, maybe Alberto is waiting up the top with a shotgun. What do you reckon?' I say joking. Well, actually, only half-joking. To act braver than I feel, I add in a melodramatic voice, 'Out here, no one would hear us scream.'

Tom groans, then takes a serious tone. 'You could be right. Maybe Alberto has lured us up here. Perhaps we weren't supposed to help ourselves to the bottles left on our table last night, after all?'

'Very funny,' I say, trying to make out the blurred foliage outside, which is getting more dense. We really don't know Alberto from a bar of soap. He does own a hunting knife. Maybe this is some kind of sick set-up. I swallow nervously.

Finally, we come to a clearing where there are a few parked cars.

'Perhaps they're Alberto's deer-hunting friends lying in wait?' Tom teases me again.

'Don't. I'm seriously starting to get spooked.'

We pull over and rug up. The owners of the cars are nowhere to be seen. Holding hands, we stumble in the dark across uneven cobblestones, eventually arriving at a gate that looks like it is part of an old fortress. I clutch Tom's hand tightly. We walk through and I hear voices in the distance. The only option is to walk towards them. They get louder. After about three hundred metres, a cluster of stone buildings appears. Tom gives my hand a squeeze. I'm still feeling uneasy. Then, outside the furthest one, a single lamp casts a glow on a sign: 'Trattoria del Borgo'. I exhale in relief.

We open the door and find ourselves inside a cozy restaurant. As we're taking off our coats, the owner, who's wearing a long black apron, whisks them out of our hands, offering us warm greetings. He seems slightly surprised by our presence until we explain Alberto sent us here.

'Ahhh,' he enthuses, then puts a hand on each of our backs. He ushers us to a table in a mudbrick room filled with black and white family photos and soft lamps. My anxiety has given way to excitement. Tom and I exchange glances—this is going to be great.

Almost as soon as we are seated he pours us a glass of the local sparkling wine called *pignoletto* which dances on our tongues like sweet champagne. Next he brings a little something to nibble on: two slices of toasted ciabatta with cured porky bits, salted and drizzled with rosemary-infused olive oil and sprinkled with parmesan. There is no charge for any of these, he explains, giving us a friendly wink. In broken English, the owner then recommends a red wine from the region, *gutturnio*. He describes it as very interesting. I describe it as brilliant. Would we like to try a few wines during the meal? Yes, we would. A collection of bottles begins to build on our table just like last night. I smile in delight. And then out come the courses.

For *primi*: veal *carpaccio* and *insalata di faraona*. I look in my phrasebook but can't find *faraona* anywhere. The owner rushes to the kitchen to ask for the English meaning and comes back holding a piece of paper.

'*Faraona* means gwee-nee-ah foh-well,' he says slowly and theatrically, his dark eyes shining.

'Gweeneeah fohwell. What?' We look at each other perplexed. He repeats it again, slower this time. After a few seconds, Tom laughs. 'Oh, guinea fowl.' He is saying it phonetically, pronouncing all the vowels separately as Italians do. The foh-well is served with a little balsamic on the side, truly the best aged balsamic we are ever likely to taste.

The owner looks proud. 'My father, he make it twenty-five years ago.'

Next he brings out *secondi*: beef cheeks braised in *barolo* and *tortellaci* stuffed with roast pumpkin and topped with diced pork. We swoon over our plates in a manner reminiscent of Pepé Le Pew after he mistook that house cat for a skunk. I mentally add all of these dishes to the menu for my last supper.

The owner comes back. 'Perhaps a very interesting *sangiovese* with the beef?'

We nod, yes, please. It's incredible. Clearly, 'interesting' means 'brilliant' in Italian. It's now 10 pm and the place is beginning to fill with locals. I suppose this late hour must be the normal time to eat dinner. A group of young guys, probably aged nineteen or twenty, sit down next to us. I watch as they pore over the menu studiously, no time for idle chit-chat. When their soup is brought out they lift their bowls to their noses, close their eyes and breathe in the aroma. Only in Italy would you see young guys wearing Formula One T-shirts sniff their *zuppa* with the earnest concentration of a master wine judge.

I am pretty full after three courses but must find room for the *dolce*. I choose vanilla gelato drizzled with the same balsamic vinegar as before. The owner insists on spooning me out a second helping. Then some local dessert wines he would like us to try before espresso, *grappa* and a few squares of local chocolate that he loves. We have eaten more food than we would normally have at two meals, but he hasn't charged us for many of the things he has insisted we taste. He kisses me goodbye on both cheeks and slaps Tom on the back with the force of a Bruce Lee karate chop. He hopes we will come back if we are in Italy again. He says he has some interesting rooms in the abbey grounds for guests.

'Tremendous,' Tom declares as I zigzag my way across the path outside.

I nod. 'God love Alberto! Who would have even thought this place was up here?' I stop and close my eyes. 'Oh, I love, love, love Italy! The food, the wines, the balsamic vinegar made by that guy's dad, the chocolates, those local guys smelling their soup, the food—did I mention the food?'

I continue extolling the praises of Italy for a bit longer, twirling giddily along the cobblestones as I do. My spirits are perhaps a little higher than they should be after all that interesting vino.

The path, which was pitch black on the way here, is now lit by small bowls filled with citronella candles. They impart a magical glow and a soft orange tang. The night is cool and crisp and the sky filled with hundreds of bright stars. And best of all? There's not a rifle-toting deer-hunter in sight.

In the car, Tom puts his hand on my knee and gives it a squeeze. 'That was the Italian restaurant of myth and legend, the real deal.' He lets out a deep, contented sigh.

We drive down the hill, which doesn't seem nearly so steep and spooky on the way back. I look across at Tom, who's tipping his head to one side in the way he does when he's searching for the right turn of phrase. It takes him a few moments, but eventually I can see he's reached a conclusion. 'There's just no other way to describe it,' he says. 'To quote Paul Keating, "That was one for the true believers".'

◆ ◆ ◆ ◆ ◆

Unfortunately, the magic of that meal doesn't linger long. A few days later, I'm lying in bed. The sound of birds and the morning bustle of the Tuscan city of Siena filters through the open window. Today, we're supposed to be driving to Todi, a hilltop village in the neighbouring village of Umbria. But I just want to stay here, under the covers.

Our lives have developed a certain rhythm. Every few days we wake up in a new bed, look at maps and guidebooks over breakfast, go sightseeing, rest for an hour or so, check the books again for somewhere to have dinner and hit the streets until bedtime. We start the cycle again the next morning, covering the things we missed the day before until it's time to leave. Then we cram everything in our backpacks, bundle them into Maurizio, drive to our next location and start again.

Since we left Sardinia, the longest we've stayed in one spot was the four nights in Savigno. We have spent the last couple of days here in Siena, with its medieval centre which has become a massive outdoor shopping mall. It's intensely crowded and crammed with high-end shops and Benetton stores. I haven't enjoyed it.

Also, the magic of going to a new place is starting to wear thin. This moving from town to town, the ritual and routine of unpacking, packing and unpacking, is beginning to make me feel like some kind of gypsy nomad. Any scrap of spare time is spent on logistics: finding laundromats and internet cafés or booking future accommodation. I didn't realise long-term travel would be quite like this. When I was back at home I would sometimes fantasise about being somewhere else. Particularly somewhere fabulous in Europe. Now I'm just craving some downtime. I thought I'd have endless hours to fill with reading, writing in my journal and vegging out. But because we're only in each place for a few days at a time, I feel under pressure to try and cram in as much as I can.

If I were at home, I'd be taking a mental health day. Tom, on the other hand, is already showered, dressed and halfway packed.

'Quick, sticks, up you get!' he pulls at the doona. 'I've told the guy we'll pick up the keys for the apartment at three o'clock and it's a pretty full day of driving.'

I groan and put the pillow over my head. 'One more hour' is my muffled reply.

'Katrina, I'm serious. You have to get up.'

I throw the pillow against the wall. 'Damnit! Just one more hour is all I'm asking. Will it kill us if we're late?'

Tom looks surprised. And annoyed. 'We don't have another hour.'

I roll over. I feel all out of kilter; the way I do when I'm hormonal.

'I'm sick of rush, rush, rushing everywhere all the time,' I rant. 'This is not fun! This is not relaxing. I just want a fucking day of staying in bed. Just one fucking day!'

I slump back down and pull the sheet completely over my head, creating a cocoon. I know I'm being irrational and losing some serious credibility, but I don't care. All I want to do is lie here, read magazines and watch DVDs. I don't want to leave this room to go and look at another frigging monument or church. And I'm over driving. Europe can get stuffed today.

And so ensues a barney between us which doesn't actually progress very far because I'm hiding under the sheets like a child, refusing to come out. Tom ends up leaving the room exasperated, slamming the door behind him. I lie and look at the wall. A half hour passes. I start to feel pretty silly. After all, we will have our own apartment in Todi for a week, one of the longest periods we'll be staying in the one spot for the whole trip. I can probably have a day of doing nothing once we get there. Good one Katrina, I think eventually. Now you're going to have to go out there and grovel. I gingerly swing my legs on to the floor and pad outside.

I approach Tom, who's sitting on the couch reading. 'I'm sorry for acting like a teenager,' I say in my humblest voice. He shuts the book slowly and raises an eyebrow. 'I guess I just want a day at home,' I continue. 'If teleporters were invented, I'd go back, have a day of relaxing and return all rejuvenated.'

Tom sighs and turns away. 'Look, let's just get to Todi and then you can do all the lying around you want,' he says. Then he looks back at me and his expression softens. 'I think we're both at the end of our tether with the travelling from one place to the next. We've probably both got travel fatigue. This is the longest either of us has ever been on the road. At the apartment we'll have our own kitchen to cook in and I don't think there's that much to do in town. It'll be relaxation city.'

I kowtow some more and we make up. With a lighter heart I pack my things and immerse myself in the rhythm of moving on once again.

A few hours later we are in the car well on our way. Tom turns off the autostrada on to a local road.

'Todi is supposed to have the most elegant piazza in Italy,' he says.

'What else do you know about this place? I haven't heard of it before.'

'Only what I saw from the photos on the internet. It's only little—a few thousand people. Our apartment is supposed to be right in the thick of the old quarter. I'm really looking forward to it.' He looks over at me and smiles. 'This is the closest we'll get to pretending that we live in Italy. We can get espresso from the same café every morning, buy produce from the market and cook up a feast each night. I think it's going to be exactly what we need to recharge the batteries before going back to France and into Spain.'

I grin back. It sounds perfect.

We don't get too much further along before we are forced to slow behind a convoy of tourist buses. And then we come to a stop. Another traffic jam. They're not uncommon on Italy's roads. I stare out at the industrial-looking farmland. 'This is still supposed to be Tuscany we're driving through now, isn't it?' I ask.

'Yep, certainly is.'

The bottleneck clears after a few minutes, and we pass through a village. I notice all the signs are in English. They're garish and are advertising set-course lunches or wine tasting. The tables outside the restaurants are teeming with foreign tourists, many of them wearing those horrible beige flak jackets stuffed with rolls of film that are so popular among middle-aged travellers. There are more coaches and quite a few Britz camper vans. 'Geez, I'm glad we're not staying here,' I say.

Then we pass an Irish pub. I gasp in disbelief. 'This doesn't feel like Italy at all!'

Thankfully, the English signs and the coaches thin the closer we get to Umbria. Soon we seem to have left the tourists behind us. Todi is not hard to spot. The countryside we've been driving through has been pretty flat, filled with lush green farms, vineyards and olive groves. Now a hill looms up out of the landscape, catching us by surprise. On top, like the icing on a cupcake, is a collection of stone buildings with terracotta roofs which, on closer inspection, are smattered with small white satellite dishes. Apart from that there's nothing to signify we're in the twenty-first century.

There are four elaborately decorated fortress-style gates at the base of the hill. They date from Roman times and are named after the cities they face: 'Romana', 'Perugina', 'Orvietana' and 'Amerina'. We drive through the last one and climb steeply past a van with a long queue outside—it's selling rolls filled with hot roast *porchetta*. A few twists and turns later we are in Piazza del Popolo, the main square. Elegant would be one way to describe it, but austere seems to be more fitting. The size of about two football ovals, it is paved with slate and surrounded by tall grey medieval buildings. On one side of the rectangular space is the Benetton store which seems to be a compulsory fixture in any Italian town. Opposite there's a deli, three espresso bars, a *pasticceria* and a *gelateria*. On the far side is the focal point: the huge Duomo with steps that slope from hundreds of years of use.

Tom pulls over. 'This is where Jens is meeting us,' he says. 'The bloke who owns the apartment.'

We don't have to wait long. A man who's been sitting on the Duomo steps spots us and walks over. Jens is a slight, middle-aged German man wearing an anorak, pressed beige trousers and polished dress shoes. He takes us just around the corner. As we walk he tells me he has a special affinity with Todi's piazza. He used to holiday here year after year when he was in his twenties and thirties, wishing that one day he'd be lucky enough to call a place as beautiful as this home. On one visit he was standing near those church steps having this same daydream, when he turned around, knocking into a local woman. They started conversing and fell in love. He married her not long after and has never left. The couple now own two apartments about twenty metres from their meeting spot—they live in the top one and the bottom one they're renting out to us.

I unpack, hanging up clothes in the cupboard and putting things in drawers, thrilled not to have to live out of my backpack for a week. At night we cook a simple dinner of spaghetti with a sauce made from fresh fungi we picked up at the greengrocer. I tear apart crusty bread from the local deli. Afterwards we walk a couple of doors down to one of the cafés and have thick hot chocolate. Already I can feel the cobwebs in my head clearing.

The attractions of the area beckon the next morning, despite my earlier desire to stay put. We visit nearby Orvieto, a slow food town that has banned any big takeaway outlets and supermarket chains, and it just happens to be market day. We buy fresh goat's feta drizzled with olive oil, still-warm ciabatta and a plum tart. Our impromptu picnic lunch is devoured in the main piazza on the steps of the Duomo with its luminescent carved marble façade. The afternoon is spent back in Todi, reading and relaxing. The slower pace gives me a chance to sort out my thoughts. I find myself drifting back to the conversation I had with Tom in Rovinj and wonder how to make sense of the whole First Big Trip Syndrome.

The day after that we explore Assisi and its Basilica di San Francesco, which is decorated with frescoes by Cimabue and Giotto. Nearby, there's a medieval abbey. We stay for a while and listen to the magical sounds of Benedictine monks chanting. Afterwards I sit on the grass outside while Tom walks around the grounds. I look at the big chunks of stone in the wall hewn by hand so many centuries ago. I think about the pews we were sitting on that were generations old. All this history makes the problems in my life seem small and insignificant.

The week drifts by. We take another day trip, this time to the hilltop village of Spoleto. It is charming, the most impressive feature the gravity-defying Porte delle Torri, a massive fourteenth-century aqueduct spanning a deep ravine. I stand at the edge. It's peaceful up here. As I look down on the woods below, I wonder whether I have been pining for things that will turn out to be pretty insignificant in the context of my entire life. Now that I am getting the chance to reflect, I'm starting to wonder if I've been overly romanticising my old life because I left on such a high. And like Tom said in Rovinj, if I went back now, things would not, could not, ever be the same.

My mood is lifted that afternoon—by the old-fashioned powers of alcohol. Jens has arranged a tour and tasting session of his friend's winery, Cantina Lungarotti. Despite the annoying Americans in our group—'Ooooohhh, yourrrr name is Katreeeena, just like the hurricaaane'—we have a very jolly time. Dinner is at a local trattoria. We eat wild boar *ragù* and platefuls of pasta big enough to feed four people. Over our dessert of vanilla pannacotta, we decide that after a few days in a row of exploring a break is in order. We'll spend the following day just hanging about Todi. The next morning, Tom goes out to explore the town. I take the opportunity to check my emails.

The only internet café in Todi is run by a fat man who tells charmless jokes in such a loud voice you can hear him down the street. He has a captive market, which allows him to charge through the nose for his facilities—about twenty-five dollars an hour. He is only here each day for a few random hours of his choosing. The rest of the time he sells real estate. Every time I walk past he has a different bimbo by his side (usually about twenty years his junior) who he is teaching English. He stops his latest lesson, which has triggered a bout of giggles from the Christina Aguilera lookalike he's tutoring, to ask me for my passport.

'Italy's anti-terror laws.' He points at an official-looking sign on the wall. 'We have to monitor every site our customers log on to and send a report to the government.'

Sounds like an excuse to look at other people's porn to me. He sees the scepticism on my face.

'I hate it more than you do,' he says, throwing his hands up in the air. 'It's endless paperwork.'

I hand him my passport and money, find a computer and log on.

I have a few new messages. I read through a couple from Mum and Dad and then I open one from my friend Josh. I notice it has an attachment. 'Thought you might want to hear how the show sounds now you're no longer there,' he writes. Down the bottom is an audio file featuring a segment that's gone to air since I left.

My cursor hovers over the 'download' button for a second. Should I be doing this? Will this just make my regrets about leaving worse? Curiosity wins.

It's about a minute long and at the end I feel confused. So I listen for a second time.

I sit there shaking my head. Yes, there's no denying it. The show sounds … exactly the same.

My old colleagues were getting people to call in with their 'wacky business names'. I know this talk topic well. We covered it many times because it always got a good response—like the hairdresser who named her salon Curl Up and Dye. It's up there with the other good talk topics such as 'nicknames you had as a child', 'best and worst pick-up lines' and 'embarrassing moments'.

I close my email and walk out. The most bizarre feeling has come over me. Suddenly, I don't want to go back.

I turn the corner and walk through the piazza, my mind in a jumble. What strikes me most is the contrast. The show sounds like it always has. But for me, already so much has changed.

I turn the key in the door and let myself into the apartment. It's the weirdest thing, but in the few minutes since I played that recording my old life feels so foreign. I don't want it back. It's completely unexpected. It's time for something new.

◆ ◆ ◆ ◆ ◆

'Happy anniversary!' Tom wakes me with a hug the next morning. 'Nine years since the day we got together, eh? Wow.'

I laugh. 'Good morning to you. You make me sound like a ball and chain.'

Prison jokes and life sentence quips aside, it actually is hard to believe we've been together for so long—and from such inauspicious beginnings.

We first met when we were both university students working part-time at a restaurant in Canberra called Bobby McGee's. It was billed as a 'themed' restaurant for hen's nights, birthdays and other parties. All the waiters dressed as costumed characters. Due to my petite size and blonde hair I got lumped with the cutesy roles: Miss Guided (surprise, surprise, a girl guide), Little Bo Peep with a crook and stuffed toy lamb and at Christmas time Mrs Claus complete with a red fur-trimmed miniskirt. Fabulous for tips, terrible for the women's movement. My ensemble the night I met Tom was a lime-coloured tutu with pink wings—I was playing the part of the fairy from *Peter Pan*. He had just come back after a year working at another restaurant to run the bar. Earlier, before I started there, he was the waiter dressed as the Scotsman with the *très* witty character name of Phil McSporran.

My first words to my future husband: 'Hi, my name's Tinkerbell. What's yours?' We got talking and I discovered he was smart (tick one on the 'perfect man' checklist), funny (tick two), studying to be a lawyer (tick three) and could sail (bizarrely enough, tick four— my criteria were very specific). Outrageous flirting followed. He'd sneak me double vodkas with grenadine to keep energy high during our shift. He would also help clear my tables. And then, after closing time, we'd run around pelting each other with ice and putting it down each other's tops. Ahhh, the romance.

Our first date was a dinner party for eight people that I threw at a place I was house-sitting. An intimate affair. Ever the smooth seductress, I asked drunkenly, 'Is this seat taken?' Then I plonked myself in his lap. Kellie, who was there for moral support, shook her head in embarrassment. Somehow Tom worked out that I was interested. He moved to Sydney not long after and we played long-distance love for a while. When I found a job in a Sydney newsroom we signed a six-month lease for a 'trial' period of living together. We even kept notes of who had bought what. A mop and bucket became our first joint purchase.

The trial became a permanent arrangement. We bought more things together. Eight years passed. Then, last September, in front of forty of our closest friends and family, we married on the shore of Sydney harbour at a spot where we used to have picnics and talk about our future together. I guess we're kind of like the punchline to a bad joke. Ever hear the one about the Scotsman and the fairy?

Even though we now have a wedding anniversary to celebrate, the date we first got together has more significance for us. Tonight, to mark that auspicious first dinner party in October nine years ago, we have chosen a restaurant in a back lane near the piazza. After a lazy breakfast, we head out to find a nice bottle of red wine to have with dinner. I leave Tom in a shop for a tasting session and wander the streets. There's a gelato store with a big queue out the door, so I join it and buy a cone with my favourite combination: chocolate and almond. I stand and inspect a decorative fountain while I'm polishing it off.

I can't stop thinking about what happened yesterday in that internet café. I feel awful, to be distracted by this on our anniversary. But it has really thrown me because the recording caused such an unexpected reaction. I know now that I don't want to go back. But the thing is, I have no idea what I am going to do next.

I bin my napkin and walk a short distance to a lookout. I can see down into the valley covered with vineyards and farms. I stare at the view but my mind is elsewhere. Why is it that since school I've felt this overwhelming drive to achieve? My twenties have been all about how fast I can prance around the career carousel. And I was doing so well. On paper I had everything I always wanted.

In front of me there's a stone ledge which has been warmed by the sun. I sit down and swing my feet over the edge. Ever since yesterday this rash of self-awareness has been prickling at me, a bit like that old demon voice. It's asking why I'm stressed and anxious when I've accomplished a lot of the things I'd hoped for.

People say stuff to me like 'you've got it all', and 'you're so together'. But success hasn't made me as happy as I thought it would. Secretly, I mostly feel the way you do after you go into a room to do something, forget what it was and stand wondering why the hell you're there. Something is missing from my life. What do I have beyond my career to be proud of? Achieving has become the most important thing. I feel my stomach sink. Perhaps that's part of why I liked having such a public job. I've spent so long with my head down pursuing career goals so I can appear successful and impressive to others that I've lost sight of what's important to me.

The sun brightens up. A farmer motors across a field on his tractor. By leaving my job and all my safety nets, I am staring my worst fears and anxieties square in the eyes. I don't like it. It's hard. No one warned me about this. I thought the most taxing thing I would be doing was sightseeing.

But it's suddenly hit me.

I'm not just going on a trip around the world. I'm finding out who I really am by saying goodbye to what I do.

At dinner that night our waiter pours our wine into big glasses. It's *barolo*, from the Tuscan town of Montalcino. I swirl the red liquid around and bring it to my nose. It smells like cherries and dark chocolate. I take a sip and force a smile. I am still feeling pretty low. In a way, I wish it wasn't our anniversary dinner. I really need someone to talk to.

'What's up?' Tom asks me.

I don't answer. I'm hoping that if I pretend I'm okay, the dark cloud will magically dissipate. But I'm afraid my frozen smile is beginning to look a little like botched Botox.

'Hey.' Tom takes my hand. 'What's up?' he asks again, more gently this time.

I dab at the rogue tear that's escaped from my eye. Traitor. 'I'm so sorry,' I spill out. 'I know this is a special dinner and everything but I just feel like shit.' I put down my glass.

Tom looks at me, concerned, willing me to go on.

'I've had, well, kind of an epiphany I guess you could call it. I've been doing a lot of thinking, you know, about feeling at a loose end being on this trip. And I've come to realise something about myself which is probably going to make you think really poorly of me.' I take a deep breath. Tom looks at me like I'm about to tell him I was once a man.

'The thing is,' I continue, 'I feel like I've strayed off course of who I really want to be. I just feel disgusted with myself. Like I have let achieving become the only thing that matters. I've put it before everything.' I stop and take a breath. 'Even us.'

I look up slowly now, scared at his reaction. But to my astonishment, Tom is smiling.

'This is one of the things I love most about you.' He takes my hand.

'What?'

'Most people are too scared to confront these things about themselves,' he adds. 'But I know that if I see something in you that I don't like, I don't have to harp on about it. You'll work it out for yourself. You always do. I could see you changing over the past year and becoming really wrapped up in your own success. But I don't think you're like that anymore.'

I am gobsmacked. I can't believe he doesn't think less of me. Instead, he's telling me how great I am.

We finish our dinner and the waiter and the chef come out and wish us a happy anniversary. We walk outside and our breath is turned to clouds of vapour in the chill. Tom hugs me close and we amble along arm in arm for a bit. Turning the corner, I see the piazza and exclaim in surprise. Dozens of cars are parked outside the big cathedral for the midnight mass. The golden light inside the Duomo is making the big stained-glass windows glitter emerald, ruby and gold. As we draw closer I hear the sound of voices joined in hymn.

We stand up on the steps, bathed in the kaleidoscope light from the windows. The angelic music swells. It's beautiful. Tom turns me towards him and lifts my chin. He gently pushes a strand of hair off my face and tucks it behind my ear. And then … he kisses me. One of those passionate Mills and Boon, weak-at-the-knees kind of kisses that, to be frank, we haven't had for a long time.

When I eventually come up for air and suggest we get back to the apartment (like, this second), I am overwhelmed with such a strong sense of love for him. I suddenly remember all the reasons why I stood in front of all those people last September in a flimsy frock while a cold wind blew and made a vow to spend the rest of my life with him. I'm so glad we're on this trip together.

CHAPTER 6

The Dordogne

ONE OF THE BEST THINGS ABOUT BEING ON A LONG HOLIDAY is that you can drink wine every night and not have to worry about being hungover for work the next morning. But we have probably taken our enthusiasm for this new way of life a little too far.

'We really need to schedule in an alcohol-free day—even if it's only one a week,' I moan as light fills our room at the leisurely hour of 9.30 am. (I still stir at 5 am, but can now go back to sleep.)

We have awoken once more with dry mouths and thumping headaches from the bottle of wine and shots of *grappa* we consumed last night, as we unwound from the long drive over the foggy mountains of Italy, through tunnels and along motorways, eventually crossing over the border. We had hoped to reach our lodgings in the Dordogne Valley, in the Périgord Noir region of south-west France, by sunset. But the travel time took much longer than we'd thought and we didn't end up pulling into the driveway of our *gîte*, or cottage, until nearly 8 pm.

As I lie here, wanting to attach myself to a drip of caffeine and vitamin B and resolving to detox, I know that tonight as we curl up beside our crackling fire, we are bound to start the process all over again. The thing that always undoes us is the fact there are so many amazing regional wines to try with varieties we've never heard of before or can't buy easily in

Australia. And I have been surprised to discover that things are so regionally specific—towns just a few kilometres apart stock completely different things. It's quite anxiety-inducing because I almost feel that I have to make haste to drink my way through the entire local line-up—after all, who knows when we'll be back? So we have developed a bit of a ritual: find a restaurant we love, ask them to recommend a local bottle shop, buy a mixed dozen, then taste our way through it each night.

This regional specificity doesn't just apply to wine. It's also the cheese, the fresh produce and even the bread which changes quite dramatically, depending on where you are. I learned that the hard way after searching the bakeries in the Piedmont town of Bra last week for the same type of bread we had in Umbria, only to be told they didn't make it that far north. I vowed that the next time I found something I loved, I would eat it until I grew tired of it.

I put this theory to the test only yesterday when we stopped at a French patisserie for lunch.

'We're on holidays—and we're in France, home of the world's best pastry shops,' I trilled as I ordered a lunch that couldn't be more different from my usual health-conscious salads: a *mille feuille* with hundreds of paper-thin slices of layered apple encased in a flaky pastry and a chocolate éclair with a gooey filling. Afterwards we went across the road to a *chocolatier* selling handmade truffles and caramels and bought a mixed bag, which we polished off in the car that afternoon.

We have also developed a pre-dinner ritual of nibbling on whatever local cheese we've picked up at the deli, something which would normally be a special treat reserved for dinner parties. Our daily tastings are now a real highlight. Satiny brie de Meaux and bitey roquefort, which would normally cost a bomb in Australia, are as cheap as Kraft singles when you buy local. And then there are the three- and four-course *prix-fixe* dinners which we justify by telling ourselves that it's cheaper to eat that way than order *à la carte*. It seems the long-running battle between my brain and my tummy has a victor—and my tummy has won.

The sunlight streaming through our bedroom window brightens so I get up, rubbing at my temples, and pad to the bathroom bleary eyed. I swing the door shut and pick up my brush off the countertop, trying to make sense of my hair. Absent-mindedly, I turn around and notice there's a full-length mirror on the back of the door. The places we've been staying in so far haven't had very good mirrors—they've either been small or made for taller people. Peering at my reflection, I flick on the light to get a better look. My hairbrush clatters to the floor as I drop it in horror.

'Fuck!'

There I am, in all my naked glory. And it would appear that somewhere between southern Italy and south-western France, I have become chubby. My thighs have lost their muscle tone, my belly's now a bakery window with spongy rolls at the front and muffin tops at the sides. My cheeks have puffed up like a squirrel's storing nuts for the winter, and my boobs—a mere cup size above flat-chested normally—have inflated so that my cup now runneth over. (Actually, that part's pretty good.) All the gobbling and gourmandising of the past few months has finally caught up with me.

Tom rushes in, looking panicked. 'What is it? Are you okay?'

'When did I become like this?' I wail. 'Why didn't you say anything? I am so enormous. I knew that my jeans were getting tight but I thought it was the damn driers at those *lavanderias* we've been using.'

I push past him into the bedroom and put on my cargo pants, which have a drawstring waist—perhaps part of the reason I haven't noticed my own creeping cuddliness. Then I slump on the bed, depressed.

'I think you look pretty good,' Tom looks at me from the doorway. 'Your boobs look fantastic. Frankly, I think you were a bit too skinny before.'

'Yes, my boobs can stay but this arse has to go. What if I can't fit any of my clothes? And what about when I get off the plane at the end of all of this? What if no one recognises me?'

Yes, what if no one recognises me? Like the time when I was seven years old and I'd just arrived home after visiting my grandparents in northern Queensland. I had spent the summer holidays there, the longest time ever away from my parents and my first solo trip in Grandma's over-indulgent care. Unlike Mum and Dad, Grandma didn't say no to lollies, chips or cakes. Every time I cleaned my plate she'd be at my elbow ready to spoon out a second helping.

On my last night, she and my grandfather took me out to dinner at an upmarket restaurant and, eyes bigger than my belly, I ordered and ate four quails. I was a very full little girl. And very portly as it turned out, because when I got off the plane Mum looked straight through me at first, not recognising her tubby daughter. When she did work out it was me, only super-sized, there was horror in her eyes. Oh, the horror. I was put on a strict regime of carrot and celery sticks for the next few months until I slimmed down. That memory has stayed with me like an internal alarm system of the boombalada that I am just a few roasted quails away from becoming unless I monitor what I eat and exercise.

I lace up my sneakers. 'We have to go walking. Now!'

He rolls his eyes. 'You're being ridiculous. Who cares if you've put on weight? You'll lose it again once you get home.'

'I just can't afford to get any bigger. I don't want to stop eating because there are so many more amazing things to try. But people are going to start humming "The Baby Elephant Walk" when they see me. My pants are beginning to chafe on the insides of my thighs when I walk and it's embarrassing and uncomfortable.' Tom looks surprised by this piece of information and, moments later, grabs his jacket.

The hamlet we're staying in has a name, Le Peytol, but it's really nothing more than a cluster of half a dozen homes. There are no fences so all the properties merge like a commune. The residents are mostly retirees—a few French and a few English, including Sue and Peter who own Les Trois Chats, the *gîte* we're staying in. It's a one-bedroom annex to their three-centuries-old stone farmhouse. You can tell they love the social interaction their guests provide just as much as the income we bring in.

We run into Peter as we leave. 'Off for a walk are you?' He leans his gumboot on the shovel he's been using in the garden. We are here for a week and will see him every morning out the front. He always stops what he is doing for a yarn—passing on local knowledge about the best places to eat (while rubbing his round belly and lamenting the richness of the food here), urging us to pick the fresh figs and raspberries in his garden or telling us about canoe trips on the Dordogne River, which we are too lazy to take. It's like having a grandfather and tour guide all in one.

Today, he's rolled up the sleeves of his crisp white business shirt and tucked it into a pair of tracksuit pants. Business on top, weekend on the bottom. The starched shirt is perhaps a throwback to his military past. He is a former fighter pilot who came here to live out his twilight years in a quieter manner. He's a short man, not much taller than I am, which affords me the chance to look down on his comb-over. Two cats and a dog play around his feet. I don't ask what happened to cat number three.

Peter points out the neighbouring houses. 'Next door is Raymond. He doesn't speak much English, but you'll see him and he'll say hello. We collect walnuts together and he sometimes takes me hunting. Up there,' he gestures to a house at the back, 'is where Celeste and Pierre live. They have a very beautiful daughter who's about nineteen. If I were forty years younger ...' He trails off and we take our cue to leave.

We take a path behind the houses into the fields, where Peter told us we could walk on trails winding through the surrounding farms.

It's ten o'clock in the morning but the sun is only just starting to filter through the mist that has rolled over the surrounding farmland during the night. No matter what the time of day, the light here has a yellow, hazy quality as if it is in soft focus. This morning it catches the dew on hundreds of tiny cobwebs that have been spun overnight, dusting the paddocks like sparkling snowflakes. We go through a tunnel of trees then up a small hill, and gaze down on a maze of country lanes snaking through lush farmland studded with storybook villages. It's all cobblestoned roads, quaint old farmhouses, pumpkin patches and castles on hills. The farmhouses in the Périgord are built from a golden stone which glows in the sunlight. I shake my head as I take in the scenery—it's a wonder the locals don't suffer from narcolepsy, the atmosphere feels so sleepy and idyllic.

In days gone by, castles must have been the new black in this part of the world. A half-hour's walk away is one of the prettier ones, Château des Milandes, bought by the American exotic dancer Josephine Baker and said to have been Walt Disney's inspiration for the castle in *Sleeping Beauty*. While she lived there during the 1940s and 1950s, Baker adopted twelve children from around the world. Also nearby is a castle at Beynac, built on an imposing 200-metre high cliff. The most recent Joan of Arc movie was filmed there and Richard the Lionheart claimed it for his digs until he was killed in battle.

We visit the Baker château and are blown away. It now houses a tribute to her life with showgirl costumes, gorgeous nude portraits and black and white photos of Baker wearing nothing more than a skirt made of glittering bananas and a cheeky expression. Then there are her bathrooms, one of which was done in gold leaf to match the bottle of her favourite perfume. I am incredibly jealous. There are fantastic gargoyles shaped like chimpanzees and pandas in the manicured gardens, and a falconry that puts on shows each afternoon. A particularly riotous part of the finale is when an eagle as big as a corgi swoops on a stuffed rabbit the trainer has glued to a remote-controlled car.

Apart from farming pumpkins and admiring the local castles, the villagers in the Périgord do a roaring trade engorging the livers of their geese and ducks. It's *foie gras* fanatacism with delis offering tasting sessions, roadside stalls selling jars of the stuff and nearly every restaurant around offering a *foie gras* degustation menu. Even the tourist postcards feature grinning farmers kneeling over some overstuffed goose with a funnel shoved down its quacker. Most peculiar. I find the thought of it a little cruel and don't indulge, even though I read a pro-*foie gras* farming article that says most of the poultry are gradually introduced to higher doses of feed—humanely, in other words. The article argues it is counterproductive to cause the animals distress because it affects the taste of the end product. I remain unconvinced—since the feeding takes place in the two weeks prior to slaughter. I imagine it would be difficult to gently ease the birds into that level of gluttony in such a short period. Then I remember my own too-tight jeans and reconsider that theory.

The following morning is a Sunday. We are woken early by the sound of cracking gunfire and the yipping of dogs. 'What the hell is that?' Tom asks. I shrug and grab my sneakers, figuring that as long as we're awake, we might as well get walking. A few moments later, we are deep in a grove of walnut trees when I hear the ricocheting of shots close by.

'Shit!' Tom cries. 'Let's get out of here.'

We hurry out to the road, hearts pounding. And that's when I figure it out: while some people play golf to relax, around here the blokes get out their rifles and go shootin'. Sundays are all about the very serious pursuit of deer and boar. By the side of the road we see a man wearing a fluorescent green vest over the top of his parka standing sentinel by a blue van. He is holding a very big double-barrelled shotgun. It's pretty scary. I'm not used to seeing people casually fingering guns as they just hang around the countryside. Frozen like a statue, he has his rifle trained on the forested hill in front of him.

'*Bonjour,*' I sing out gaily to break the ice and alert him to our presence. He blinks, then without moving from his position, slides his eyes sideways towards me. I beam and wave, a little too enthusiastically. He gives a curt nod. We walk fast until we get to the corner, then sprint as though our lives depend on it. Perhaps they do.

I double over panting once we've reached the safety of our *gîte*. 'That guy could have murdered us, bundled us into the back of that van and no one would be any the wiser.'

Later, when we tell Peter about it, he explains the local hunters have a special code with the rules of engagement passed down from father to son. Each hunting group is divided into different ranks. The man we saw would have been one of the more junior members whose role is to wait by the roadside ready to shoot the prey when the other hunters flush it out of the woods. Over the next few years, if he proves himself, the hunting group will vote to promote him and he will be trained by the more senior members until he progresses to being part of the core team. And so it will continue as his teenage son joins him and the tradition is passed on. That's the way this secret men's business has been done for centuries.

'All that talk of wild boar and venison is making me hungry,' says Tom. 'How about a leisurely Sunday lunch?' I suck in my stomach and convince myself that my morning walk (and mad sprint) has tipped the Jenny Craig scales of justice slightly in my favour.

◆ ◆ ◆ ◆ ◆

It's late in the afternoon when we finally leave the restaurant. Twilight is beginning to fall as Tom negotiates the curved roads back to our *gîte*. Feeling sleepy and content, I stretch out in my seat.

If I were back in Australia right now, my Sunday afternoon would have been spent feeling depressed and grumpy about having to get up at 4 am the following day. I watch as the last of the light catches the red roofs of the farmhouses and think once again about my chat with Tom in Croatia and the epiphany moment I had about returning to work.

What Tom said to me was spot on. I have forced the change. It's snowballed into an avalanche of other changes which have caught me completely off guard and have been painful to confront. I love having the luxury of breathing space to think, to get some perspective, clear my head and figure out what I want from life. Wouldn't it be great if this holiday feeling could last forever. The germ of an idea begins to take seed.

'Let me just put something out there,' I say, turning to look at Tom. 'Instead of going home at the end of all this, there is another option. It's a little bit left field, but it's something we talked about a long time ago.'

'Yes?' He slowly raises an eyebrow.

'Well, this overseas experience doesn't really have to end after six months, does it?' I reach over and stroke his hair. 'The idea that I've got is this—you've got a British passport and we're married now, which must give me some entitlements. So,' I suck in a deep breath, feeling the thrill of butterflies in my stomach, 'instead of going home to Sydney at the end of the trip, why don't we move to London?'

CHAPTER 7

Spanish steps

THEY SAY THAT A WOMAN ALWAYS KNOWS WHEN SHE becomes pregnant. It's part of her inner psyche, a female intuition that signals when there's a new life growing inside her. My gut feeling is that I'm not. But ever since we arrived in Spain, in Toledo, I've been having other gut feelings that signal that I might be. Like last night, when we went to a tapas bar near our *pension* and I caught a whiff of the cured legs of *jamón*, hoofs still intact, hanging from the ceiling. Tom barely made it out of the way as I rushed to the bathroom to dry-retch. And there was that same nausea yesterday morning and again today when I woke up. This is not the only sign that I may have a tortilla in the oven. I have also missed my period, I keep having dizzy spells and have absolutely no energy.

Toledo, a biggish town of about seventy-five thousand which is forty-five or so minutes south of Madrid, wasn't on our itinerary. But now that we have ended up here as a result of poor planning, I'm glad of the chance to spend a few nights in a place I hadn't expected to see.

After farewelling Sue and Peter at Les Trois Chats, we spent a week touring the Basque country just over the Spanish border, wandering around the beautiful beaches of San Sebastián and marvelling at the space-age Guggenheim Museum in Bilbao. Then we were hoping to stay a couple of nights in Salamanca. Tom had fond memories of it and wanted to see what it is like now. But Halloween took care of that. I've always thought of the holiday as one for kids, American kids at that, but it seems the residents of Salamanca feel differently. All the accommodation was completely booked out for Halloween festivals. Fearing an uncomfortable night in Maurizio, we consulted our map and it turned out Toledo was one of the few places left on the way to Seville, our next stop, where the hotels weren't chockers with trick-or-treaters.

As unprepared for the language as we were for our accommodation options, we spent most of the long drive listening to a Spanish language CD. Clearly it was made for Brits heading to the Costa del Sol as it focused on such useful phrases as 'one lager please', 'I'd like a jug of sangria' and 'this food is too spicy'. It kept us entertained enough through the hours of driving, first through the mountainous landscape of the north with grass so green it looks like astro turf, then through seemingly endless miles of dead-flat plains that are typical of Spain's interior. Just as we were about to start climbing the walls with boredom, we saw a smallish hill breaking up the landscape. Further up was the grand city gates of Toledo, surrounded on three sides by a river.

As Robin often explained to Batman, this town is very holy. It has mosques beside synagogues beside cathedrals. Captured by the Romans, the Visigoths, then the Arabs, Spain's former capital became an intercultural bubble-and-squeak and is thought to be one of the few places where Arabs, Christians and Jews lived in relative harmony (for a while at least). We are staying within the city walls in an area riddled with slanted alleys lined with buildings of an unusual blend of Arab and Gothic styles. This is apparently very exciting for architecture buffs but is causing us to get lost.

'Bloody hell. The guidebooks say they designed the medina to confuse invaders,' Tom says, after we take yet another wrong turn into a lane with barely enough breathing space for both of us. 'You can certainly see how that happened. All of these lanes look the same. Look,' he fingers a series of long grooves carved into the sides of the walls, 'scrape marks from the cars that misjudged the distance. Those poor buggers.' We laugh, remembering that pesky roadside step in the Sardinian hill town.

We find a small greengrocer and buy apples for a mid-morning snack. I chomp on mine thoughtfully as we walk out.

'Everyone smokes, even more so than in France,' I say. 'Did you see that woman who served us? She was puffing away while she was handling the food. She didn't even take her fag out of her mouth to weigh our apples. And all the women here seem to speak in really deep, husky voices.'

'That would probably be the nicotine effect,' Tom laughs.

I have also noticed that Spaniards seem to be a rowdier, less reserved bunch than the French. They have no qualms about openly staring at me, and everyone's very touchy feely. They push past me in the street, elbow me out of the way as I stand at the counters to be served, and waiters and shopkeepers give me mini-hugs. They look as though they embody a zest for life—many sport the round bellies of enthusiastic eaters and they yell happily and heartily to each other across the streets or from apartment windows. Apart from Wednesday and Thursday nights, when they take the evenings off, Spaniards seem to treat after dark like it's party central. We have taken to wearing earplugs to bed to block out the noise of people going to restaurants well after midnight, having passionate arguments on the road or singing at the top of their lungs outside our hotel balcony at 3 am.

We pass a shop that is so crowded people look as though they are fighting to get in. There are Spaniards and non-Spaniards alike lining up to get to the counter. I look up at the sign: 'Toledo Mazapán'. Aside from being famous for being the home of the painter El Greco (there is El Greco everything here—cafés named after him, T-shirts, plates and spoons sporting his image), Toledo is also famous for being marzipan enthusiasts what Périgord is to lovers of *foie gras*.

I squeeze past a group of people and peer through the window. I have a tradition of buying my dad a little tray of glossy marzipan sweets shaped like brightly coloured fruits every

Christmas. It all started when he filled my six-year-old head with the story that Santa was a marzipan nut and I would be guaranteed fabulous presents if I left him a large plateful with a double scotch. I figure Dad would get a kick out of receiving the crème de la crème of marzipan, so we join the queue. I watch the dozen or so women behind the counter in white aprons and chefs' hats arrange ornately decorated *delicias*—discs of marzipan buttered with splodges of sweetened egg yolk then folded into soft half-moons.

'Marzipan is basically just almonds and sugar,' I say to Tom as we wait. 'But I'm pretty sure neither of those crops is grown here. It looked like it was all olive trees and grape vines to me. Why the hell is marzipan such a local specialty?'

As it turns out, there's a simple explanation. Anywhere in the world where there's an Arab influence you'll find good confectionery. I find out later that when the Arabs arrived in Toledo at the beginning of the eighth century they stocked the town with sugar and almonds. It seems the custom has stuck. Or perhaps it's just that the dads of Toledo tell their kids porkies about Santa too? Spaniards take their *mazapán* so seriously a law has been passed by the government dictating its ingredients.

The highest quality, the one I'm buying now, has to be made from at least fifty per cent almonds. There's a frenzy being whipped up by the hordes in this shop. Some of the older women are ordering dozens at a time and staggering out with armfuls of white boxes. What are they going to do with it all?

The sickly sweet smell of all that *mazapán* has made me feel green around the gills again and, after making my purchase, I have to rush outside to gulp down some air.

'Could you be?' Tom asks, looking nervous, and then gives a definite shake of his head. 'No,' he concludes taking a mental check to reassure himself, 'we've definitely been careful. It's impossible. Isn't it?'

'Well, technically, it's not impossible,' I say. 'The pill's only supposed to be ninety-eight per cent effective or something and

I've also heard about people who got pregnant even though they used condoms.'

Tom's eyes turn saucer-esque. 'Not reassuring.'

A few shops down, there's a chemist. We decide to end the speculation and buy a pregnancy test. Everything is behind the counter, except for a set of scales, which calculates your weight for twenty euro cents. I pull in my stomach and sidestep the scales, deciding ignorance is bliss for now. I ask the woman at the counter, dressed in a severe looking white coat, if she speaks English.

'No,' is her unapologetic reply.

'Shit,' I say, thumbing through our phrasebook. 'Medical section, medical section. Where is it? Ah.' I find it and look up the word for pregnancy: *embarazo*. Yes, I certainly would be red-faced if it turned out I was up the duff after using contraception. There's nothing in here for pregnancy test though, so I decide to improvise, putting together the words for 'pregnancy' and 'test'.

I clear my throat. '*Deseo intentar embarazo?*' I ask. Her eyebrows shoot up and she looks from Tom back to me, astonished. I say it again, lisping the 'z' like they do on our language CD. She starts laughing hysterically. What have I said? I wonder as my cheeks start to flush. Tom looks as confused as I am. The other people in the shop are looking at us now too, quietly laughing to themselves. The pharmacist calls out another woman from the back room.

'I can speak little English,' she says to us. What a relief.

'Fantastic. What I was trying to ask for is a pregnancy test,' I say, aware now that everyone in the store is listening. '*Deseo intentar embarazo*. Is that how you say it?' I ask, pointing at the words in my phrasebook. She cracks up too and the pair of them laugh so hard, it looks as though they may need to avail themselves of the incontinence pads on the shelf behind them.

'No,' she finally gasps, dabbing at her eyes. 'What you just say is "I want to *try* pregnancy"!'

Damn phrasebooks. Test might mean two different things in English but *intentar* clearly only means one in Spanish: to try. She probably thought Tom and I had mistaken her chemist for a honeymooner's hotel.

We leave meekly, test in hand, and go straight back to our room. We need to know the answer right away.

'Imagine if you were,' moans Tom. 'No more wine or soft cheese. Oh God, I've just realised you've been eating and drinking heaps of that sort of stuff over the last few weeks. What if you were pregnant then? Not a great start to life for a baby.'

I lock myself in the bathroom and undo the wrapper. I have never had to take one of these before, so I have no idea what I'm doing. The instructions are all in Spanish except for a sketchy diagram showing a woman with black lines spurting from between her legs on to a stick. I guess that's supposed to be wee then. What if I miss? Gross. Feeling very icky, I hold the plastic stick by its end like it's a poisonous snake and take aim. One second, two seconds, three seconds, and done. Now I just have to wait a few minutes. Two lines means preggers, one line means I'm home free.

I go out and sit on the bed beside Tom and watch as he drums his fingers nervously on the bedside table.

'I'd have to have it. I mean there's no reason not to.'

'It wouldn't be all bad,' Tom agrees, 'I'm thirty-two now—that's a good age for becoming a dad.' He drums his fingers some more.

The clock beeps. Time for the moment of truth. I go into the bathroom and take a deep breath. The stick is on the basin top. I am shaking as I pick it up. Could this be the moment I'll tell my future child about? Finding out about his or her existence in a hotel room in Toledo? The little display screen is glinting at me under the lights, teasing me to take a look. Bugger it, here goes. I pick it up. One line.

'I'm not pregnant,' I shout out to Tom in a flat voice. I must just have a bug. It's funny, but I feel strangely disappointed. I certainly wasn't trying to get pregnant, but the thought of it didn't fill me with dread. In fact, I have surprised myself by starting to warm to the idea. All through my early twenties I was adamant I didn't want kids at all, telling anyone who would listen that I didn't have a maternal bone in my body. In the last few years, that has gradually started to change. Now I find myself looking at babies in shopping centres and thinking 'cute' instead of 'hideous'. But there's always been the worry of finding the 'right time' to take time out of my career to raise children. I guess it's only now the career focus is starting to subside that the thought of kids is becoming appealing. Tom comes in and gives me a big hug.

'I was starting to get used to the idea,' he says. 'I mean, I'm glad we're not—it would be good to plan for being pregnant and eat all the right foods and everything—but it wouldn't have been so bad.' I nod, thinking how strange it is that my thoughts on something I used to be so passionately against have changed so much. Perhaps it's all part of growing up.

As I leave the bathroom I catch sight of my newly rounded figure in the mirror. It's time I stopped eating for two.

The next day, we pack up Maurizio for the drive south to Seville. Tom taps the dashboard. 'He's holding up well. Ten thousand kilometres clocked up in the last two months.' A group of pedestrians skittle in front of our car and he honks the horn to clear a small path to let our car through the narrow street.

'Ummm, are you sure you don't need me to get out to guide you?' I ask nervously as we inch our way past another set of scrape marks on the wall. 'We seem to be the only car using these lanes. I'm not sure they're meant for anything wider than a donkey.'

'No, it should be right, I'm thinking of Sardinia. Don't worry. I'm just going to take it very slow.' He gives the horn another beep as we enter a crowded square out the front of a church thick with tourists who, not unreasonably, feel they should have priority.

People scurry, staring at us like we are insane for even contemplating driving on roads as slippery and narrow as these. I wind down my window and see an American tourist gawp at us in shock. And then—maybe because he has spotted Maurizio's French registration markings or perhaps it's because he can see the sizeable wine cellar on our backseat—he turns to his companion and exclaims in that quiet dignified manner that American travellers are renowned for, 'There goes a very brave Frenchman!'

◆ ◆ ◆ ◆ ◆

Every time we hit a town that we're staying in for more than a couple of nights, we scope out the bars and restaurants that come most highly recommended and then keep going back to our favourites. I didn't realise how much of a creature of habit I was. Perhaps it is because we don't have a home base so we're craving routine in any form.

We've been coming to this tapas bar for the last three nights we have been in Seville. And it is highly likely we'll come back here at least two of the four nights we have left. We picked this place out as our favourite the day we arrived. There seems to be one bar for every *Sevillano* and many of them have loads of character. But, to us, this place has an air of authenticity that sets it apart from the others.

Bar Las Teresas is small and moody with chocolate furniture, vintage bullfighting advertisements on the walls and black and white signed photographs of long-gone flamenco stars. It's cosy and warm, the sort of place you can settle into for the night. Just around the corner are the Andalusian capital's two most recognised monuments, the Alcazar and the tallest thing in town, the Giralda Tower. Apparently the guy who converted the Giralda from an old minaret into a cathedral bell tower also built thirty-five ramps inside so he could ride his horse all the way to the top. Horses still hang around outside the tower entrance shackled to open carriages festooned with flowers and filled with tourists on sightseeing jaunts. Unfortunately, this means that all the major attractions smell of horse shit. In fact, all of Seville has a peculiar acrid stench, like animal urine and burning tyres. It sears the inside of my nostrils and catches me in the back of my throat. It's a strange contrast, because apart from the stink it is a really beautiful and stylish place.

Each time we come to Bar Las Teresas we sit at the same high stools at the bar. But even though this is our third night in a row and we're being served by the same stern-faced sixty-something men clad in starched white shirts, black bow ties and white aprons, they have barely acknowledged us. One strides over silently to give us the menu on a small card. These same barmen, who have faces of stone when they see us, transform into jovial uncles at the sight of their regulars, who are treated like long-lost family. Hugs are meted out to young couples, men are greeted with kisses on both cheeks and the bar's resident eccentric—a camp seventyish man with slicked-back hair, wearing a blazer and cravat, heavy Elvis Costello-style glasses and a gold pinky ring—gets affectionate pats on the back as he stands by the bar each night French kissing his fat-as-a-sausage cigar.

We have tried smiling at the bar staff but still haven't managed to crack their brusque veneer. That's despite the fact we've left tips each night and even ordered the special *platos* like *ibérico jamón*, one of the priciest and highly prized cured hams. Their tapas is fantastic and the atmosphere is so convivial, yet I am painfully aware we are outsiders sitting in our own silent bubble at the far end of the bar. It's churlish but I love this place and I want the old blokes to love us too. So tonight I am using the last weapon in my arsenal.

The barman approaches to take our order.

'Do you have any Pedro Ximenez?' I ask in Spanish, referring to the syrupy-sweet sherry that's produced in the region of Jerez in the south.

'*Sí,*' he grunts, as he wipes away the total of our previous order from the countertop and chalks in a new one. At many tapas bars, the bartenders miraculously manage to keep a running tally of who's ordered what in their heads. At others, they keep tabs by counting up the number of toothpicks from the items you've eaten. Either way, I marvel at their ability to stay on top of it during peak hours when there could be hundreds of people in the bar.

We have discovered there are two ways of ordering tapas. You either choose from one of the *platos* displayed on the counter, which contain ready-made items such as stuffed tortilla or paper-thin *jamón* wrapped around squares of melon. Or you can order items off the board which can be quite fancy, things like slow-simmered beef cheeks, *patatas bravas* (fried potatoes in a spicy sauce), omelette with *gamba y hongos* (shrimp and mushrooms), or roast rabbit glazed in sticky balsamic vinegar.

The barman gets his knife out and wipes it against his apron as he waits for me to order. It's an impressive knife with a long thin blade which he uses to slice to order the cured hams that hang from the ceiling. Displayed behind him on the wall are the old knives whose blades have been worn to the point where they can no longer be used—the ghosts of tapas past. One of the knives is dated 1984, but I think this bar is at least two hundred years older than that.

'*Sí*, Pedro Ximenez,' he repeats again, giving a curt wave at the shelf of bottles behind him, while looking over my head to break into a warm smile as another group of *Sevillanos* arrives. Enough. I get ready to lock and load my big gun of international diplomacy.

'*Qué usted recomienda?*' I ask, praying I've got the pronunciation down.

'Eh?' he says, putting away his knife.

'*Qué usted recomienda?*' I repeat.

'Hmmm,' he says tilting his head, and then he brightens, saying in that rapid-fire way which is habitual for Spaniards, '*Sí, sí, sí, sí, sí!*' as he pulls down a bunch of bottles from the shelf and lines them up in front of us. He is actually beaming. And then … he speaks to us in perfect English.

What did I say that melted the ice? Why, the phrase that pays. It worked a treat in Alba when Tom said it in Italian ('*Che cosa suggerite?*') and was lovingly looked after by a stunning *signorina* who gave up an hour to select a perfect mixed dozen of wines for him at a bottle shop. The same words resulted in an Umbrian restaurateur and his wife farewelling us with hugs and kisses after we used it during dinner, then in France ('*Que recommandez-vous?*') turned a rude Frenchman manning a cheese van into a charming conversationalist, carving us off slice after slice of his wares to try.

It's so simple it's ridiculous. It means 'What do you recommend?' That's it. We have learned to say it in every language so far. Waiters, store owners and provedores are completely bowled over that you're putting your trust in them and doing it in their own language. Time after time we have asked and watched them soften immediately, taking on their responsibility with a puffed-up pride. By saying these few magic words, we have been urged to try things we would never have dreamed existed.

We leave on a cloud, clutching the piece of paper on which the barman has written the names of all the different sherries he let us taste (many of which were on the house) but are brought back to reality when we pass a couple of English guys wearing blue soccer jerseys. 'We're just ditherin', we are,' one of them says in a Liverpool accent. 'This is just like Amsterdam i'nt it? Wot are we doin' coming down 'ere? Let's just stick wiv wot we know.' They turn on their heels and we follow them for a bit past a few Zara clothing stores—there seems to be one on every corner—before watching them go into a street where there's a brightly lit bar themed as ye olde English pub. Spilling out on to the road in front is a flotilla of footy hooligans.

It's pure chaos and reminds me of an episode of the reality television show called *Airport* about a hapless git who flew to Italy to watch his team, bought a ticket to the match from a scalper on the plane, got pissed as soon as he hit the ground and spent the night sleeping on a street in a blanket of his own vomit. Now picture about five hundred blokes just like him, all wearing blue Chelsea jerseys for tonight's match against Real Betis and bleating out club songs in the streets while Spanish police form a barricade around them. Even though Seville is considered to be the tapas capital of Spain with hundreds of funky bars, all these numbskulls have headed straight for the only English pub in town.

We beat a hasty retreat back to the hotel and stick in our earplugs. Luckily, we are cocooned in oblivion by the time all the footy fans come back from the stadium to drink more pints and set off firecrackers in the streets. Perhaps there is a God and he hates the lager lads too. Chelsea lost.

Now that we've mastered the real-deal tapas bar, I'm keen to experience the second of Spain's most famous attractions: flamenco. I have just finished reading *Duende: A Journey in Search of Flamenco* by Jason Webster. He left England to go and live with a troop of gypsy *flamencos* in Andalusia to find true *duende*, the magic or spirit of flamenco. Like him, I didn't want the tatty tourist experience and this afternoon I think I have found the genuine article.

Most flamenco performances in the big cities are put on for the tourists, so they tend to have a whiff of the circus about them. In many of the major centres spruikers will wander the streets, handing out brochures showing photos of places with a 'party' atmosphere where you get a free drink on entry. The dancers at these establishments wear stereotypical flamenco gear: fringed shawls, roses in their bunned hair and gaily flounced dresses of red and yellow polka dots. I want something more authentic. After walking the streets and trying to translate listings in the street press, I spotted a small sign for the Centro de Cultura tucked away in a tiny back lane. On a big wooden door is a poster, written in Spanish. There is a black and white photo of a beautiful dancer with 'Flamenco 10 pm' underneath and today's date. I hurry inside and buy the last two tickets.

We take our seats fifteen minutes before the performance. The room is already full. It is a small space, no bigger than a classroom, but has extremely high vaulted ceilings from which a series of coloured Moroccan lanterns has been suspended. The soft glow of dozens of candles flickers against a trellis of flowering jasmine vines which twist from floor to ceiling and perfume the air. We are seated in a U-shape around a small wooden platform that serves as the stage. In front of it there's a wide copper bowl filled with floating flowers. The candles and the Moorish architecture give the place a feeling of sacredness and we all murmur in low voices. The lights dim and you could hear a pin drop. No photos, we have been told, and definitely no videotaping.

Two musicians take their place on chairs by the side of the stage. The singer shuts his eyes and begins in a strong, impassioned voice. The guitarist, who crosses one leg over the other, resting his instrument on bended knee, starts playing. His eyes never leave the singer to whom he looks for cues as to where the song is going. Both men are in their thirties. The singer looks rougher and more street savvy, giving a hard edge to his desperate melodies. He wears a chunky silver ring on his thumb which flashes when he claps his hands in soft rhythms. His eyes remain shut when he sings, but he expresses himself through hand gestures, touching his chest with his palms and opening his hands outwards as if sawing through the air in front of him.

The song ends and the room darkens. A single spotlight in the centre of the stage illuminates a female dancer wearing a chocolate brown dress. She is petite but curvaceous, with womanly hips and dancer's legs clad in black fishnet tights. Her black hair, which is in a low bun, shines under the light. The tempo of the guitar becomes faster and she smacks her rump in time, flicks her hips, pulls up her top skirt and swishes it provocatively around her waist. Yet somehow, she manages to look regal. It's the way she holds her head—chin aloft, high and proud—an expression of intense concentration and fury, her eyes narrowed and lips pursed.

I straighten in my chair as out comes a young Antonio Banderas. He stands under the spotlight and closes his eyes.

The expression on his face is something between anger and orgasm as he slowly lifts his black shirt above the waist of his suit pants. The middle-aged woman sitting next to me gives a little gasp, her hand fluttering to her mouth. Back on stage, Banderas Junior clutches the fabric so tightly it looks as though he might rip it to expose his chest and the knotted tie he's wearing against his bare skin. He is breathing hard through his nostrils, his shoulder-length curly hair moving up and down as he lets air in and out. He splays his fingers and lets go, running his hands up and down his stomach and thighs.

Then, an impassioned animal wail starts. Softly at first, then louder and louder until it fills the room, reverberating off the walls. I realise it's coming from the back of Banderas Junior's throat. His feet begin to move, thumping the ground like a metronome. His white boots kick up swirls of dust around the tiny stage, creating a magical effect in the spotlight. And then he's stomping his heels, faster and faster, until it looks like he is either having convulsions or is in a minor earthquake. The female dancer starts clapping to match his rhythm and the guitar strums soulfully in time. The movements of his feet begin to blur, the guitar riffs build, the clapping gets so fast it sounds like castanets and then suddenly he breaks out of his reverie and launches into a series of lightning fast turns on stage. Thump, *thump*, thump, *thump*, thump. Over and over again. He connects with the stage so hard, he sends the beat pulsating right through our chests. The clapping, thumping and the throbbing of the guitar reach their crescendo and then … silence.

'*Olé*,' the woman says in a soft voice soaked with pride. Banderas Junior stands feet and arms wide apart, chest heaving, looking sated, beads of sweat on his forehead. The small audience of about fifty people erupts into stadium-sized applause.

I have never felt so moved by a dance performance. Tears prick my eyes as I stand and join with the clapping. Then a small green light catches the corner of my eye. It seems not everyone dug the *duende*. The light is coming from the screen of a mobile phone held by a bored-looking teenager who remains hunched in his chair—not even looking at the stage— as he busily thumbs out text messages to his mates.

◆ ◆ ◆ ◆ ◆

A few days later we leave the bright lights of Seville behind and trade it for a tiny place that's just perfect for doing pretty much nothing at all. In a week's time we're going to Morocco. But before that, we are having some downtime in a village called Gaucin in the south of Spain, just an hour's drive and a short car-ferry ride away from Morocco.

Sleepy Gaucin is one of the area's famed *pueblos blancos*, or white villages. I had no idea southern Spain was home to little whitewashed towns. When I see it for the first time aloft a ridge overlooking a deep green valley, it reminds me of those cookie-cutter photos of Greek island villages I've seen on the walls of souvlaki shops. The Spanish versions are set amid lush mountains with craggy peaks that have forts or castles perched atop. Formerly a Roman stronghold, there's also evidence of the town's Moorish history, from the tubes of harissa and jars of saffron in the greengrocers to the sneak peeks you get from the street into internal courtyards with mosaics of north African tiles and fountains.

In the nearby town of Ronda, the Carmelite nuns still make sweets from recipes they continued to bake in secret when the Christians booted out the Arabs in the 1400s. They sell these goodies from hidden side entrances at convents and churches. You just need to know where to look. On a day-trip there, the locals pointed us to a tiny door, leading to an even tinier room where there's a buzzer. Footsteps sound and I hear a voice from behind the wall asking what we want. From a list on the wall, we order a packet of Tortas de la Virgen, which turn out to be thin fennel-seed biscuits the size of saucers sprinkled with granulated sugar and cinnamon. We put our money on a wooden lazy Susan device set into the wall and seconds later it does a 360-degree spin with the biscuits and our change in front of us. I never see the nun's face.

After a few days of exploring Gaucin we decide there are only two signs of acquiescence to modernity: an abandoned discotheque on the edge of town with a sign showing silhouetted dancers from the era of spandex trousers and Barry Gibb, and the gradual replacement of donkeys with quad bikes ridden by the town's younger citizens. Apart from that, life is as it's always been. We are woken by the crowing of roosters. An old man in our street rides a donkey to some mysterious place every morning then leads him back into his house through the front door at night. There are no supermarket chains or big hotels and the farmers still bring their wares to the local markets.

All the buildings are identical: white with green wooden shutters hanging over the doors. The only way you can tell if one is a shop or not is by watching for a procession of people going in or out. Shopping can take the entire morning or afternoon. There is just the one person serving behind the counter and you have to ask for things to be passed to you. The town's population is mostly elderly, so invariably the seventy-something woman in front wants about three thousand pieces of *jamón* sliced for her or twenty-seven individually wrapped lollies for her grandchildren.

I've been enjoying thumbing through the Spanish cookbooks in the kitchen at the unbelievably fantastic place we're staying in—a 300-year-old olive mill that has been converted into a holiday villa. After so many nights of eating out I am relishing the chance to cook up a storm. The local markets have been our daily port of call for fresh produce. We buy a freshly killed rabbit which still has little bits of fluffy white fur around its ankles. The butcher picks it up by the hind legs and lays it down on his chopping block. Bang, bang, bang! He sections it with his cleaver, finishing with a final executorial chop to the head.

As he bundles it all up in a bag, I catch his attention.

'*Non, por favor,*' I plead, pointing to my own head. He chuckles, but sets the piece aside. Cleaning out a rabbit's innards is one thing but having to look at its pretty little head, which looks rather like a cat's without ears and has a pursed mouth like a parrot's beak, is another entirely.

After returning home and marinating poor headless flopsy for tonight's dinner, we've been sitting, as has become our late afternoon custom, in front of the big open fire in the living room of the villa. The November chill is sending temperatures into single digits further north and it is beginning to bite down in this part of the world too. We have just stoked up the fire to keep us toasty into the evening when someone (read me) stupidly raises the question of when we are going to climb the bloody high mountain that looms over the top of Gaucin. We have admired it as we potter around town, promising to tackle it 'later'. But as I wriggle my toes in front of the warmth wondering how to change the subject, Tom decides later is now.

'But it's going to get dark soon,' I protest. 'And we don't have a map—it's not like any of those other walks we've done.' Before we arrived we bought a book of walks you can take in the region. They all have quirky names such as The Walk of Melanie and the Tiger (no sign of tigers or girls called Melanie) and The Walk of the Cork Cutters (again, false advertising). But nothing of this mountain they call El Hacho. Nonetheless, Tom's mind is made up. 'How hard can it be? Don't be a wuss. I'm sure we'll find the trail easily.' So, grumbling and dragging my feet the ten minutes it takes to get out of town, we make our way to the base of Gaucin's answer to K2.

About an hour later we are above the tree line in a landscape so inhospitable not even the goats are dumb enough to clamber up here. The top of the mountain looms. We are only halfway up El frigging Hacho. It should be renamed El Oucho on account of its groundcover of shrubs with thorns like hypodermic needles that jab you with the force of a hepatitis injection. We are also lost. And I have had enough.

'If there isn't a path up there, Tom, I swear to God I will kill you and leave your body for the vultures!' I shout as he searches ahead for the trail. I look beyond the thorns at my feet and catch an eyeful of the view. It's actually pretty spectacular. I can see Gaucin spread out like a fan on the ridge below before the land drops away into a series of hills and valleys stretching to the coast. Dozens of glinting windmills on a distant rise form the wind farm the locals protest against with bumper stickers, claiming it kills migratory birds. Herds of goats are drinking from bathtubs scattered in the middle of paddocks far below me. Further south the setting sun illuminates the imposing Rock of Gibraltar and beyond, the strait separating Spain from the Rif Mountains of Morocco.

I take a step forward to get a better look, and ... 'Shit! Goddamnit!' I feel another stab to the back of my calf. 'Have you found the trail yet?' I yell.

Another evil prickle penetrates my sock. I rub the top of my foot and lament how inappropriate my lycra yoga pants and Converse trainers are for tackling rugged terrain. Overhead, spiralling in the currents, is a baker's dozen of raptors with wingspans of well over a metre. We have probably only got about ten minutes before the sun sets and I feel a lump of fear rise in my throat and a rash of renewed annoyance for being up here. If I ever make it out of here alive, I may write to the author of that book we got and suggest this be called The Walk of Katrina and Her About-to-be Divorced Husband.

'I've found it,' Tom calls out. 'You just have to scramble up here a bit.'

I look ahead of me. Between me and the tiny sheep trail he's spotted lies a thick fleece of the angriest looking thistles I've ever seen. And they are all looking at me as though I've disrespected their mother.

Later that night, as we lie in our villa's deep bath soaking our shredded legs and drinking wine, talk turns to the subject I raised in the car in southern France a few weeks ago and which hasn't really been dwelt upon since. London.

'Should we do it? Should we move there at the end of all this?' Tom asks.

I can't remember much about London, but I figure there are so many expats there, it must be extremely similar to Australia. And, yeah, people talk about the grey weather. But how bleak can it be? As nervous as I feel about moving to a country where I won't know anyone, the prospect of making a fresh start is really appealing.

'Yes,' I say. 'Our house is already packed up, so it should be a relatively easy process. We can just sell off some of the things we don't need, some of our old furniture, that kind of stuff, and put the rest in long-term storage.'

'But neither of us has jobs,' Tom points out.

'Look,' I reply, 'I want to keep testing myself, pushing the boundaries, taking chances.' I twist the tap with my foot, letting more hot water in.

'But not only do we not have work, we don't even have a place to live,' Tom says.

'Well, yes, there's a risk we may end up jobless and homeless. But I doubt it. Not if we're prepared to work in bars or whatever to get by. I think we should do it.'

'Hmmm,' Tom says, looking wistful. 'I do love the idea of being a few hours away from anywhere in Europe. We'd have some pretty amazing weekends of travel.' He takes a deep breath. 'Shit, everything sensible in me is saying we shouldn't. But maybe it's time to break out of our comfort zone?'

'Let's go for it,' I say, smiling. We clink our glasses.

I take a sip of my *sangiovese*, the second bottle we have opened today. Damn. Those Italians sure know how to make a mean drop of red. Here's hoping we can buy lots of great Italian wines in London, too.

CHAPTER 8

Sheep's head soup and all that

THE FIRST TIME I HEAR IT, WE ARE STANDING ON THE rooftop of our *riad* surveying the sprawl of the dusty medina below. We have only been in Marrakesh an hour, arriving late in the afternoon. It's our first proper stop in Morocco.

The sound begins as a faint muffled wail, a little like Tarzan's jungle call. Then similar cries echo from different points all around the city. It becomes a deep hum, like the loud buzzing of bees, from every direction. Then it bristles thickly in the air, filling it physically. I listen harder and realise the buzz is actually made by voices. It comes from loudspeakers on minarets around the medina and as I stand there it builds to a shimmering crescendo. I shut my eyes and concentrate on the babble. I can make out a few words, which at the moment have no meaning.

'*Allahu Akbar, Allahu Akbar.*'

I later discover this means 'Allah is the greatest'. It is part of the call to prayer ritual which occurs five times a day: at dawn, midday, mid-afternoon, sunset and dinnertime. This is when the holy men of the mosques call their members to drop whatever they are doing and pay homage to the big guy

sheep's head soup
and all that
119

upstairs. All this feels so different to Spain, which we left two days ago.

The night before we departed Gaucin my brain was in overdrive about what to expect. I imagined a land of extreme poverty, but also one of romance, mystery and exotic spices. There's also the idea of Morocco as a scary place, a concept perpetuated by my former workmates. 'Why the hell would you want to go there?' they quizzed me when I ran through our itinerary. And, 'Have you got a death wish?' Despite my laughing it off, they wouldn't let up on the scare tactics, recounting stories of 'friends of friends' who'd had their hotel rooms robbed, or contracted a weird tapeworm after riding a camel in the desert.

As the clock flipped over into the hours before dawn, my mind raced with questions. I have never been to an Arabic Islamic country before. How much would I have to cover up— would I be expected to put a scarf on my hair and could I wear T-shirts without causing offence? I have heard that donkeys and horses share asphalt space with trucks and motorbikes and aren't required to carry lights at night. How are we going to go driving on Moroccan roads? And will I be able to go sightseeing safely on my own or will I have to stick by Tom's side?

So it was with bleary eyes that we left Gaucin and El Oucho behind, drove south past Gibraltar and boarded the car ferry that took us across the strait. It was a short sail to Ceuta, a chunk of land on the tip of Morocco, still part of Spanish territory. Aside from the glut of petrol stations—you can get some of the cheapest fuel and duty-free in the world there—the architecture, language and vegetation were not much different from the Spanish mainland.

The petrol station price boards served to highlight the gender differences between Tom and me.

Tom: 'Wow, you can get really cheap diesel here.'

Me (not paying much attention to my surroundings, as usual): 'Really? Maybe we should stop. I need a new pair of jeans.'

After the resulting explanation, which left Tom chortling and me feeling a tad ridiculous, we continued along the coast until we reached the border of Morocco proper, marked by a tunnel of grim-looking booths flanked with machine gun-toting police. As soon as we slowed down we were accosted by men wearing Jedi knight-style hooded robes the colour of mud, all thrusting forms at our car. Rolling down the window a little I could hear fluent French pour from their mouths. I stayed in the car while Tom went with one of the men, who had shown him an official-looking tag identifying him as an agent of Morocco's Department of Tourism.

About fifteen minutes later Tom gestured for me to join him at the window. An official was poring over our forms.

'Here. You,' the man barked, pointing at the place where my occupation is listed. 'Journalist? Who are you a journalist for? TV? Newspapers? Write down exactly where you are journalist.'

I listed my last employer as a point of contact. I couldn't help but feel nervous entering a country where the press is regarded with suspicion and my occupation seemed to be a dirty word. Perhaps the guys at work weren't giving me a bum steer about this place after all.

Back at the car, another official conducted a brief search. He lifted the boot and we held our breaths, thinking about the bottles of Italian wine we had stashed in there. But his inspection seemed more for show and he waved us on, looking bored.

As we pulled out to leave, a man who helped Tom fill out the forms leapt in front of us with a hat in his hands, blocking our path. 'Something for Mohammed?' he pleaded, tucking away his bogus government ID. We'd barely been in Morocco for thirty seconds and already, just like the famed mirages of the desert, nothing was quite what it seemed.

As soon as we crossed the border, the landscape, people and level of affluence changed. Suddenly there was rubbish blowing along the rocky dry ground, camels sitting on the side of the road and everything was tinged with brown dust. The paddocks

sheep's head soup
and all that
121

were over-farmed and eroded. Livestock grazed right up to edge of the motorway and sheep roamed the sandy beaches. Every other motorist on the road to Casablanca seemed to be driving a beaten-up Mercedes. Well-fed policeman stood at roundabouts randomly pulling people over. As soon as they saw our French plates and white faces though, they waved us through. After twiddling with the dial to search the radio stations I discovered the people in this country are obsessed with disco. We drove to the best of The Weathergirls and KC and The Sunshine Band.

The arid countryside was flecked with a string of satellite towns. People were out of their houses drinking mint tea by fold-up tables at the side of the road, standing with suitcases and thumbs out to hitch a ride on trucks loaded precariously with wood and livestock, gathering around shops that had carcasses hanging in the open air and smoke billowing from barbecue plates, or just standing in groups in otherwise empty fields. We passed a man riding a motorbike with a goat sitting behind him. His little billy seemed to be quite enjoying the ride. Straddling the back seat, serenely surveying the countryside.

We spent the first night in an unremarkable hotel on Casablanca's industrial outskirts and set off for Marrakesh the next morning. In the distance we saw the imposing Atlas Mountains. The pollution and dust turned the clear sky into a washed-out icy blue and the faint silhouette of the snow-capped peaks blended right in. It was daunting to think that in the days to come we'd be driving right over the top of them to get into the heart of the desert.

After lunch a couple of young men on motorbikes appeared, tailgating our car, flashing their lights and signalling for us to pull over.

'What the hell?' Tom said, looking worried. 'Do you reckon we've got a flat tyre or something?'

'No,' I replied. 'I've read about this. It's a bit of a ruse to try and rip off tourists. Apparently these guys get you to pull over to the side of the road. Sometimes they try to take you to their cousin's hotel for commission. But I've also heard about people being robbed of everything they have.'

One guy pursued us aggressively for about twenty kilometres. My stomach flip-flopped every time his friend, riding pillion, tried to catch my eye. 'Don't look at them,' I urged Tom, as he rapped on our window. Even though we had the doors locked, their persistence made me feel vulnerable. Finally they gave up.

It felt safe to look out the window again. That's when I noticed an oasis of lush palm trees in the middle of the desert. It seemed like a mirage, as though the trees have dropped from the sky onto the honey-coloured sand. And rising high above the flat plains was the tall minaret of the Koutoubia Mosque, the landmark many a lost tourist uses to get their bearings in the Marrakesh medina. We had arrived.

After driving in circles for twenty minutes trying to work out the Arabic signs, we decided not to risk doing battle with the tourists and donkeys. We left our car with one of the blue-jacketed men guarding an open-air parking lot on the outskirts of the old city and paid him a few hundred dirhams to watch over Maurizio for the week. Grabbing our backpacks, we went in search of our hotel behind the high mudbrick walls.

As we ducked and weaved our way through the streets, we discovered that Marrakesh was a full-on boxing tournament for the senses. It assaulted us at every turn. The first thing we noticed was the stink: it was equal parts fried food, sewage and rotting garbage. The next was the beggars. Small children ran alongside us, tugging on our sleeves hopefully and calling out, '*un dirham, un dirham?*' There were old men in rags who threw themselves at our feet and held out empty bowls. And most heart-wrenching of all were the women who looked up at us with mournful eyes as they breastfed their babies in the gutter, pleading, '*Mademoiselle, Monsieur, s'il vous plaît?*'

We pressed against the walls to avoid being bowled over by overlaiden carts drawn by horses and donkeys, their backs bowed under the weight of dozens of heavy sacks. Their owners walked alongside, whipping them with lengths of cane. And then there were the salesmen. Men yelled at us, first in French, then in English, to come into their carpet shop, eat at their restaurant or let them guide us around a monument. By the time we reached our hotel, I was desperate for an escape hatch.

I was hopeful that our *riad* was going to provide it. Because it was Tom's birthday in a few days' time I had booked fancier accommodation than usual, at a traditional Moroccan home that had been converted into luxury digs, to celebrate.

'The map says it's supposed to be here,' I told Tom, as we surveyed a row of huge unmarked doors tucked between a shop selling copper sinks—yes, they sell everything including the kitchen sink here—and another with rows of brightly coloured dip-dyed scarves. 'There's no sign,' I said, looking around. 'This could be anything.' I pulled a rope attached to a big bronze bell and it clanged a few times. Then the door opened to another world.

'*Bonsoir, Madame, Monsieur.*' A beautiful young woman with a sequined headscarf and colourfully embroidered leather slippers greeted us at the door, holding out hennaed hands for our bags. The doors clanged shut and we were spirited away inside. We had left noisy, gritty Morocco behind for an oasis of opulence: courtyards with birds twittering in the orange trees and beautiful mosaic fountains in which rose petals and candles floated. She led us past rooms filled with silk cushions and rich carpets, and daybeds with curtains billowing gently in the breeze. As she showed us around, she explained that every room was decorated according to a different spice, such as ginger or cinnamon. We were shown to the paprika suite, where a gleaming silver pot of mint tea awaited us.

After unpacking, we go up to the roof terrace where we stand now, still caught up in the magic of the call to prayer.

Suddenly my reverie is broken by someone shuffling along the concrete. A morbidly obese woman is lumbering along and sighing heavily. 'Not this bleedin' thing again,' she whinges in a British accent, heaving herself on to a daybed. 'Day and night this racket goes on. Why can't they do their bleedin' praying in silence like the rest of us?' She gives another snort and plugs herself into her iPod. I almost have to physically pick my jaw up off the ground.

◆ ◆ ◆ ◆ ◆

The next morning, I leave Tom behind in our room and venture out alone to buy some water. This will be one of the only times I'll dare leave his side for our entire Moroccan stay. That's because the moment I hit the grimy, hustling street I become a beacon for unwanted male attention

'*Mademoiselle, Mademoiselle!*' the men shout at me from their stores. Others leap from chairs where they've been snoozing to run alongside me calling out, '*Bonjour, bonjour.*' Then, when I pretend I don't understand them, 'Hello miss, hello.'

My face burning, I put my head down, only to almost walk straight into a teenager riding a bicycle. He makes loud kissing noises and tries to touch my hair. I swat his hand away. Under a dusty awning is a small shop with bottles of water on the counter and I hurry over. There are a number of older men sitting on the path outside and I can feel their eyes on me as I make my purchase. I look at them and give a shy smile and a nod. They narrow their eyes, staring at me with contempt. I wonder what I have done wrong. I am wearing long pants and a long-sleeved loose top—certainly nothing that I thought would cause offence.

Wandering around the gardens, souks (markets) and backstreets of Marrakesh over the next few days, I find that no matter where I go, exuberant male attention follows me. I take to covering my hair with a scarf, but still I am harassed and stared at, especially by the older men. Later I read that it's frowned upon for young men and women to socialise together

sheep's head soup
and all that
125

before marriage, but Moroccan men see western women as an exception to this rule. They pester us relentlessly. And, indeed, if Tom leaves me alone for one second, every man in town seems to swoop, wanting to talk to me and touch me. It's pretty confronting.

But my discomfort soon turns to indignation. I see families on outings, the women in burkas walking a few paces behind their husbands. I watch one woman wearing a chuddar, so heavily cloaked there is not an inch of her flesh showing to the outside world. The slit for her eyes in her veil is covered in mesh and, as she picks up her child, I see she is also wearing gloves to cover her hands. This modesty is in stark contrast to the behaviour of the men. They unzip their trousers, relieving themselves wherever they stand. Men seem to have carte blanche to do as they please, and they enjoy themselves smoking and drinking tea at the male-only cafés and restaurants. I realise how much I take my liberty for granted.

As the days go on though, I start to see that, in small ways, the social norms are changing. The current king, Mohammed VI, is seen to be a champion for women's rights and in 2004 he passed the Mudawana, a new family code that bans husbands from divorcing their wives verbally (they used to be able to just 'tell' them and that was that). It also means that women are no longer legally required to be obedient to their husbands. But many say this is not enough. Moroccan women are still considered minors under the penal code and have high rates of illiteracy and unemployment. The liberals argue it is difficult to liberate women without giving them the means with which to exercise freedom. Still, the king's wife provides a bold new role model for the modern Moroccan woman. She's a university graduate in her thirties who is photographed in Chanel, not chuddars, and wears her long hair loose.

I am reflecting on all of this while Tom and I drink tea at a café near our *riad*, when I see another group of young burka-clad women bustle by with their heads down. My eyes drift down to their feet. 'Look at that,' I whisper to Tom, pointing. There, beneath their drab beige robes, is a flash of fishnet stocking on one and a snippet of leopard-skin trouser-leg on another. I can't help but smile. You go, sister.

◆ ◆ ◆ ◆ ◆

On our last night in Marrakesh we decide to see what the Djemaa el Fna, the local version of Times Square, looks like after dark. Flanked on one side by the souks and on the other by hotels and café terraces, it is the busiest piece of real estate in the entire continent of Africa.

The Djemaa is a tourist attraction but it's still used just as much by the locals. And it's completely different depending on when you visit. We have been before during the day when it's a circus of curiosities with everything and everyone competing for our attention. Small crowds with rapt expressions gather around toothless storytellers, acrobats perform tricks, and witchdoctors smear oil on people's foreheads, gesture to the heavens and do the big sell to their audience. There are sluggish cobras, which lie stubbornly on blankets while snake charmers wheedle them with recorders, and hedgehogs and monkeys straining at leashes.

After the sun goes down, the storytellers and witchdoctors go home and the Djemaa becomes a giant white-tented open-air food hall. Tonight we pick our way through the back streets past the market stalls piled high with dates, dried apricots and figs. As soon as we round the corner into the square, I am hit again with the smell: blood, raw meat, faeces and freshly cooked flat bread. Breathing it all in is an unsettling sensation of being simultaneously attracted and repulsed.

In front of us are big vans that have been converted into stalls with fresh produce displayed on shelves and trestle tables set up out front. As we walk by, the cooks inside the open-air kitchens hold out big bowls of couscous, *tagines*, and chicken and lamb *brochettes*, trying to tempt us.

sheep's head soup
and all that
127

'You come to our stall, we are number one!' shouts one man who's emerged from the front of a van to block our path.

'*La shukran,*' I say, the Arabic phrase for 'no, thank you'. He drops his tea towel on the floor.

'Omigod,' he exclaims in English, wide-eyed with mock amazement. 'You speak this language? Sit, sit.' I shake my head and try to dodge him, but another operator grabs us with an almost desperate intensity, crying, 'You come back to number twenty-seven! Tonight, later, tomorrow—just remember number twenty-seven!'

Further along we see a stall selling *bisteeya*. We ordered it the other night when we went to a restaurant in a converted palace for Tom's birthday. It's pigeon braised until tender and sweet, then stuffed inside a filo pastry parcel along with ground almonds and creamy lemon eggs and decorated on top with criss-crossing icing sugar and cinnamon. I found it had the curious quality of being sweet and savoury all at once while leaving the texture of peanut butter in my mouth. Surprisingly delicious. Next to the *bisteeya* seller is the stall no tourist dares eat at: the sheep's head stand. The customers look up at us curiously as we watch them devour everything but the eyeballs.

We eventually settle on bowls of *harira*, a hearty soup of lamb and tomatoes, which we eat on a bench crowded with Moroccans. Small boys stand patiently behind us holding plastic bags, begging for leftovers. I give one of them two bread rolls and his face lights up like I've given him a toy. Afterwards, we follow a group of men to another stall. The owner gestures me closer and, from a big fudge-coloured mound, scoops a tiny bowlful of soft paste out and gives it to me. I eat it using my fingers and look up at Tom. 'It tastes a bit like gingerbread dough,' I say, pleasantly surprised. I think it might be a sweet called *sellou*, which is flavoured with anise and cinnamon.

We go to bed after midnight, full and satisfied, looking forward to our drive over the Atlas Mountains and into the desert the next day.

Tom pulls the blankets up. 'We can probably sleep in a bit,' he says, 'the drive isn't that long.'

'Mmmmm. I'd like that a lot,' I reply, looking forward to a late start.

My eyes feel like they have barely closed when I'm jolted awake with a start. What is that unrelenting noise? It's so loud. I check my clock: 5.15 am.

The noise gets louder and begins to take on meaning.

'*Allahu Akbar*,' it says. And then louder still, '*Allahu Akbar*.'

Ah. The first call to prayer for the day. The loudspeaker sounds like it's right outside our door.

The cry is echoed by others around the city and I groan, putting my pillow over my head.

The phantom voices build. '*As-Salatu khairun min an-naum. As-Salatu khairun min an-naummmmm*.' (Prayer is better than sleep, prayer is better than sleep.)

Really? Perhaps, in hindsight, I was a little quick to judge that British woman and her iPod antics after all.

After leaving Marrakesh later that morning, the landscape quickly changes. As we climb the steep foothills of the ranges, it goes from flat sandy desert to soil the colour of spilt claret. Within a few hours we are in thick cloud among the snow-capped peaks. The temperature, which had been a warm twenty degrees in the city, drops steeply and soon we have to turn the heater on. Rocky outcrops jut from either side of the road.

Even though we are some distance away from the metropolitan area and in extremely inhospitable countryside, there are still people everywhere, waving us down or standing in front of our car then stepping away at the last minute, trying to sell us something. It has to be the world's biggest roadside department store—the range is incredible. Many vendors

sheep's head soup
and all that
129

advertise their wares by holding them out towards oncoming vehicles. There are men clutching flapping chickens by the ankles, small children with bags of walnuts, teenagers holding gemstones or rocks split open to show off their bright red crystallised centres, women sitting at long tables with homemade signs saying 'fossils' and families selling a million and one clay pots and *tagines*.

We reach the desert town of Ourzazate just as night is falling. It is a dusty dive of a town whose only claim to fame is the Atlas film studios on the outskirts where flicks such as *The Living Daylights*, *The Last Temptation of Christ* and *Gladiator* were filmed. It's one of those places that makes you feel as though you are truly in the middle of nowhere. So it is with some surprise that I spot an internet café on the way in. I make a mental note of it, thinking I should really let my old workmates know about my change of heart some time soon. It's all well and good to dream up a life change while sitting in a bath tub drinking red wine, but there are practicalities to contend with. I go to sleep feeling uneasy.

The next morning I wake early, struck by thinking-induced insomnia. Tom is still asleep, so I sit at the small desk by the window holding a notebook. It has several paragraphs already scribbled out. I watch the first rays of morning light brighten the palms and the desert outside, trying to find the right words to close the chapter on my old life and embark on a new one. I know as soon as I send that email our decision not to go back becomes definite. The sun travels higher into the sky and I still sit there, feeling unsure.

After breakfast, we go to the basic-looking shop with computers that look as though they hail from the era of Commodore 64s. Here goes, I think, taking a few seconds to compose myself. I start typing.

Hey there,
I remember sitting there not so long ago telling you I was so

sure I'd come back, but I guess time away changes your perspective on things.

The travel has been fantastic and it's made me want to try a different way of life for a while. So, Tom and I are planning to live OS for a couple of years. We'll probably settle in London, because it's easier for us both to find work and use it as a base for more travel. I hear they are open to having Aussie accents on air, so who knows? There's always busking.

I wanted to email you as soon as I knew for certain as we'd talked about my possible return.

Thank you for always being so supportive of me, for your friendship and for being such a delight to work with. I don't miss the hours, but I do miss your company.

Katrina

I hesitate for more than a few moments and then finally press 'send'.

Back in the car, I wind down the window. My hands are shaking and I feel physically ill. Tom looks across at me.

'Are you okay? You're not carsick again, are you?'

'No,' I laugh, faintly. 'I just feel all weird after sending that email. I've got a nervous feeling in the pit of my stomach. But I guess it's an excited kind of nervous.' Tom gives me a reassuring smile.

We leave nondescript Ourzazate behind and the scenery is transformed into the fabled desert of *Lawrence of Arabia*. Even the name of the stretch of road we are on sounds like something of myth and legend: The Road of One Hundred Kasbahs. It lives up to its moniker too. The caramel desert is dotted with ruin after ruin of crumbling walls, some with turrets intact, all the rich colours of terracotta and salmon. There isn't a village or dwelling in sight. Just mile after mile of barren land, which shimmers like water under the heat of the beating sun. I watch as a pack of wild dogs feast on the carcass of a donkey. Up ahead, a robed man rests against a rock as he watches over a herd of camels. 'God, this feels

sheep's head soup
and all that
131

so primitive,' I say. 'It's like we've travelled back about a thousand years.'

We drive closer. The camel herder has something in his hands. Is he carving something out of wood? Or making decorative jewellery to sell at the *souks*? I crane my neck to get a look at him as we pass. When I figure it out, I can't believe it.

'No way,' I say, shaking my head.

'What?' Tom asks

'Guess what that guy is doing?'

'I have no idea. What?'

'He's text messaging on his mobile phone! Civilisation's not so far away after all.'

My jitters from this morning still haven't gone. I reach over to the glove box to grab a lolly to chew on, hoping it will ease my nervous tension.

I've always done the right thing, I think. Ever since I left school, I've taken all the right steps. It would have been easier and more predictable to stay in Sydney, get a mortgage and have a baby. I don't really know what London is like. Will I find work and make new friends? Will I start missing my old life again?

Those questions are put on hold as we while away the next few days exploring the Dades and Todra Gorges. They are set in valleys that seem utterly incompatible with the rest of the desert landscape and are extraordinarily beautiful. All of a sudden the desert becomes small hills which turn into cliffs cut through with swathes of red and cream, like streaky bacon. Beyond them are valleys filled with olive trees and palms. In the centre lie the gorges, which you can drive straight through. We seem to be the only tourists visiting at this time of year and locals look at us curiously from their doorways. Their houses are built of mud, exactly the same colour as the landscape, making them almost invisible. We dodge camels and donkeys on the road. Kids sing out '*bonjour*' to us as they play soccer in the dirt, some asking for '*un dirham*', but laughing—knowing there probably isn't a hope in hell of getting it. In the towns many of the buildings are in such a state of severe disrepair they look as though they have been bombed.

Gorge explorations completed, we begin the drive to Erg Chebbi, the biggest Saharan sand dunes in Morocco. For lunch we stop in a town called Erfoud. At a small family-run restaurant I order the local specialty, a lamb *tagine* with forty-four different herbs and spices served with eggs simmering on top. After driving for hours, we are beginning to play on each other's nerves and our exchanges quickly turn snappy. I storm out to the car to get some alone time. A split second later, nearly all the local men in town appear at my side.

'Miss, you buy carpet from me? Number one quality.'

I take a deep breath and shake my head, willing them to go away, but somehow they interpret it as encouragement.

'Maybe you come to my shop, Miss.'

'No, you come to mine. I have very cheap price.'

Eventually Tom feels sorry for me and comes out to unlock the car. As we go to leave, the same men lean through our windows telling us we are going the wrong way to Merzouga, the town on the outskirts of the dunes.

'The road you want to take is closed. You take me with you,' one says. 'For fifty *dirham* I'll show you other way.' Fortunately, we've read that this is a common scam, so we shake our heads.

'Where you from?' asks another.

'Australia,' Tom states, beginning to pull away.

'Koala, kangaroo! Shrimp on barbie! G'day cobber!' he cries.

After arguing with me through lunch, Tom's patience has worn thin. 'Please don't,' he says in his best don't-mess-with-me voice through gritted teeth. 'Australians don't actually talk like that, you know.'

As we motor off, I look in the rear-view mirror and have to stifle a laugh as the man's face droops in shock.

We don't have to travel too much further before broad belts of fine white sand begin appearing on the edge of the road. Then I

sheep's head soup
and all that
133

see the dunes rising up in the distance like a shimmering flamingo-pink bushfire. Their beauty distracts us from our bickering and we drive the rest of the way in awed silence.

All the hotels are squared up along the edge of the dunes and we have to drive over sand and rocky gravel to get to them. Tourism seems to be booming here—every place we come across is undergoing expansion. Just as it begins to get dark, we find a place that has a vacancy and unpack our bags in relief. Afterwards, we explore the grounds, hardly believing our luck. The hotel's gorgeous—it's set in an old kasbah amid a maze of flowering gardens and courtyards with ornate fountains and sculptures. But things that seem too good to be true usually are. We discover later the hotel's staff seem to be suffering some kind of crisis of confidence. They are desperate for praise, as often as possible.

That night at dinner, in between attempts to sell us camel treks or trips to their uncle's carpet business, we are frequently asked to affirm it's 'very nice room?' or 'very, very nice food?' We get up to go to bed and are buttonholed again. 'You go to dunes in the morning?' asks a young man wearing long black robes.

I tell him yes, we will be.

'Very beautiful, yes? Very nice dessert?' he asks eagerly.

Tom and I look at each other questioningly. But we didn't eat dessert. We only had the main course.

He points outside and repeats, 'Very nice dessert?'

Then it dawns on me. 'Oh,' I say. 'You mean "very nice desert?"'

'Well, in fairness,' Tom whispers as we walk away to our room, 'I struggled with that one at primary school, too. And I don't speak Arabic and French as well.'

The alarm wakes us early the next morning and we set off to climb the dunes and watch the sun come up. The moon is still high in the sky and the sand is slightly pink in the pre-dawn light. We trudge past a group of tents belonging to a

Berber family and stop a short distance away. We're now surrounded by sand on all sides. It feels like we've got the dunes completely to ourselves. I unlace my sneakers. The sand is so fine it has come through the narrow mesh on top and now my shoes are full of apricot-coloured grains.

A few minutes later I hear voices behind us. I turn around to see two young men dressed in bright blue robes with gold embroidery around the neck and sleeves. They have black scarves wrapped around their heads turban-style.

'*Bonjour,*' they call out. We sit and talk with them for a while and discover they are fluent in French and English. I tell them we are from Australia. One of them gives me a smile with rotting teeth. The sun is now beginning to make its journey over the highest dune and we get up to leave, eager to catch the full sunrise, but they pull out a cloth bag from beneath their robes.

'We have fossils and sculpture we make,' they say, lifting out objects for us to see.

'They are very nice but, no, thank you,' I reply.

They ignore me and begin to lay down about twenty objects in the sand at my feet.

'Please look. We make,' the taller one says.

'No, thank you,' I say again. 'We just came to look at the dunes.'

'Please, Miss. Look. Maybe you want something,' he repeats.

'What I want,' I say, dusting the sand off my jeans and moving away, 'is to spend some time alone with my husband.'

'No, look. Here. I think you buy something,' he says, his voice rising.

'Please respect my wishes.' I am trying to be assertive but polite.

That's when they snap. 'You cannot understand this in Australia,' the tall one shouts, 'we are poor people.' We walk away, but they continue yelling at us as we go.

To avoid any more encounters, we decide to move much further up into the dune complex. It takes quite a bit of effort, climbing up and over summits about ten metres high. We crest

sheep's head soup
and all that
135

a tall one, find a good position and settle down. From here I can peer straight over the top of all the peaks, which seem to stretch on for ever. There are so many different smooth, sculptural shapes it's like being atop a giant meringue.

The only sound is the faint seashell roar of the light wind. The coil of tension I have been carrying around since sending the email the other day slowly starts to unravel. The sun spills a creeping glow over the dunes, turning them the colour of orange juice. A breeze picks up sand off the face of one of the dunes and drifts it forward, making new patterns as it goes. It ripples across the flat surface, carving a design as though a snake has wriggled through it. I draw my knees up and marvel at where I am now. This place feels so far away from anywhere and everywhere. From Sydney, from London, from the modern world.

Another whisper of air swirls through the dunes, but this time it feels like it's blowing through me, smoothing my thoughts, changing their patterns. I don't fight it. I like this changing feeling. I open myself up to the sensation and let it ripple through my consciousness. I don't think I have ever felt calmer.

An hour or so passes and the sun tracks its way through the sky. Tom and I sit together in peaceful silence.

'It's like being in hell,' says Julie in a matter-of-fact manner, 'but you certainly feel clean afterwards.' It's one week later and I'm leaning against woven cushions in the breakfast room at our *riad* in Fez. Julie, an English woman we've befriended, is describing her *hammam* experience from the night before.

'What's so bad about it?' I ask her. 'I've always wanted to go to a *hammam*. Being scrubbed, massaged and steamed sounds pretty pampering to me.'

'Do you think you'll go?' she says, raising one eyebrow.

'Yes, if the one you went to is authentic. I don't want to go to a tourist *hammam*. I want to go where the locals go.'

She pushes a strand of ash-blonde hair behind her ear with a delicate flick of her wrist and chuckles.

'Oh, well then. This is authentic all right. I don't think you'll be disappointed.'

Julie and her husband John, a handsome couple in their fifties, are in Morocco on a buying trip, which must be music to the ears of all those carpet-sellers. I've enjoyed chatting to them because I haven't encountered anyone who speaks fluent English for about a week. We've driven through the affluent Swiss chalet-style village of Ifrane, stayed in the old capital of Meknes and spent a few nights in the current capital of Rabat. The last was most notable for its numerous billboards showing the king in movie-star poses. In one he was on a jet ski, in another he was on horseback, and I even saw a shot of him and his toddler son wearing matching outfits.

John and Julie have been in Fez slightly longer than the few days we have spent wandering around here. In that time I've discovered it has a mystique and exoticism that Marrakesh lacks—mainly thanks to its dark and maze-like medina. Over two hundred thousand locals, many clad in hooded cloaks, live and work here. Ornately arched city gates enclose the old walled town inside an outer ring of centuries-old cream coloured walls with massive ornately carved gates. Inside, the medina's snaking alleys are punctuated with ancient mosques and dozens of tiled drinking fountains, which are inlaid with *zelij* designs, mosaics of blue, white and orange stars, considered the most divine of Allah's creations.

Fez is set in a valley and is bisected by a river, which I suppose was once pure and majestic but is now fetid and polluted. I watch timeless scenes of daily life—the haggling in the markets, the hammering of tools by silversmiths, potters and mosaic artists. But for all its exotic allure, I am about to discover that this is a city where animals are expendable, small boys are dipped in vats of chalk and pigeon poo is smeared on handbags.

I have a soft spot for animals, particularly dogs, and I have been finding it a little confronting to get my head around the way they are regarded here. Though I have steeled my heart against the constant site of the poorly treated horses and donkeys staggering along with ribcages protruding through skin and abscesses from regular whippings, there have been two scenes which I have found harder to take.

The first occurred when we parked Maurizio near a construction sight. I had just shut my door when I heard the sickening high-pitched scream of a creature in severe pain. A dog, snoozing under the shade of a tree, had been hit by a brick dropped by one of the workmen. It zigzagged around in panic, the grey fur on its head streaked red with blood. Still yelping, it eventually went to cower under a nearby car. I was distraught and looked around to see if anyone would help it, but no one batted an eyelid. The construction workers continued on as if nothing had happened. I ran into a shop to get the dog some food and water but when I came back it was gone. Then when we arrived in Fez I saw a small white horse, its back bent under the burden of a dozen or more sacks, drop dead right in the middle of the street. I had to cover my mouth to choke back a sob, but the owners quickly converted death into opportunity. Without skipping a beat they tied up its hooves and dragged it off to the nearby tanneries.

These same tanneries have become a tourist drawcard. It's responsible for all the brightly coloured goat, cow and lamb skins that get made into the leather slippers known as babouches, the bags and the jackets sold in street markets. But oh my god the sniff. Definitely not beautiful. Set on the far side of the river, you can smell the tanneries well before you see them. It's a ripe, just-stepped-in dog-poo, rotting-meat, haven't-showered-for-three-years kind of funk that follows you around and seems to impregnate everything nearby. We decide to see the main tannery up close, and as we walk there I have to cover my nose with my sleeve to stop myself from gagging.

The canny locals have capitalised on the tourism appeal by turning all of the buildings providing a view of the tannery pits into leathergood shops. We decide to be guided by the man on the street who hassles us the least and are taken up three narrow flights of stairs into a big room where belts, jackets and handbags hang from the ceiling. Out the front is a long balcony where I can see over to the surrounding hillsides and the skyline of Fez's outer suburbs. Stretched out below the railing, squeezed between the old buildings, is a honeycomb of more than a hundred round clay wells.

'The men use same technique since the fourteenth century', says a rangy man who's introduced himself as the store's owner. He puts his cigarette to his thin, mean mouth and takes a long drag. 'Over there, near the river, that is where they take skins first. They use water and lime to get rid of fur which is used for weaving. Then they take here,' he points to the closest vats, which are several metres deep and stained bright blue, red and gold, 'to the wells of indigo, henna and saffron.'

'Where does the smell come from?' Tom asks.

'Here in Morocco, special gastronomy is *bisteeya*.' We nod.

'Children raise pigeons and sell to restaurants for the meat,' he continues, 'and then they collect droppings and bring them here. For dye. They also use blood, urine, excrement.' He waves his hand dismissively. 'You know, pieces of animal we don't want.'

Like that poor little horse, I think.

We stand and watch for a while longer and I start to notice a harsher, more chemical smell. I point to the network of wells at the side, which are covered in a thick white paste. There, I can see a teenage boy treading on the skins as though he's crushing grapes while another man holds him by the shoulders.

'What are those wells for?' I ask.

'They are the chalk pits. The men can only do a few hours there each day because it makes them sick here.' He points to his chest. 'But they wear protection—gumboots and gloves.' I look again but can't see anyone wearing any such things.

sheep's head soup
and all that
139

'It is very important trade passed down from father to son,' he says quickly.

'At what age are they allowed to start?' Tom asks.

He looks shifty again. 'Oh, maybe ten, nine.' His voice wavers then, and I can tell the boys are much younger.

After our tour, Tom haggles him down on the price of slippers and a bag we pick out as Christmas gifts for our family. The store owner relents after twenty minutes of claim and counterclaim, telling Tom, 'You bargain like Berber', before ushering us to the back of his shop. He pulls aside a curtain to show us a room where—surprise, surprise—he has carpets for sale.

'Very good quality,' he assures us. 'I make good price for you.'

We leave, laughing. I wonder how many tourists buy carpets they don't want just to get some peace?

◆ ◆ ◆ ◆ ◆

The next afternoon, I pack a towel and a cake of soap in my bag and follow the directions Julie has given me to the *hammam*. After twisting down a few blind alleys, I find myself at a doorway next to a café. Several tables of men stare at me as they sip their mint tea. I feel a bit nervous. This is the first proper outing I have had without Tom since we've arrived in Morocco. I look at the sign, which is in Arabic and French, and work out that during daytime hours only female customers and their children may enter. After 7.30 pm the *hammam* is reserved for men only. I have been told that for the local women, *hammams* are the equivalent of girly slumber parties— a chance to catch up on gossip, be pampered and let their hair down. For men, hammams are comparable to the pub. It's where they go for a yarn, to broker a business deal or to get away from the missus.

I knock and a partition in the wooden door slides open. A wizened old face appears, giving me a toothless smile. The door is unbolted and the woman gestures at me with a crooked finger. I am led into an area that looks like the changing room of a rundown swimming pool. The concrete walls are dank, the floor tiles broken and dirty. A day spa this certainly ain't. The woman points at my clothes and motions for me to remove them. I strip down to everything but my underpants and clutch my soap and shampoo, shivering.

A few moments later I hear the sound of flip-flops smacking against the wet floor and look up to see a matronly woman wearing a blue scarf wrapped around her head like a dishrag. She's naked but for a pair of ragged underpants. Her enormous breasts have dark chocolate nipples the size of mandarins. They sag to her navel and swing as she walks. She gabbles something at me in rapid Arabic and tucks my arm firmly in the crook of hers, leading me to a set of big double doors.

Inside, it takes my eyes a few seconds to adjust to the dim light and the thick steam. When they do, I see an orgy of flesh spread out before me. Everywhere, walking, lying and sitting, are naked women with latte-coloured skin and the buxom figures of Renaissance-era models: voluptuous thighs, full bosoms and ample stomachs with multitudes of fleshy rolls and folds. I am the only non-Moroccan woman here and, though I may have put on weight, I feel as slender as Kate Moss by comparison.

The noise is uproarious. Women are yelling and laughing to one another across the room, babies are crying, children are screaming and there's the constant sound of water being sloshed in and out of buckets. The attendant leads me into the furthest of three interconnecting rooms and pushes me down by the shoulders, forcing me to sit on the tiles. And then she walks off.

I continue to hold on to my toiletries and wonder what to do next. Up above is a high domed ceiling with cut-out squares covered over in blue, green and yellow plastic, and in front of me a line of women traipse back and forth to a wall of taps at the far end to fill up their buckets.

sheep's head soup
and all that
141

Five minutes pass and I still have no idea what I'm supposed to be doing. I haven't seen that woman again. Do I wait for her to come back? Or do I just go and get a bucket and start washing myself? I get to my feet and start towards the taps. Suddenly she appears from nowhere and gives me a stern shake of the head. No. She gestures with her finger. Like a bad dog, I obediently slink back to where I was.

After only ever observing Moroccan women covered head to toe in robes, it is fascinating to see what they really look like. Beautiful women with plump lips and thick eyelashes lather bars of henna into hair which reaches almost to their waist. Friends scrub the backs of friends, mothers wash young daughters and daughters use flat combs to untangle their mothers' hair.

Then, without warning, the woman with the blue dishrag is back. A bucket in one hand, my arm in the other, she hoists me off the ground and leads me into the next room. She strides confidently forward in her thongs while I take baby steps behind her trying not to slip. Some of the women stare at me as we go by and I feel like the new kid at school. I surrender to it, shrugging my shoulders and grinning like a fool. To make matters worse, I realise I am wearing the world's most inappropriate underwear: a red G-string with bright green cherries on the front. Super.

When we reach the wall, the attendant sits down cross-legged, dragging me with her. She gestures for me to put my legs in a wide V shape and then, presumably because I don't do exactly as she wants, pulls me by the heels so I skid along the tiles on my buttocks. She wrenches my legs either side of her body and clamps my right foot under her armpit so my calf is pressed against her heaving bosom. Then she takes a cloth and, using one hand, starts scrubbing me industriously along the inside of my thighs, in between my fingers and toes and around my breasts in big circles while I lie there stunned.

Oh my god, I think, trying not to appear fazed. Then I'm pulled back up again and taken into the next room where she unexpectedly tips an entire bucket of cold water over my head, leaving me gasping like a fish.

'Massage,' the attendant says next, depleting her vocabulary of its only English word, and I'm pushed to lie face down on the tiles next to two small children. I watch them stare at me curiously as she soaps up my back. The kids giggle when my cheek is mooshed into someone's flip-flop and the force of her lathering pushes my head against the wall.

And then, just when I didn't think it could get any more humiliating, she reaches in between my butt cheeks with her index finger, scoops out an errant piece of soap and flings it against the wall near my head. From the corner of my eye I see something leave. What was that? Oh, just my dignity.

About an hour later I walk back on to the streets of Fez, shell-shocked. Tomorrow we leave Morocco and, I have got to admit, I'm not exactly sorry about that. Over the last three weeks I have experienced the most severe culture shock I've felt travelling anywhere. But I have also seen some of the most stunningly beautiful and diverse countryside in the world. And though I haven't been all that mad about the gender imbalance, the experience of having to relinquish control and of being at the whims of others has been humbling. I must say I've never felt more privileged to be a woman from Australia than I do now. While I may fret about career choices, at least I've got opportunities to fret about.

As I wander back to our *riad*, there's an orange glow in the medina as the lanterns in the street are turned on. I reach up and wring out my ponytail, which is still dripping from the bucketing I received earlier. Yes, I think, Julie was right. If there is a hell on earth, that *hammam* may well be it. But, boy, I certainly do feel clean.

CHAPTER 9

Searching for a spot of sunshine

I HAVE A PERPETUAL PROBLEM WITH LATENESS. TO BEGIN with, I was born a whole week later than I should have been. I was late walking down the aisle at Kellie's wedding when I acted as her maid of honour, having to sprint to get to the altar before her. And I was once so late to my first job as a radio newsreader, the news theme had started while I was still driving to work. Luckily for me, I've met my Siamese twin in the lateness stakes. Tom. Last year, we were late for our own wedding together. This was particularly lucky, because my mum was late too. Had we arrived on time she would have missed the entire ceremony by a good half hour. These things must be genetic.

Today, Tom and I are joined at the hip again as we take Maurizio on his final run, testing the outer limits of his ponypower in a display of acceleration that's making the poor little car shudder with gasket-straining effort. We're racing along at speeds that would be considered obscene on the autobahn, let alone this 130-kilometre-per-hour stretch of freeway on the Costa del Sol. But we have no choice. We must get to the train station on time so we can hand Maurizio back to the rental company and make our connection to Madrid.

Maurizio has been the mainstay of our lives over the past three months and it's going to feel funny saying goodbye. We have clocked up 13,200 kilometres together and he's taken us to places we would never have been able to go as ordinary tourists. We just hope the rental car inspectors don't look too closely at the paintwork and find that memento of his adventures in Sardinia.

You would think we'd be used to it by now, this lateness thing, and just factor it into our lives like an involuntary tic or a pissed uncle who you have to make allowances for. But, no, whenever we are late—which is often—we are always so damn surprised and outraged, like it is never our fault.

'What's the time?' Tom quizzes me for the third time in as many minutes. This gives a hint to the reason behind his tardiness. He refuses to wear a watch.

'It's ten to twelve. What time does our train go again?'

'Twelve fifteen.' He pushes on the accelerator even further. A sign for Malaga whizzes past in a blur, I have just enough time to make out the numbers. Forty kilometres to go.

'Why did we decide to go to that stupid post office this morning?' Tom rants. 'We should have sent all our Christmas presents yesterday afternoon. We had more time then. I knew we shouldn't have spent all afternoon drinking with Liz and Dean.'

After arriving back in Spain from Morocco, we have just spent a very pleasant couple of nights with two Australian friends of ours who live in Marbella. Yesterday, after showing us Antonio Banderas's restaurant, simply called Antonio, Liz and Dean took us to a questionable nightclub, which they insisted they had only visited once before despite knowing the bartenders a little too well. We ended up downing more shots of vodka than is sensible while watching bored-looking teenage podium dancers in barely-there hot pants jiggle their bits to the best of Nelly and Shaggy.

'If we miss this train we're screwed,' Tom says. 'There isn't another one until tomorrow. We'll have to buy new tickets and it would stuff up all our other connections to Barcelona and Rome.'

We speed up even more. I take a look at the dashboard and get a shock. Let's just say Maurizio is now bettering the top speed stated in the Renault Modus manual.

Amazingly, we screech into the car park with two minutes to spare. The rental car guys are waiting for us and we practically pelt the keys at their heads as we grab our gear and sprint for the platform. There's no time for tearful farewells or remembrances of times past with our trusty companion. 'Bye Maurizio!' is all we have time to yell behind us as we take off. 'Thanks for the good times.' We leap on to the train a half-second before it pulls away from the platform and collapse into our seats, huffing like the couple of unfit, overfed heffalumps we now are. And, just like that, the first part of our trip is over and the cities tour has begun.

◆ ◆ ◆ ◆ ◆

We arrive in Madrid to discover that it is both the festive season and frigging cold. Morocco had been relatively balmy and it had also been devoid of Christmas paraphernalia. Here it's only early December but it seems like Santa has binged on yuletide cheer and done a technicolour yawn of neon candy canes and bon-bons down every street.

We dump our bags in our foxhole of a hotel room. We can just swing a cat in the bedroom but even a kitten would hit the bathroom walls. We learn soon enough that most hotel rooms in European cities are tiny. We also discover that Europeans overcompensate for winter by making all their indoor areas feel like saunas. From a fashion perspective, this poses quite the conundrum as I have to devise outfits for two completely different environments: four jumpers, a sheepskin balaclava and hot water bottles strapped to my feet to nip out and buy a paper, while inside all that's required is a fig leaf and a smile.

We are travelling to six major cities in the twenty-four days between now and Christmas Eve when we fly to Washington, a very lean average of four days in each place. Just enough time to see all the major landmarks, get a feel for the local flavour, find the best places to eat and drink and then do each of those two things rather heartily. At least this is what we are telling each other now when, really, we're kind of kicking ourselves that we didn't allow for more fat in our timetable.

Having shadowed Tom all over Morocco, I am itching for some alone time. We vow to spend our days in Madrid sightseeing solo and then meet up at night. This way, we'll hopefully have something more to say to each other at dinner than 'pass the salt'. Conversation has stalled so badly in the last week that when we do speak we often comment on exactly the same thing. 'Why bother even talking at all?' has become our joking catch-cry and we have even started taking books to the table at meal times.

After breakfast the next morning, I take my backpack with a bottle of water and an apple and plug in my iPod. With a spring in my step I walk past the Christmas markets at the Plaza Mayor, where the inquisitors used to carry out public punishments, and down to the Puerto del Sol, the square bang in the centre of Madrid's CBD. Oh, to be free once again to do as I please. Madrid is prime-rib carrion for culture vultures and I intend to gorge myself silly at the modern art museum Reina Sofia and the Prado, which features Picasso's *Guernica* and big, big canvases by El Greco, Velázquez, Rafael and Goya.

There is internet access at our hotel and later I decide to bite the bullet and check my inbox. I have been avoiding the internet cafés since I sent the email to my colleagues back in Sydney. I hold my breath and open my account. I have seven new messages. Three of them are from work. I bite my lip and pray for kind words, thinking that if I were them, I would be a little indignant given my insistence that I would definitely be returning. But, as I read on, I go positively weak-kneed with relief.

I totally understand what you're saying and of course respect any decision you make.

I envy your ability to travel without deadline; I would like to do it myself one day.

Please let us know when you're coming back. Thanks again for all your hard work and loyalty to us over the years; it will never be as good!

I log off feeling wistful. In a way, if they were angry it would have been easier to put it all behind me. Reading their gracious emails has brought on a rush of warm feelings and a twinge of regret that I won't be working with them again. Especially now they have been so darn decent about it.

The next day I take my lunch amid the autumnal leaves of the Parque del Buen Retiro, Madrid's botanic gardens, and marvel at the peace and quiet. It's wonderful to be in a place where I can sit on my own without interruption. Later, as night falls, I refuel with a quick snack standing at the counter of one of the many Museo del Jamon stores, where hundreds of *jamóns serrano* hang from the ceiling. The different types of *jamón* are all listed on a board and vary wildly in price. At the Bill Gates end of the spectrum is *Jabugo*. Apparently it is cured in mountain snow and made from the meat of pigs that have eaten nothing but acorns, giving it a nutty flavour. I go for something a little more at the bankrupt Michael Jackson end. Though I find it a little hard to get my head around, I am told I must eat the white ribbons of fat in the paper-thin slices of meat. I stuff a piece in my mouth and am surprised at how the fat offsets the salty dryness of the meat, making it taste silky and creamy.

I'm learning to adjust my eating routines to fit in with the Spaniards', which is why I'm eating a little snack now. If Tom and I go out to dinner at our usual time of 8 pm, we'll be the only ones in the restaurant. *Madrilenos* typically don't eat until 10 or 11 pm, so the only way I can make it to the dinner table without gnawing off my own arm in hunger is to try and eat five meals a day. It's a pastry for breakfast, then perhaps a little wedge of tortilla at 11 am; a *bocadillo*, or small sandwich, at

3 pm and a bite or two of tapas around 6.30 pm with a few drinks. Then I'm primed for dinner by 10 pm. I am told many Spaniards manage to find room to squeeze in a sixth course for the day: *chocolate con churros*.

Tom has already discovered Spanish hot chocolate, which he has declared the reason why winter was invented, but we are yet to try it *completos* with *churros*, the long doughnuty fingers which are made specifically for dunking. The most famous place in town for this fabulous gluttony is Chocolateria San Gines, where queues have been forming out the door for more than a hundred years. It's only open between the hours of 6 pm and 7.30 am and it's a local convention to go out on an all-night drinking binge, or *juerga*, duck in for a cheeky *chocolate con churros* on your way home, rinse off the nightclub fumes in the shower and go straight to the office.

Tonight we have decided to make an evening of it and take in a double-bill of native specialties, beginning with dinner at the place where Ava Gardner is said to have taken her toyboys. In between having affairs with Howard Hughes and George C. Scott, Gardner got loved up with the matador Luis Miguel Dominguin and actor Mario Cabré, dining with them in the front room of Calle de la Bola. We arrive just after 10 pm and are seated out the back with the other tourists. Like them, we order the dish this place has been known for since Gardner's time: *cocido*, or bullfighter's stew.

A big enamel jug is brought to the table and the waiter strains the broth off the stew into a bowl. This soup is the starter. There is a layer of oil about half a centimetre deep on top of a broth so beefy and rich it makes me feel sick. I can't eat more than a few mouthfuls and get a stern raise of the eyebrow from our middle-aged waiter. Next, the rest of the jug's contents are poured out on to a plate: custard-coloured chickpeas, a hunk of *jamón serrano*, another of pork, a nugget of gelatinous beef and, most disgustingly, a big spongy slab of white fat. To garnish this delicious treat, the waiter then scoops two big spoonfuls of boiled cabbage on top. No wonder matadors feel the urge to stab things with swords. I'd be really angry if a dish this awful was named after me, too.

Afterwards, we walk up the end of a seedy looking alley to find Chocolateria San Gines. It's all bow-tied waiters and velvet settees inside. The thick, thick hot chocolate is kept on the counter in an urn and stirred with a motorised paddle so it doesn't set solid. We get two mugs and a plate of freshly fried golden *churros*. These are about thirty centimetres long and as thick as a jumbo jelly snake. Tom picks one up and inspects it. 'They don't have any sugar or cinnamon sprinkled on the outside,' he says, disappointed.

'Maybe the batter's sweet?' We tentatively dip the *churros* into our cups. Tom chews a few times and makes a face.

'Yuck,' he says.

'Really?'

'Yeah.' He puts the rest of it on the plate and pushes it away. 'It's savoury and weird. Like dipping a French fry into hot chocolate.'

On our last day, I am on my way to see El Palacio Real, the royal palace, which is said to have more rooms than any other in Europe, when a statue in a small courtyard between two buildings catches my eye. It looks so realistic I am compelled to stop and stare at it for a while. It's a life-sized bronze cast of an old man, fashioned so that it looks as though he's peering over a railing. I am wondering who this person was and why he's been immortalised, when another old man, a real one, with a smart woollen scarf, coat and peaked hat, shuffles over to join me.

'*Hola*,' he greets me, pointing to the statue and giving me a crinkly-eyed smile. He rests on the railing next to me, life imitating art. In Spanish, he asks me where I'm from and if I speak his language. Australia, I tell him and, no, I don't.

'*Francesa*? *Italiana*?' He asks hopefully.

'No,' I shrug helplessly, feeling ignorant. 'Only *inglesa*.'

He laughs at this and points to his chest: 'Only a little *inglesa*.'

He then attempts to tell me, using bits of Spanish, Italian and French, the story of the statue: who it is and how it came to be here. It is sort of like listening to opera—even though I can't understand the words, I know exactly what he means.

He ends his story dramatically. 'And now,' he halts for emphasis, '*muerta*!' To illustrate his meaning he makes a choking noise, widens his eyes, hangs his tongue out the side of his mouth and clutches his hands to this throat. We both burst out laughing and I reach out and pat him on the arm. He takes my hand and squeezes it affectionately. I am utterly charmed.

'*Gracias*!' I say and he shuffles off, turning around once to wave at me from up the street.

It was just a small thing and it's likely he will have forgotten all about it in five minutes' time. But that will probably stand out as a highlight when I think back on my time in Madrid. It is the serendipitous moments like these, the random conversations, that affect you the most and stick in your mind long after the tourist landmarks are forgotten. Crossing the language barrier to share a joke with someone and making a connection with a complete stranger—that's the kind of stuff that gives travel its magic.

No sooner do we get off the train in Barcelona the next day than a stomach bug I contracted from a rogue serving of couscous somewhere in Morocco re-emerges. I end up being bedridden for three out of the four days we're here.

From what I do see I notice that Barcelona is funkier than grand, regal Madrid. It's the first time I have seen a real 'city' beach where apartments and restaurants are built right up to the edge of the sand. On the cold sunny Sunday when I finally feel well enough to sightsee, I find a favourite hangout for groovy locals, who sit and chill with their newspapers and beers, chatting to friends. We take a cable car trip that runs from near the Olympic park across the port and offers great views of the city and coast. Even though we were all crammed in like sardines, Tom and I get a prime window possie and are able to see the snaky green strip of Las Ramblas filled with buskers and market stalls, a big whale-shaped sculpture by the sand which is all glittering and golden, the port and its Darling Harbour-style complex, and the big wooden ramps where luxury cruisers the size of small hotels are built.

That night, we are wandering around the Gothic Quarter—which really does look the way it sounds, all medieval buildings with gargoyles and things on top—when I hear the strains of reedy fairground music. Around the next corner in a square is a group of ageing locals who are holding hands and dancing in front of a cathedral. Dozens of people have formed circles, some with just four or six, others in groups as big as thirty. They concentrate as they slowly step in time to the music, doing a point-step-step-point in one direction, before holding their arms up and leaping the other way. The energy and size of the leaps vary depending on how old they are. They are all wearing their ordinary weekend attire and some have stripped off their jackets, scarves and handbags, which are piled up in the centre of the circles. I discover later they are doing a Catalan dance called the *sardana*, which locals have performed on Sunday nights in this same spot for decades. I feel lucky to have stumbled upon it and huddle next to Tom to watch as the mist settles in, happy to be a small part of this tradition tonight.

◆ ◆ ◆ ◆ ◆

Twenty-four hours later and the scene couldn't be less idyllic. After two train rides and a plane trip, we have barely been in Rome an hour when we find ourselves embroiled in a very public marital spat in the middle of a busy street. After Tom legitimately complained how he had done most of the organisation for our trip, I promised to pull my weight and book all the hotels in the cities. But I've been, well, maybe a little slapdash on the details—let's face it, details can be boring—such as double-checking that the addresses listed in our guidebook from two years ago are still current. Now we're standing outside a bar which I guess once upon a time used to be a hotel.

Tom is fuming. 'I thought you knew where this place was.'

'I did. I mean, I do. Here, in this guidebook, it says it's supposed to be right here. How was I supposed to know they've moved?'

'Well, you could have checked their address when you emailed them. That's what normal people would do.'

The hairs on the back of my neck bristle. Normal? And then … the gloves are off.

A series of verbal explosions follows, with a few 'don't speak to me like thats' and various expletives added for good measure. Because we don't know anyone here and naively assume that no one can understand us, we are really letting rip. I'm usually described as 'soft-spoken', but I don't think many people have seen me when I get really mad. I don't make a practice of yelling and screaming in the middle of the street, but I'm frazzled from travelling, it's dark, I'm cold. And when you're at the end of your tether there is a strange satisfaction in taking out all that frustration on someone else.

Suddenly, a young man wearing an apron emerges from the bar looking very distressed. 'No, no, no, no, no,' he says, wringing his hands. This stops us in our tracks. We must have really gone too far to ruffle the normally fiery Italians. He takes us by the arms and leads us inside, where his wife uses the phone to call the operator—I also have the wrong number for the hotel (yes, yes, I know!)—then rings the place and gives us the new address. We jump in a taxi, waving embarrassed goodbyes.

The next few days pass comparatively calmly. Rome is a take-your-breath-away kind of city. It has ruins and monuments that make you go 'wow' at every turn. I get a cricked neck from constantly looking up at all that antiquity, but then discover the view down at street level. Everyone is trying to outdo each other in the glamour stakes. Even the policemen ooze sexuality as they patrol on flashy motorbikes wearing big mirrored sunglasses and uniforms they must have been sewn into. Many of the women are supermodel-slim, meowing around town in luxuriant furs and tight jeans tucked into knee-high boots. I feel positively frumpy by comparison and am growing very tired of my travel wardrobe. There are only so many things you can do with a black top and scarves.

We visit all the usual suspects. At the Forum we pause at Caesar's temple where history buffs still leave flowers, we listen to an orchestra playing in the freezing cold by the Spanish Steps and we queue with the masses at the Vatican. Despite the wintery weather, we also go to the place considered to serve the best gelato in all of Rome and perhaps Italy, Il Gelato di San Crispino. They only serve in tubs because 'cones interfere with the flavours'. I have a scoop of pannacotta with chips of seventy per cent cacao flecked through, while Tom has ordered dark chocolate and whisky.

A few moments later he stops.

'What is it?' I ask.

He's recognised something. 'Wait here,' he tells me and disappears around the corner. I stand, licking my spoon, wondering what he's up to. A second later he is back, smiling as though he has a surprise. 'I thought this was where we were,' he says, remembering the spot from when he visited as a teenager. He leads me by the arm down an alleyway, and as we turn the corner, the streetscape opens up to a piazza.

'The Trevi Fountain!' I exclaim. It's luminous in the late afternoon light and so dazzlingly beautiful my eyes fill with tears. The gelati momentarily forgotten, we dodge past the rose-sellers lining the steps and throw a few coins in to ensure our return.

Another day is spent going from one famous espresso bar to another, seeking out Rome's best coffee. We start with the city's oldest, Antico Caffè Greco. Chopin, Wagner, Byron and Goethe have all reclined on the red velvet chairs here. I get a terse language lesson at another renowned establishment, Caffè Eustacia, when we finally get inside after standing in a queue which weaves out the door. I place my order in Italian and the bow-tied elderly barista barks, '*Due espressi!* Not *espresso*,' as if he is lecturing a small child. Shocked by his forcefulness, I laugh and shrug my shoulders to lighten the moment. But he remains stern, pointing a finger in my face, saying, 'No', and repeating his drill to teach me the correct plural.

Later I go out on my own and find the place which possibly makes the best coffee in all of Rome, La Tazza D'Oro, which translates as The Golden Cup. Right in front of the Pantheon, it's crowded with Romans who lean against the bamboo walls inside and spill out on to the steps. I may have only just learned the correct way to order it, but as I stand at the bar sipping my chocolatey-tasting espresso I smugly congratulate myself for at least learning to drink coffee as the Italians do. Particularly when two American girls, who have asked for cappuccinos, mistake me for a native. 'Imagine being able to drink coffee like that.' One of them points me out to her friend, speaking in English right next to me but assuming I can't understand.

'Wow,' the other says, fluffing out her hair and looking at my cup. 'It's so strong, so little! So Italian!'

I have to turn my head so they don't see me laughing.

On our last night, we decide it would be nice to have dinner at the bar where we had the big blue the night we arrived, just so they know we didn't end up killing each other. We go inside and take a seat, peeling off our layers of coats, scarves, jumpers and gloves. It's full of trendy young things drinking wine as jazz plays in the background. The young couple who helped us out spot us from behind the bar and come over to greet us like long-lost friends.

'You-ah find your hotel?' His dark eyes look at me earnestly as he takes my hand in both of his.

'Yes,' I say, giving an embarrassed laugh. 'Yes, we did after all that. *Grazie.*'

'We were so worried about you,' says his wife, who has taken off her apron and is wearing a tight black woollen dress.

'Yes,' he nods. 'We-ah thought you might-ah get divorce.'

Tom and I laugh heartily at this as if they're a couple of wags. Divorce? Why, that's just crazy talk.

But then again, we still have to travel together for another two and a half months.

The young Italian woman on the other side of our table puts her spoon down and shuts her eyes. '*Bellissimo, bellissimo,*' she sighs in rapture. I look across and notice that she has just taken her first mouthful of *ribollita*. This dish, literally 're-boiled', is made by baking left-over minestrone layered with garlic-rubbed toasted bread. It can take up to three days to prepare, but the plates at our table are slurped clean in mere minutes.

We travelled from Rome to Florence two days ago. So far, we have seen the Uffizi, the leather markets, the Ponte Vecchio and walked up to Piazza Michelangelo to watch the sunset. It's now Sunday and we have one more highlight to enjoy: the long, long lunch. Scenes of family banquets from movies like *The Godfather* and *Big Night* have made me yearn to be part of a real Italian feast. I think I've found it.

The restaurant we're in, Il Latini, is one of the best places to try Florence's most famous menu item, *bistecca fiorentina*, massive T-bone steaks grilled over wood. We were warned it is a popular place for local families to get together on a Sunday so we searched the back alleys last night until we found it and made a reservation for lunch. When we arrive today, a good fifteen minutes before the doors open, there are already about 150 people outside with the desperate look of those queuing at soup kitchens during the Depression.

The waiter seats us at a big communal table in the middle of six rowdy young Italians on holidays. Even though we can barely communicate with each other, they embrace us into their party, pouring us glasses of Chianti from the large bottles in the middle of the table. A couple of glasses later, the waiter comes over, explaining in half-Italian, half-English, that there is no menu and he will just bring us whatever is good. '*Perfetto!*' we cry. Perhaps we should slow down on the Chianti. As well as the *ribollita*, he serves us a platter of house-cured prosciutto and *salame*, small rounds of *crostini* spread with chicken livers, then a plate of tomatoes and *bocconcini* followed by spinach and ricotta ravioli in tomato *sugo*. Then we need to undo our top buttons because the *bistecca* has been dehorned.

The waiter delivers one steak for every two people. Each one weighs a kilo. The outside is rubbed with olive oil, salt and rosemary and perfectly charred. The inside has only received a breath of heat so it's on the rare side of blue. The meat is incredibly tender and of such high quality we wonder whether the restaurant has its own cattle farm. After one bite, the slim blonde woman to my right, who's barely eaten a thing so far, puts her fork down saying, '*basta, basta*' (enough).

Just relax, lady, I think as I watch her. But I stop short of judging her too harshly. I realise that's how I used to be.

Like a lot of young women I know, I have always been pretty image-conscious and afraid of putting on weight. So I carefully monitored what I ate and dragged myself out of the house to exercise even when I didn't feel like it. Whenever I looked at a block of chocolate, a bowl of ice cream or even butter and full cream milk, I would think 'bad', but a bowl of fruit and muesli or pretty much anything else low in fat or sugar would earn itself a diet gold star. After denying myself all week, on a Sunday night I might eat some chocolate. But then I would end up eating the whole block because I'd feel frantic about not being able to have it again until a whole week later. Maybe this secret fear was a hangover from the time I ballooned as a seven-year-old? I expended an awful lot of energy thinking about food and exercise. I may have been slim, but I wasn't having much fun. Tom didn't like it much either, the way I'd scour menus for the least fattening thing and insist we share dessert, or not eat it at all. But a lot of my friends acted this way too, and we would compare notes on how 'good' or 'bad' we'd been that week as we huffed along on our power walks.

It is only since being on this trip and letting my hair down a bit that I have realised it was a pretty unhealthy mindset. When I first arrived in Europe I was genuinely alarmed to discover that most cafés don't—or won't—serve skim milk and I would look at all the creamy buttery dishes on the menu wishing for a salad. I fought a battle with myself, wanting to try all the yummy cheeses and breads but knowing what that would mean for my waistline. Then, the one thing I spent years being terrified of actually happened. I put on weight. So far it's something in the order of six kilos, but who's counting. Some time after leaving France I stopped fighting it and just relaxed. It actually wasn't so scary after all.

I don't look disgusting as I had feared I would, just a little curvier than normal. My cheeks have filled out and my stomach has a few rolls on it, but my hair is shinier than it's ever been and my skin is positively glowing. So what if I have outgrown some of my clothes? I know I'll probably lose the weight again when we get home and don't eat out every night. But for the first time in ages, I feel I've got a healthy relationship with my body. Now, I have dessert every day—but I often don't feel the need to gobble it all down because I know that I can always have more tomorrow.

After our main course we get chatting to Mario and Sofia who are visiting from Sicily. 'The best place in the world. *Numero uno*,' Mario enthuses. He looks to be in his twenties. He is well-groomed in a self-conscious way with prominent labels on his clothes and too much hair product. His girlfriend looks sweet with a low-cut pink jumper and a crucifix on a chain. Mario's friend sitting next to him, with the skinny blonde, is from Carrara.

'Carrara is a very beautiful place,' Mario says, grinning while pretending to stroke a growing Pinocchio nose. 'But *Sicilia*. Aaaah, *il mio dio.*' He stops and his face takes on a dreamy, faraway expression. 'In my town there is a *molto*—how you say in English?—*amazing* biscuit. You have to try the wine and the food. The *limoncello*, *arancina*—the best!'

I eye off his lean form. 'How do you stay so slim with all that delicious food then?'

'We go to gym, sometimes two hours every day,' he replies. 'And I try and stay away from that biscuit.'

At the end of the lunch, after our new friend proposes various toasts to the 'kangaroos', we hug and kiss goodbye and stagger out carrying a week's worth of food and wine inside us. No wonder Marlon Brando became twice the man he used to be by the end of the *Godfather* movies. The endurance you need to get through a big Italian feast like this, it should be made an Olympic sport.

It's been two days since we left Florence and we've been exploring the streets, parks and cafés of London. I'm supposed to be imagining all of this as my future home. Instead, I'm having silent moments of utter panic. London is definitely not Australia. Which is obvious, really. Only I kind of thought it might be. For a start, there are so many Australians living here—something like six hundred thousand at any given time. We share many cultural reference points with the UK: both have Queen Elizabeth as our head of state, both have the Westminster system of government and, for some weird reason, both watch *Neighbours* and *Home and Away*. Willingly. But Australia never gets weather like this.

It is *omigod* cold. The icy wind knifes through my clothes then crawls into my joints and twinges like a toothache. Then, by contrast with all the quiet reserved Londoners I have met, I am loud and garish and feel as ocker as Paul Hogan. I've discovered this by just being my normal self, saying 'hi' to shopkeepers who recoil in fright like I'm trying to sell them something and laughing out loud at jokes in the street while everyone else scurries along silently. Also, where is the sunshine? And the trees? The sky is so low it appears as though it presses down on the very tops of the austere white terrace houses and in mid-winter it's getting dark at four in the afternoon.

I haven't said a word of this to Tom's sister Jess, who has embraced the city as home. Or Tom, who's busy talking to people about where he might be able to find work. A small part of me is changing my mind about that grand plan we made in Gaucin and wishing for a way out. Still, first impressions can be wrong. I vow to try and find a bright side among all the bleakness.

We dine up the top of the OXO tower with my oldest friend Katie, who's been here for four years working at a big investment bank. She gives it to us straight. 'I'm not going to lie to you,' she says. 'Winter here is horrible if you're from a warm country like Australia. I sometimes spend all weekend in bed. It can be hard to make friends. I've found that even now my friends are all expats.' She takes a sip of champagne and looks at the view across the Thames. It's winking with Christmas lights strung along the shores. 'It's really all about the career opportunities,' she continues, 'which are fantastic if you're prepared to put in the groundwork. And the travel. To be able to get on a plane and be in Europe in less than an hour— well, that's pretty magic.'

I look across at Tom. 'Yeah, I've got to tell you, that's a huge part of the appeal for us,' I say.

She wrinkles her nose. 'The only problem is everyone I know tends to work such long hours here that, come the weekend, all you want to do is chill out,' she says resignedly. 'To be truthful, sometimes jumping on a plane is the last thing you feel like doing.'

Jess takes us on a tour of the chichi parts, doing the big sell. We lunch at a trendy café where 'Salman Rushdie sat at the table next to us last weekend', Jess tells us. She shows us Primrose Hill where she regularly sees Jude Law and Sienna Miller and we take a brisk morning walk around Kensington Gardens and the Portobello Road market. On our last day we drive through the countryside to Oxford and have a pint of warm ale in a real English pub beside a roaring fire. It's really very charming.

But try as I might to picture myself walking around these places as a bona fide resident in a few months' time, I just can't see it. It's so different to how I imagined it would be. I wonder how I'll get my head around the places, people and popular culture I've never heard of before. Who on earth are Cat Deeley and Ant and Deck? What is a chav? A sense of growing disquiet bubbles in the pit of my stomach. It's normal to be a little concerned, but I'm wondering if maybe I rushed into making this decision without pausing first to ask myself why.

The problem is, I've told everyone. It's locked in. I wonder, this desire to start over in London—is it because I want to avoid my demons? The prospect of having to reconstruct my life if we were to move back to Sydney terrifies me. I have no idea where I'd work or what I'd do. By staying overseas I don't have to think about it. The adventure continues. I'm also worried that if I go home I'll revert to the person I used to be. If everything around me is the same, how can I be different?

I am no closer to any answers as we leave to catch the early flight to Paris.

◆ ◆ ◆ ◆ ◆

'Happy birthday!' It's my brother, ringing me on my mobile, just as we reach the boarding gate.

'Hey, Ben. You're the first family member of the day to call.'

'When do you go to my favourite city?'

'I'm just getting on the plane. I can't wait. I've made a booking at this very chic Parisian bistro for dinner tonight and everything. I've even got a new dress.'

'Well, if you're going to the Louvre,' Ben instructs, passing on his wisdom from several trips to Paris to visit his girlfriend who is studying there, 'don't line up like a chump at the entrance with all the Americans. Find the shopping centre underneath. Walk through it and there's an entrance which goes straight upstairs. You can dodge the whole queue. And then, rather than getting on those touristy boats where you have to hold a phone up to your ear like a sap …'

'Ah, thanks,' I interrupt. 'But I really have to go. They're calling out our names now.'

'Okay. Well, happy birthday. You're ancient now! Remember what I said about the Louvre. Oh, and you'd be a sucker if you went drinking at the bars outside of happy hour.'

On the plane, I think about my brother's 'ancient' jibe. I'm surprised to be this age yet still feel so young. My mum was practically a kid herself when she gave birth to me. I can recall her thirtieth birthday vividly because I was nine years old. On that day I remember thinking, 'Oh my god. Thirty. That is so past it.' But she seemed so much more responsible and grown up than I am. She was on to her second marriage, owned a house and had two children.

The lead-up to turning thirty has prompted a stocktake of where I'm up to. What I've achieved, what I haven't, if I'm the kind of person I want to be, what I want to do with my life. I'm reminded again of my friend's comment about now being 'your potential'. This idea used to fill me with blind panic. Now that I have got the big three-oh by the scruff of the neck, I feel like that process of 'finding myself' might be drawing to some kind of conclusion. Getting off the career treadmill has allowed me to pause and think. I look across at Tom, who's dozing in his seat. Up here, as we fly across the Channel, it's extraordinary the difference I feel since I flew over nearly four months ago. I'm much more comfortable with myself and I'm beginning to really like the idea of who I am. And the fact that I'm about to celebrate in one of the world's most glamorous cities, well, that certainly helps.

An hour later and we're standing by the luggage carousel at Charles de Gaulle airport watching the bags go around. And around. And around. Until there are only two lonely suitcases left. Neither of them is mine. Tom's backpack was one of the first to come out. But my bag has gone AWOL. Two airport attendants pull up in a motorised buggy and grab the two unclaimed pieces of luggage.

I approach one of the men and begin in my best French, '*Excusez-moi, s'il vous plaît …*'

'Finished!' he cuts me off.

'But …'

'Finished,' he repeats sniffily, making a horizontal chopping motion with his hand. Then, still glaring at me, he stabs his finger at a sign that says '*Bagages Perdus*' and has an arrow pointing in the direction of the lost luggage counter. He turns his back on me, wiping his hands of any further responsibility. Don't you know it's my birthday, you horrible man?

An hour, a long queue, three forms and several frustrated exchanges with indifferent 'customer service' representatives later, we come to the conclusion that my bag and I will not be reunited today. In fact, the airline can't say if a reunion is on the cards, ever. It slowly dawns on me exactly what this means. I have been left high and dry in the style capital of the world. This is the city where even poodles wear haute couture and I am dressed in a sloppy joe with stains on it and my oldest jeans. As my eyes travel further south I remember I am wearing—*quelle horreur!*—*chaussures de sport* (sneakers). I put on my daggiest outfit this morning because I was planning to have a shower and get changed as soon as we got to our hotel. I wanted to look fresh for the day. I groan again as I realise I don't even have any make-up with me. Or the new dress I had bought especially for the fancy restaurant.

In the months before we left Australia, I had bunged on a bit of a 'princess' routine whenever the topic of my birthday came up. Since I wouldn't be able to have the requisite big party with friends and family, I set about creating the perfect night in Paris as a substitute. While Tom rolled his eyes, I researched all the fancy-pants restaurants and eventually booked a table at Allard, a famous Left Bank bistro which promised to have Parisian ambience by the ladle-full. I also developed some very firm ideas about how I would look on this auspicious night, hence the new dress.

At no stage did my carefully thought out plans involve a stained sloppy joe. Maybe this is some kind of divine punishment for behaving like a spoiled brat about all this birthday business. Tom gives the woman behind the counter the number of the place we're staying and asks her to call if my bag ever does show up.

After moping for a few hours, I decide to make the most of what's left of the day. We are in Paris after all. We cross one of the stone bridges over the Seine, moving fast to keep warm in the cold, grey weather. I am in the middle of blathering on about something when I look off to the left and see an unmistakable shape through the mist that makes me stop, mid-sentence.

'Oh, it's the Eiffel Tower! I think? Sort of.' I can only see its criss-crossed metal feet. The low-lying cloud has gobbled up everything else. It's still a thrill to see a part of this most famous of icons in real life, right in front of me. We wander around the Tuileries, oohing and ahhing at the sculpture garden.

Later that afternoon I cover my stains with my pashmina and drag Tom to the ultimate place for the chinking of china, the Ladurée *salon du thé*. We feast on the to-die-for macaroons. There are so many flavours it is difficult to choose, but I end up selecting dark chocolate, raspberry, vanilla bean and salted caramel. I am in seventh heaven as I take in my surroundings, a living, breathing example of Parisian chic. The walls are decorated with bright birds of paradise flying through a tropical jungle mural. The lamps are the shape of palm trees and our fellow female tea-sippers are dripping in diamonds and Chanel. Even the Maltese terrier at the next table has a diamond collar.

Back at our room there is a message under the door to contact reception. The man at the front desk is not only friendly but speaks perfect English. 'Katrina Blowers?' He looks at me expectantly. I nod. 'I have good news. The airline called this afternoon. They have found your bag.'

'Fantastic,' I cry. Here comes my dress. And here comes my make-up. 'Did they say when I could have it?'

'Well,' he pauses. 'That is the bad news. It is still in London. And they won't be able to get it on a flight until tomorrow.'

My face falls. 'Oh. Well, at least they've found it, I guess. But tomorrow? *Merde.*'

I think about going shopping for a new outfit, but it seems such a waste to have to buy new shoes, stockings and a dress for just one night. Especially when our savings are only flowing in one direction.

Tom looks me up and down. 'Could you wear what you've got on?'

I snort. 'I doubt they'd even let me through the door. And I'd feel uncomfortable all night. I only want to do the whole fancy dinner thing if we're going to do it properly. Let's just cancel it.'

'We could always go tomorrow after you get your bag back.'

'I don't mean to be precious, but tomorrow won't be my birthday anymore,' I sigh. 'It wouldn't be the same.'

So, despite the best laid plans, my thirtieth birthday dinner becomes crêpes from a roadside cart in Saint Germain. We stand under the street light devouring crispy batter filled with ham, egg and gruyère cheese wrapped in a paper napkin. On the way here, we happened to pass by the restaurant we are supposed to be going to and peered through the window. Inside, the table lamps cast a sparkling glow on the elaborate jewellery and sequined cocktail dresses of the diners who were feasting on duck *confit* and twice-cooked soufflé. I take another bite of my crêpe, adding melted cheese to my stain collection. Suddenly, I don't care about missing out on it all.

'Happy birthday, gorgeous,' Tom grins at me and raises his crêpe as a toast. I raise mine in return and am consumed by a fit of giggles.

'Look at us,' I eventually manage. 'Out of all the options, all the possibilities, all the research and agonising about trying to create the perfect night. I never thought I'd spend my thirtieth birthday dinner eating takeaway on the side of the road in jeans and sneakers.'

But there's nothing else I'd rather be doing and no one else I would prefer to be spending it with. My husband, the soft street lamps of Saint Germain and the best damn crêpe I've ever tasted. This is more than enough for me.

We wipe the grease from our hands and go in search of a bar with a not-too-strict dress code so we can down a few thousand martinis for dessert. I turn my head and take one last look behind me at our dinner spot as Tom puts his arm around my shoulders and shepherds me around the corner. It's a birthday moment I'll never forget.

CHAPTER 10

A brand new start of it

'HAIL MARY, FULL OF GRACE, THE LORD IS WITH THEE ...'

Paris is several hours behind us. As we fly to Washington DC I turn around again to look at the fifty-something woman who's in the aisle seat behind me. She's dressed in the black clothes of a Spanish widow. A good or bad flight comes down to the lottery of which passengers you sit next to. Today I have drawn the wrong numbers. This woman won't stop praying. Her benedictions were mouthed silently at first, the clicking of her rosary beads drawing my attention to them. But now her Hail Marys are getting louder and more rhythmic, as though she's rapping for the Lord.

'Blessed art thou among women ...'

Whump! Once again, the plane bucks like a mechanical bull.

I look to Tom for comfort, but he's somehow sleeping soundly. This is the worst turbulence I have ever experienced. Flight attendants sprint up the aisles snapping tray tables shut. I check their faces for signs of panic but their expressions remain mask-like.

The plane hits another pocket. It makes me jiggle in my chair so violently my fillings feel like they're about to pop out. The flight attendants buckle themselves into seats next to the emergency doors. I take some deep breaths. This is not good.

Crack!

I jump as a piece of luggage falls from the overhead locker. One of two flight attendants braces herself against a seat to pick it back up. The plane does a series of brisk bunny-hops, throwing her off balance. I look up to see the ceiling rattling.

'And at the hour of our death …'

Then suddenly the turbulence clears. I relax my hands. The flight attendants unbuckle themselves and straighten out their uniforms. The plane is so stable and quiet now, it's like nothing ever happened. I wonder if it will last. A short while later, the seatbelt signs are switched off and there is a flurry of activity as passengers form queues for the toilets.

An hour later it is still peaceful. I seem to be the only person awake. My religious friend is all Hail Maryed out and her chin nods against her chest. Tom continues sleeping like a baby, albeit one who wears a mask and earplugs. He has missed the excitement entirely. I flick through all the cooking shows and *Friends* reruns on the entertainment system, relieved by the tranquillity.

We have two and a bit months left of our journey. Until now our itinerary has been fairly planned. The European and Moroccan legs were all we really focused on, leaving whatever happens in the months after Christmas and New Year as a vague addition. We've talked about South America and Southeast Asia as possible next destinations, but exactly where is anyone's guess. Luckily we've got a couple of weeks in the United States to figure it out.

We'll be staying with Greg and Wil and I can't wait to spend some time lounging around their home. After so long away I'm really beginning to crave familiarity and I miss all my family and friends. Particularly now that it's Christmas Eve. This longing has been intensified by an email I read during our brief stopover at Heathrow. It was from Kellie and her husband. There was no message in it, except for the words in the title: 'Merry Christmas Aunty Katrina!' And an attachment.

I opened it up thinking it might be a silly photo of their dog Mussie wearing reindeer ears. To my surprise, it was an ultrasound picture. There, in fuzzy black and white, was the image of a baby no bigger than a walnut. I started blubbering like a twit in the middle of the airport lounge. But my happiness was also tinged with the regret of not being there to share such a big moment in my best friend's life. And now that we are moving to London, I realise I won't be there for the birth either.

I tilt my chair back and rearrange my blanket. This homesickness is very reminiscent of how I felt when we first left. Let's hope seeing Greg and Wil will cure it.

◆ ◆ ◆ ◆ ◆

The middle of Washington DC is possibly the most stylish Christmas-ey place in the world. There are no tacky neon reindeers or gaudy nativity scenes here. All the old-fashioned terrace houses around DuPont Circle, where Greg and Wil live, have chic wreaths on their doors and sumptuous decorations adorning their stoops. Even the big stone lions that guard many of the city's bridges sit pretty with fat velvet ribbons tied around their necks. There is a chill in the air but, unfortunately, I don't think we'll get a white Christmas tomorrow. The daytime temperature is a balmy ten degrees Celsius. Not exactly snow-friendly.

We arrived late at night to find our friends' three-storey apartment filled with homey cooking smells. Wil was all flushed cheeks and corkscrewed hair as she gave us floury hugs. She had been channelling Martha Stewart in the kitchen, baking bread. The enthusiastic welcome and their place, which is so comforting it's womb-like, have made us as placid as a couple of newborns.

It's Tom's first trip to the States. On our first walk, I enjoy his surprise at small cultural points of difference. 'Look, newspapers in a vending machine on the side of the road. Check that out— it's a genuine bagel shop. Just how many different doughnut brands do they have here?'

A brand new
start of it
169

Wil and Greg drive us to Arlington National Cemetery, the first of the city's many tourist sites and monuments we'll see. I notice there are lots of AIDS awareness posters on billboards around town. Wil explains that something like one in twenty DC residents is now HIV-positive. Which is one of the highest rates in America. I am shocked. It seems incongruous that people living here, in the hub of the world's superpower, among all these edifices to wealth, power and grandeur, would be victims of an epidemic normally associated with poorer countries.

'ABC …' I recite, pointing out the text on a passing poster. 'What does that mean?'

'Oh.' Wil looks unimpressed. 'That's Bush's big idea to manage the crisis. It's an abstinence-until-marriage message. A is obviously "abstinence", B is "be faithful" and C means "condoms".' She meets my eyes in the rear-view mirror. 'The Bush administration's spent something like a hundred million dollars on programs that are all about waiting until you're married and then not cheating once you are. That's their AIDS solution.'

'Isn't that a little naive?' I ask. 'Not to mention that it completely ignores drug use.'

'This is the US. The abstinence message is pretty popular here, you'd be surprised. You get a lot of celebrities talking about it too.'

We spend a bit of time wandering around Arlington, which is truly stirring. Visitors continue to leave notes and flowers on JFK's grave. We also pass a few older people pausing to offer prayers. It's sobering to think the rows of white headstones represent actual people—more than three hundred thousand in total.

Afterwards, to shake off our sober moods, we go into the city in search of lunch. Eventually we pick a café that's part of a big chain offering 'home cooking'. A sign on the wall reads 'Food like Mom wants to make'.

'Wow,' I shake my head. 'Doesn't anyone cook things from scratch anymore?'

Wil looks up at it and smiles. 'That sign kind of says it all. There's no incentive to cook here. In some supermarkets the only things you can buy are pre-prepared or instant meals.' She laughs. 'The people at my work can't believe I actually bake my own bread and cakes. But you should see how unhealthy all the stuff is. Have a look at the ingredients list next time you buy something. There's this thing called high-fructose corn syrup, which is about ten times more evil than ordinary sugar. It's in just about everything. No wonder so many people get diabetes.'

There are a million reports about America's obesity crisis but I have to say, at street level, it's not noticeably worse here than anywhere else. It's not until I go looking for something healthy to eat, say a sandwich or a salad, that I come face to face with the American attitude to food. Nearly all the cafés and restaurants are part of franchise operations and the food is super-sized, pre-packaged, chock-full of preservatives, salt and sweeteners, and smothered in sauces. I don't just get a salad. I get every ingredient I can think of soused with deep-fried croutons and a creamy dressing all in a tub the size of a shoe-box (for one). Want a sandwich? Try a half-metre long sub filled with meatballs. The Starbucks culture is practically religion. People walk around with takeaway coffee cups the size of a vase grafted to their hands. And even the supermarkets are shrines to junk food. In one store I see an entire aisle dedicated to corn chips.

'I read something once that summed up America beautifully in just two words,' Greg tells me later. 'Sheer profligacy.'

I am all for moderation, of course. Except for one day of the year—Christmas. We wake up to discover Wil and Greg have stuffed our socks with Australian chocolates and lollies and placed them on the hearth. The snow hasn't materialised but we spend the day snuggled around the fire anyway, thrilled to experience a Christmas that doesn't fall during a stinking summer. We indulge our tradition of eating chocolate for breakfast, morning tea and just a few more squares for lunch. Then the four of us somehow find room for champagne and a

A brand new
start of it
171

roast dinner. The phone rings all day with wishes from home and we stream Australian radio via the internet. The accents, food, wine and music bring a little touch of Down Under to DuPont Circle. By the time I go to sleep, my cheeks hurt from smiling so much.

Between Christmas and New Year we do little more than sit on our friends' squishy couches watching DVDs and reading magazines. Tom has borrowed a book of Greg's about trekking in Patagonia and has been reading it eagerly. Unfortunately he seems to have developed a disturbing enthusiasm for going there in the New Year.

At Tom's urging, I read the itineraries. There are two treks in the area, a shorter, easier one called The W, where you can stay at heated lodges (my eyes light up at this one) and a longer one dubbed the Paine Circuit, or Circuit Grande, that involves camping in remote glaciated areas and is recommended for those with an advanced level of fitness. Of course Tom wants to do the Paine Circuit. At first I think he's joking. It sounds like something you would do for one of those Amazing Race reality TV shows. Only we wouldn't have the enticement of prize money. But he's serious. I point out the bits where it says we'd be camping in glaciated mountains, it would be freezing and that at one pass experienced trekkers have 'come to grief'.

'I'm sure it would be beautiful,' I say, 'but can't we do the shorter trek? It sounds really good. The longer one just seems like madness. We're neither experienced nor fit enough.'

Tom just responds with lines like 'you only live once' and 'don't live your life in fear'. I decide to drop the subject for now, hoping that like a kitten chasing a butterfly he will soon lose interest.

On the rare days when we feel bad about slothing around, we force ourselves outside. We travel on the space-age subway and do the mandatory pressing of the forehead against the White House gates. Then we go to the Mall and stare in disbelief as Americans photograph their kids striking goofy poses in front of the moving Vietnam Veterans' Memorial. Wandering around the tributes to American history, I'm struck by how much it feels like the Forum in Rome. These markers are so enormous, they are like religious icons.

Then, just as we are in serious danger of needing to be surgically removed from the couches, it's New Year's Eve. Tomorrow we leave Washington for a week-long trip to New York. But tonight there's a party to go. It's being thrown by none other than the son of Jalal Talabani. That's right, this year we're going to be singing 'Auld Lang Syne' with the son of the Iraqi president.

On the way over, Greg briefs us about Talabani Junior and his wife. He says they are about our age, really friendly and recently married. Junior has lived outside Iraq for a while and was educated overseas. The majority of guests here tonight will be Iraqi officials, their children or, like Greg, from the foreign diplomatic corps.

We pull up at a modest house in one of Washington's trendier suburbs. Unremarkable, except for the beefcake men with wires in their ears patrolling the perimeter of the front lawn. There are more inside, lurking in the shadows of the hall. Should I be nervous? Exactly who and what are these secret service types protecting us from?

I smooth down my shirt and pants. I have dressed conservatively, remembering my experience in Morocco and not wanting to offend any Iraqi cultural sensibilities. I needn't have worried. As we walk in the door I am overwhelmed by the cleavage. There are bosoms hoisted up in round melon shapes that are anatomically bewildering, bosoms spilling out of red satin dresses, bosoms peeping from deep V-neck lines that threaten to expose them completely and bosoms bouncing to R 'n' B in the living room where space has been cleared for a dance floor. Whatever modesty might prevail in Iraq is not present here. Tom and Greg stand goggle-eyed by the door as though they've been hypnotised.

The finest bosoms of them all belong to the hostess, who is all curves, flashy teeth, dark hair and eyelashes. Smiling, she takes our coats. Her husband comes over next to welcome us to his home. In a soft voice with a slight British accent he urges us to help ourselves to champagne. I take a moment to look around the room. No one I know can afford to throw a party like this. There are ice buckets filled with bottles of Veuve Clicquot, a table groaning with fancy canapés and, in the centre, a chocolate fountain. An actual wellspring bubbling with liquid couverture. Mmmmm. Silver platters dotted around the room are loaded with truffles, which I recognise are from an exclusive *chocolatier* in Paris. We bought some for Greg and Wil but could only afford a box of twenty. They are so expensive it makes you cry. Here there are hundreds of the damn things, just scattered around the room.

Greg spots a few people he knows and ushers us over. As we shake hands, he explains they work at the White House in policy-type positions. They all talk about work stuff. Even though it's New Year's Eve, they were in the office until a few hours ago, they say. They lament how they will have to work tomorrow too.

The night goes on and I meet more faces. It's the same story. Everyone is in their late twenties or early thirties and all they talk about is work. Or what they want to do next. They're all so damn perky and focused. The party is a networking opportunity.

After so long away from the career loop, I feel very left out. Especially when each new person I meet has the same opening question: 'What do you do?' When I tell them, 'Um, nothing right now. I'm travelling', their eyes glaze over with misapprehension. Then they're off. They've seen someone more interesting on the other side of the room.

A few more hours of champagne and small talk passes, and then it is time for the countdown.

'Ten …'

'What's your New Year's resolution?' yells an American woman I've been chatting to for the last five minutes.

'Nine …'

I pause.

'Eight ...'

'Uh, don't know,' I shout over the din. 'Haven't figured it out yet.'

'Seven ...'

But I'm thinking maybe I should try not to get so stressed about work stuff.

'Six ...'

Yes, that would be good.

'Five ...'

I look around the room for Tom. 'What's yours?' I ask.

'Four ...'

'To cut out carbs,' she hollers back.

'Three ...'

'And to get a promotion,' she adds.

'Two ...'

I force a 'fabulous!' expression on my face.

'One ...'

Tom appears at my side with a fresh glass of champagne. 'Happy New Year!'

He locks me in a hug and we kiss to celebrate a shiny new marker. A moment when we imagine things can be better. When we all make promises to begin anew. A moment when every one of us resolves—with the best of intentions—that this is the year we will quit our bad habits.

◆ ◆ ◆ ◆ ◆

I am in New York, in the Metropolitan Museum's Egyptian galleries, sitting on the stone steps of the Temple of Dendur. Tom is next to me. Outside the tall windows in front of us the lights from the yellow taxis pierce the afternoon grey, illuminating the skeleton trees on Fifth Avenue. Where we are inside is noisy. Visitors mill around us, posing in front of the tall columns of the reconstructed temple and trying to read the hieroglyphics. But I'm not paying attention to any of this. I'm too busy crying. I've just told Tom I want to go home.

A brand new
start of it
175

It all started a few days ago on New Year's Day. After fielding the career questions the night before, I woke up to see it was also on the minds of a few people back in Australia. In my inbox were emails from industry acquaintances who hadn't heard about our London plans and were fishing to fill staffing holes for the year ahead. When was I coming back and would I consider some opportunities?

I replied no, explaining my plans to move overseas. But I was relieved I hadn't been forgotten about. Then, I panicked. Not forgotten about—yet. Surely, it's only a matter of time. What the hell was I doing? Seeing all those driven, successful people at the party reminded me of what I'd left. I wanted to be like them again. And it scared me that I wouldn't. *The biggest mistake of my career.* My old colleague was right—these are supposed to be the consolidating years. I'm crazy to be knocking back opportunities that are landing in my lap. In London, my experience might not mean anything. No-one will have a clue who I am. I'm about to waste the next few months travelling when I could be doing some interesting work and building up contacts before we move.

'I want to get my fill of sunshine and beaches before we move to London,' I tell Tom now. He looks down at his hands. 'Besides, I've seen the things I really want to see most—Italy, Paris, New York. You go ahead to South America without me,' I say. I can't meet his eyes, so instead I hunt around in my bag for a tissue. 'You can do the trekking you really want to do without having to compromise your itinerary because I'm a big wuss,' I smile weakly. 'And I'll meet up with you in Sydney in two months' time.'

'But it won't be the same,' Tom says quietly. 'This is about us travelling together. I don't understand why you feel like this all of a sudden.' His face crumples. He runs his fingers through his hair. It's gotten long now after so long away. 'I'm not ready to go back home yet,' he says. 'I thought that there was so much more we wanted to see. South America for a start, and then we've talked about spending the last month travelling through Hong Kong and Cambodia. Aren't you interested in doing that anymore?'

'I think I'm spent,' I reply, and look at the ground again. 'I don't want to keep bringing you down. And I just can't shake this feeling that I'm throwing everything away.' We stay there talking for hours. Tom keeps asking me to give my decision more thought. Eventually I reluctantly agree. He just looks so disappointed. We decide to spend the next few days apart, so I can have some thinking space.

I walk out of the Met alone and into the spitting rain. The weather matches my mood. I decide to find a café and warm up for a while. As I cross Fifth Avenue I pass a woman gabbling obscenities into her mobile phone. It makes me smile despite how I'm feeling. I have never heard so many people talk like they're in an episode of *The Sopranos*. In this city the word 'fuck' is an adjective. New York's babies must be born burping up attitude.

The rain starts coming down harder, so I duck into a nice-looking café in a back street. Shaking out my coat, I see this place doubles as a gallery. Grabbing a newspaper from the magazine rack by the counter, I order a coffee and take a seat by the window. Outside, the street is slick with puddles that are growing in size by the minute. The afternoon light is gloomy from the low-lying thunderclouds.

My coffee arrives and I start flicking through the paper to distract myself. When I get to the features section a headline catches my eye. 'The Quarter-life Crisis', it says.

'Our twenties and thirties should be the best years of our lives—so why do so many of us feel like we're going nowhere?' The piece is about the growing number of people my age who are worried about their life choices and future direction, worried they are spending the best years of their lives being frustrated, delaying kids, travel and house buying, and putting in sixty- to eighty-hour weeks to get ahead in careers that leave them feeling unfulfilled. But they keep at it anyway, wanting to be seen to have the 'perfect' job, relationship and life. Eventually it all comes to a head, usually around the age of thirty. For this generation the 'quarter-life crisis' has replaced the 'mid-life' one that prompts fifty-something men to have affairs and to buy sports cars.

Wow. A quarter-life crisis. I do know quite a few people that could be going through that. I can remember conversations with some of my most successful friends about how they wonder 'is this all there is?' Telling me they grind their teeth in their sleep because of stress. Other high-profile people I know have confided to me that they have panic attacks from the pressure they're under. I would never have imagined it to be true by looking at them— they seemed so together. But then, that's what people always said to me. And half the time I felt like I was losing the plot from having so many balls in the air.

Dinner that night is tense. Tom and I spend the evening making small talk, skirting around the elephant in the room. It is almost a relief the next morning when we go our separate ways for the day. Tom is off to the American Museum of Natural History. I decide to spend the morning looking around the Lower East Side. We're staying near the old World Trade Center site. Directly opposite is the designer discount store Century 21. I shake my head when I see it, remembering the woman I met at the New Year's Eve party. 'Sure, Ground Zero was sad,' she told me earnestly. 'But I got the most amazingly priced Armani suit from, like, right across the road.'

I jump on the subway and spend a few hours ducking in and out of vintage clothing shops in the East Village. All my good shopping karma comes at once when I spot a pair of Manolo Blahniks in my size for eighty dollars. I pay for them with the shaky hands of a fashion junkie and think about how I have hardly bought anything new these past few months. I used to go shopping all the time, out of boredom or if I was having a bad day. I think about my clothes in storage at home. Some of them still have their tags attached. Why did I buy clothes I never wore?

Maybe I was affected by that thing my friends used to talk about, the 'golden handcuffs' syndrome. When you stay in a ho-hum job that pays well so you can buy a lot of stuff which you think will make you happy. Was I doing that? I walk out of the store, clutching my shopping bag. No, I don't think so. I liked what I did. I turn a corner and stop to look in the window of another boutique, but I can't get the idea out of my head.

Two shops later it suddenly dawns on me. I was bound by golden handcuffs. Different ones. The gold was more status and self worth than money. Is this why I found it so hard to leave and why I want to go back now? Status and self worth. Is a successful career the only road to those things?

That night, Tom and I go and see a movie. It offers a reprieve, because we don't have to talk. I feign tiredness afterwards and tell him I need an early night. I lie there blinking, long after the lights are turned out. Tom is curled away from me on the other side of the bed. It feels like there's a gulf between us. As I listen to him breathe, I realise how high the stakes might be. I'm breaking the commitment I made to 'get on board'. This trip's been good for us, too, spending so much time together.

We've learned things about each other that we didn't have a clue about. For example, I wasn't aware that he doesn't like to eat breakfast without showering first (we've rarely had breakfast together for nine years). I didn't know that he's a brilliant photographer or that he knows all sorts of nerdy things about computers. Tom didn't have the foggiest that I'm into art and sculpture, that I carry a notebook in my handbag at all times to scribble in or that I pick all the dried fruit out of my morning muesli. Just little things, really. But stuff you want to know about the person you share your life with.

We've also reconnected. Before this trip I don't think either of us realised just how much we'd drifted apart after so many years of existing at separate ends of the day. Although I was starting to wonder what we had in common anymore. We didn't spend much quality time together. On my days off I was often so tired and grumpy that we'd end up arguing over stupid little things. The truth is we'd kind of lost our way. Now that we're so much happier I don't want to lose him again.

Thinking back to the Met a few days ago, I remember the hurt on Tom's face when I told him I wanted to go home. If I left now, what would that mean for us? Would the damage to our relationship be irreparable? Might it be the end?

I get up early the next morning and decide to just walk the streets and see where they take me. We've got another three days here and have agreed that until I've figured out what I want to do we will only spend nights together. It is a rare sunny winter's day but still chilly enough to need gloves and a thick coat. I love how the cold weather makes things feel mysterious, with people peeking out from under their hats and steam snaking out of manhole covers.

It's not long before my spirits are lifted by the buzz. This city has such a distinctive personality. It's more crowded, noisy and exciting than any other I've been in. It's like a totally cool best friend, albeit a schizophrenic one with tourette's. It's gritty with a filthy subway, resident rats and large homeless population, yet glamorous with its achingly stylish bars and boutiques. It's mythical with a Gotham skyline, but familiar from all the instantly recognisable landmarks. There's something or someone to pique your interest at every turn. Yes, it's a cliché that's spawned a million T-shirts, but I do love New York.

At lunchtime, I try and pass myself off as a local at Pastis, a fabulous bistro straight out of *Sex and the City*. Until I give myself away by sneaking a look at my map. Then I take the subway to spend the afternoon exploring Central Park. I walk through big open green spaces, around statues and fountains and down squiggly trails that lead into thickets of trees. The park is eerie and feels all but abandoned.

I plonk myself down on a bench near the open-air ice skating rink and start munching on an apple. The peace and quiet is nice. I sigh deeply and rest my head on the back of the seat. I'm so tired. Which is odd, because I haven't worked a day in months. But even though I've been away for so long, mentally I feel like I've still been on duty. I guess that's because I've spent a lot of my time worrying. I sit still for a moment, trying to sort out the fears I've had since leaving Australia. There's a definite theme there. I've mostly been stressing about the things I think I should be doing at the moment instead of this trip. Tom hasn't been obsessing about any of that stuff, he's just been enjoying himself. What's wrong with me?

I take another bite. Hang on a second. I know what it could be. I groan inwardly. That article about the quarter-life crisis, about people I know. It wasn't just about them. It was about me too.

I put down my apple core and try and recall the crisis symptoms. Wanting to be seen to have the perfect life, feeling frustrated and unfulfilled, with fears over future direction. The article might as well have used me as a case study. What's my life become? A 'To Do' list by forty? I've already ticked off graduating from uni, travelling the world, getting a great job, finding 'the one' and marrying him. What's next—more promotions, a house, new car, a baby and then getting my figure back in eight weeks? Why?

I try and figure it out. I guess the more on that list I tick off the more validation I get from those around me. I've wanted people to think I 'have it all'. I feel so pathetic. Why do I give a fuck what others think? My life should have more substance than that.

The wind picks up. It's getting cold. Don't feel so bad, I tell myself, a lot of my friends do it too. Yeah, Katrina, but you've been ticking boxes faster than anyone you know. And that list overtook what really matters. You've been in too much of a rush to tick the next box to appreciate what you've got. Like your relationship. You've been putting it second to all that other 'stuff' you think is important. If you went home now, you'd be doing it again.

I sit up and wrap my scarf around my neck. That's it. I see what's happening. It's so obvious. I've become so consumed by what I think I 'should' be doing that I never ask myself if I actually want to do it. Like, why on earth would I want to jeopardise my relationship and give up travelling the world with the man I love so I can go back to Sydney for more work and a few more contacts?

There's not much daylight left. I stand up and sling my bag across my shoulder. There is one thing I should be doing now and it's something I want to do very much. Find Tom.

A brand new
start of it
181

I walk quickly towards the glow of Columbus Circle.
I'm done with ticking boxes.

◆ ◆ ◆ ◆ ◆

That night we go on a bar crawl around Greenwich Village.
Working things out in my head has left me feeling wonderfully
light-hearted. Tom is surprised as I drag him from place to place.
We follow a list of 'secret bars' a friend has given us to venues that
don't have signs on their doors. Many of them are in residential
streets and it's not until you press a buzzer and are let in through
thick velvet curtains that you realise there's a lively crowd inside.

Now it's 2 am and we're queuing for the diabetic-coma
inducing cupcakes at the Magnolia Bakehouse. We wander
out, each licking a mound of fudgy icing that's twice the size
of the cake beneath. The brightly lit cafés and restaurants are
still full of people eating and drinking. Snatches of jazzy
music, conversation, smells of wood-fired pizza and cigar
smoke waft from open doors and softly lit courtyards.

'Hey,' I say, linking my arm through Tom's.

'Mmmm?' He leans into me.

'About the rest of this trip. South America. Cambodia. Hong
Kong. All of it. I've done a lot of thinking.' I hug his arm closer.
'And the thing is, I'm one hundred per cent sure that seeing this
through with you is something I want to do. I've asked myself
what I'd regret more at the end of my life. I doubt I'd die wishing
I spent more time consolidating my career, but I'd definitely
regret not finishing this trip with you.'

We stop at the corner to wait for the lights. Tom turns
towards me looking half-thrilled, half-hesitant.

I cough and meekly go on. 'Um, look. If I haven't blown my
chances already by being an enormous pain in the arse, please.' I
bin my cupcake wrapper. Then I wind my arms around his neck
and look into his eyes. 'Please,' I repeat. 'Do you think I could still
come with you?'

CHAPTER 11

A rock and a hard place

'THE PAINE CIRCUIT. IT LOOKS LIKE IT SHOULD BE PRONOUNCED the way you say "pain". But here it says you say it more like *pye-knee*,' I remark, mostly to myself. I put down the guidebook I'm reading and wander over to Tom. 'Would you like me to make you a cup of coffee, honey?'

I'm still on my best behaviour after being given yet another get-out-of-jail card last week. 'Yes,' Tom had stated simply to my question that night as the traffic whizzed past us on Bleecker Street.

'Yes?' I was hopeful he meant it, but also thinking I would have ditched me so long ago.

'Yes,' he repeated. Then he fixed me with one of those 'I love you, but I really need you to make good on this commitment' looks.

It's been a week since then and when you are trying to keep out of the doghouse, it is a good idea to sit, stay and roll over. So, after returning to Washington, I thought it would be wise to cave in to Tom's wish to trek the harder trail in Patagonia.

I put aside my grave doubts about whether either of us is physically or mentally prepared. At least we now look the parts. Yesterday Greg took us to a huge camping warehouse store where he and Tom spent several hours like kids in a toyshop, playing with all the outdoorsy gadgets. We left with enough gear and freeze-dried food for an Antarctic expedition.

If and when we get out of Patagonia alive we have decided we will spend a few days each in Santiago and Buenos Aires, then scoot up to see the Iguaçu Falls. The plan is to leave this part of the world after that and fly to Hong Kong before spending a few weeks in Cambodia with friends. Finally, we reckon we will have earned a week of chill-out time with hammocks and cocktails on a nice beachy resort in Thailand. And then home. It's amazing to think that all of this will soon be over. Typical. It is only now that I've decided I really want to be on this trip that it seems to be rushing to a close.

The next few days are spent packing up all the heavy winter clothes we won't need. Apart from on the trek, it'll be nice and warm in South America and Asia. Coats and boots go in a giant box to be shipped to London. After that we hug Greg and Wil goodbye, sad to leave their place which has felt so much like home. A day and a half of flying time follows before we land in the southern Chilean town of Punta Arenas. We are staying here tonight to get over our jetlag before going to Puerto Natales, a smaller town that is the base for expeditions to the Torres del Paine National Park. From there it's a two-hour bus ride to the place our trek begins.

The airport at Punta Arenas is really just an enormous shed. As we wait for our bags to come out on the sole conveyor belt, I catch a glimpse of myself in a tinted window. Oh dear. My eyes are trying to escape their sockets on stalks, my hair looks like you could cook chips in it and my pants have coffee stains on them from a turbulence incident while I was trying to eat breakfast. I look like a half-sucked lolly. I'm so glad there's no chance of bumping into anyone back home.

I'm halfway through telling Tom I am going outside to find us a taxi, when I hear a voice behind me. 'Excuse me. Are you Australian?'

I turn around to see a couple about our age grinning at me.

'Er, yes,' I answer hesitantly. The woman looks pretty and fresh despite coming off the same flight as us. She sweeps her curly brown hair off one shoulder.

'Sorry to interrupt,' she says. 'But we've been travelling for the last three months and you're the only other Australians we've met. It's just so exciting to hear familiar accents.'

They introduce themselves as Hamish and Rachel. After discovering we're heading in the same direction—there really aren't too many other destinations here in back-country Chile—we decide to share a cab. They have been deprived not only of Australian company but also of anyone who speaks English and are in the mood to chat. It turns out they live in the Sydney suburb next to ours. They have taken a year off to tour all of South America.

I'm telling them about our trip and the trek we're about to go on when Hamish starts smiling broadly.

'What?' I ask him.

'I've just figured out who you are,' he says.

'Um, really?' I feel my cheeks get hot.

He nudges Rachel. 'It's Blowsy from the radio! You're Katrina Blowers!'

I nod, embarrassed.

'What a coincidence! I should have realised as soon as you told me your first name and where you were from. We used to listen to you every morning. My alarm was set to your seven o'clock news bulletin,' Rachel adds.

'I had to pull my car over to the side of the road to hear your final show,' Hamish says, 'it was really emotional.'

'Yeah, it was pretty emotional for me too,' I say, and we all laugh.

Great, I think. So much for this half-sucked lolly not bumping into anyone.

That night we sleep for ten hours. When we get to Puerto Natales in the morning we hire things like sleeping bags and mats to supplement our trekking equipment and buy more food supplies in tins and packets. We have to be entirely self-sufficient on the Paine Circuit, which is over a hundred kilometres and takes about eight days. The first part is the most difficult and isolated. The camp sites on this section are pretty basic. Some have small shelters manned by wilderness types who live there for the summer, collecting camping fees from trekkers. A couple sell supplies, but the stock, which is delivered by horseback, is not to be relied upon.

My previous trekking experience is pretty limited. I have been to Nepal, but that was practically a five-star resort experience by comparison. We were part of a group with a trek leader, a big team of porters and a cook. We camped, but our tents were set up for us. There were five meals a day with desserts, including chocolate cake, and mugs of steaming tea were delivered to our doors in the morning. Sherpas lugged our bags, leaving us with nothing heavier to carry than cameras.

I toss and turn in the pre-dawn hours, dwelling on what's ahead. I am sure there are some people who wouldn't find this trek in the least intimidating, but it will be the most demanding thing I have ever done. I'm worried about the weight in my backpack, which is laden with food and camping gear. I am taking my mobile phone for emergencies but it probably won't work. When we get back, I have decided to leave it off for the rest of the trip and only check it once a week. I don't need to be contactable anymore. I'm on holidays.

As I lie here I think too about the twenty-five kilometre walk into the park tomorrow, having never walked that far before in one day. Hopefully the countryside will distract me. It's a UNESCO biosphere reserve and has also made the list of *National Geographic*'s 'fifty places to visit in your lifetime'. I'm not too sure what the other forty-nine are, but at least I'll have knocked one over before I croak. Unless that moment comes on this trek which, joking aside, is not beyond the realms of possibility.

I roll over, thinking now about the weather conditions. It's said that on this walk you can be standing on a block of ice in torrential rain, see blinding sunshine about fifty metres away and then turn a corner to be buffeted with gale force winds. The highest point, Paso del John Garner, is the most perilous. That's the bit where the books warn trekkers have 'come to grief'. If the good weather holds, we should reach there on day four. The sun comes up and I'm still awake.

Clydesdale-sized llamas gallop alongside our bus, kicking up dust as they strain their long necks to race us into the National Park. It has just gone ten in the morning and for most of the three-hour journey from Puerto Natales we've been dozing on seats covered in velvet with the stuffing coming out. Rachel and Hamish are sitting in the row behind us. They are trekking the shorter W trail, but unfortunately our paths won't cross since, by the time we reach that section, they'll just be finishing.

The bus skids to a halt and we are dropped off in a dirt car park. We swap email addresses standing in the brilliant sunshine.

'Good luck,' Rachel says. 'I definitely expect you to email a photo of yourselves at the finish point.'

We help each other hoist on our packs before extending our new trekking poles. Then we're off in different directions. We take a gravelly uphill road to find the beginning of our trail.

The sky overhead is a royal blue but thick snow clouds swirl around the tops of the row of mountains in front of us. I look up at them with a sense of foreboding. Mostly we will be trekking in a wide circle around their perimeter. But there are two occasions when the trail takes us right up in the thick of them, the first when we cross the highest pass and then when we traverse a valley to see the *torres*, or towers, the park is named after. As the cloud clears briefly, we catch our first glimpse of them, three finger-like towers of granite poking up between the craggy peaks. They are unlike anything I have ever seen in nature—so smooth and vertiginous they are almost like skyscrapers. It's warm, so we've stripped down to T-shirts. But the wind whips through the long biscuit-coloured grass and buffets our ears with a deafening whirr.

We are barely two hundred metres down the track when my back seriously starts hurting.

'I have to stop,' I wheeze, unsnapping my chest strap.

'What, already? We've only just passed the sign marking the beginning of the trail,' Tom says.

'My back. It's killing me already. I think my pack is too heavy. I have things poking into my spine.'

Tom looks unimpressed, but helps me get my pack off. We sort through all the contents, putting them in piles on the grass.

'I don't know.' I chew my lip as I stand with my arms crossed, surveying the big mound of food, camping equipment and clothing I have stuffed into the pack. 'It's so heavy. I'm in pain and we've only just started. My legs are shaking just from walking up the hill to this sign.'

'What have you got this in here for?' Tom pulls out my thick leather-bound diary. 'And surely you could have found a thinner book to take with you?' Now he's holding the novel I'm currently reading, which could double as a house brick.

'I need both of those. There's no way I'm not going to write in my diary to document a trek like this. And the book, well, there's not going to be much else to do for the next eight nights.'

'Well, what are we going to do?' Tom explodes, his frustration at my weeks of whinging and whining about this all being 'too hard' finally coming to a head. 'You need to tell me right now, *right now*, whether you can do this. It's no good if we go a few hours in, or even go to the first camp tonight and you decide it's too heavy and you can't go on.'

'But …' I try.

'There's no turning back then,' he continues 'We'll have wasted an entire day and we don't have days to spare.'

'I …'

'Just tell me this second whether you're up to this.' He has his hands on his hips now. 'Because right now, we have the choice of walking back down this path and doing the W Circuit with Hamish and Rachel.'

'How can I tell you whether or not I can do this?' I shout, my irritation reaching boiling point too. There's no one in sight so I figure I might as well let loose. 'I have no frigging idea what's ahead,' I go on. 'I don't know how long it's going to stay flat like this. I don't know how quickly my pack will get lighter as we eat our food. And I don't know how much fucking pain I'm going to be in!'

Tom turns away, exasperated.

'But really, babe,' I continue, still emotional but quieter, 'how the hell should I know? How can I answer that?'

Tom kicks a rock on the ground for a while. 'This is serious, honey,' he says in a low voice. 'We're trekking into wilderness here. You can't just decide after a few hours that you want to stop. After all this planning, all this research. Bloody hell. I thought you'd practised wearing your pack around the hotel room?'

'I did!'

There's more rock kicking, then he tries a different tack. 'Listen, maybe we should do the W. It would be a huge shame to have gotten this far, but if you can't do it, you can't do it.'

His reverse psychology works.

'No way.' My voice rises again. I set about repacking my things. 'I will not be a quitter.'

We eventually work out a deal where Tom takes some of my heavier things, including, quite reluctantly, my book and journal, and I set my jaw in my best impersonation of a determined expression. Off we go again.

Fortunately, the weight swap works well enough. The pack is still incredibly heavy but manageable. The worst of the pain is in my hips where the straps from my harness feel as though they're creating bruises. Oh, and my hamstrings are twanging like too-tight guitar strings. Bah humbug. For the rest of the day, every step I take I do a mental inventory of each food item in my pack and evaluate its worthiness. By the time we get to lunch, I've virtual-binned half the porridge, a third of the chocolate, half the sugar (there is a big bag of it to disguise the taste of the porridge for Tom, who hates the stuff), all the nuts and all the tuna, and I am seriously considering auctioning it off to fellow campers.

The wind continues to hammer us for the rest of the day, but the scenery is amazing. Now I understand why this place has such a reputation. We walk along gently undulating hills covered with pale swaying grass. Then through meadows carpeted with small white wildflowers so thick they look like snow. They fill the air with a syrupy perfume. Fuzzy bumble bees the size of ten-cent coins buzz around them, the weight of their amber-striped bodies making the stems of the flowers double over whenever they land. We pass glacier-fed rivers the ice-blue colour of wolves' eyes. And there is the constant presence of the ice-capped mountains to our left, reminding me of where we will be in a few days' time.

Our first camp is in the middle of another pretty meadow. The caretaker is a man shaped like a boulder who lives alone in a basic one-room shack. Inside is a pot-bellied stove, which we gravitate towards to warm our hands. He greets us in broken English and asks where we are from. 'Kangaroos!' he cries cheerfully when we tell him. Damn that animal and its hopping ways. The recognition earns us a free piece of tasty walnut cake though, which he delivers to us on plates, smiling and making boing-boing noises.

Another couple, Rich and Candy, are sitting at the small table nearby reading a book. They are American, in their early forties and are wearing the clobber of trekking veterans: Gore-Tex jackets and pants, high-tech moisture wicking tops, bandannas around their necks and boots that look as though they've seen some serious action. Rich, the more outspoken of the two, is wiry and fit with craggy features and one of those lazy eyes that makes you unsure where you should be looking. Candy is the homely type with shoulder-length chestnut hair. We sit for a while in silence as we eat our cake. I notice that Rich is reading a thick book that's all pages without a cover. As he finishes a chapter, he tears it off and passes it to Candy.

'That's an interesting way to share,' I comment.

Rich looks up from his page and strokes his patchy greying beard. 'These sorts of measures are essential when you're doing a trek of this nature,' he says, staring at me intently. I decide to focus on his right eye. He picks up my thick novel, which I've brought in with me, and gives me a look as if to say, only a rank amateur would dream of carrying something this enormous.

Instead he announces, 'It's all about economy of scale in these circumstances. Candy and I learned that some years back when we did the Appalachian Trail. Didn't we, Can?' She nods.

Rich leans his head back against the corrugated iron wall and continues. 'Yessir. Six months that took us. Camping out every single night. The trail stretches from Georgia to Maine and is over two thousand miles long, touching on fourteen states.' Candy buries her nose in her book again. I think she's heard this story a few times before. 'The best thing about a hike like that,' he goes on, 'is that it allows you to reconnect with your instincts. You remember how to sense tiny changes in the weather and your surroundings. Whether it's going to rain or storm, if there's water nearby. They're senses we all have, always have had, but we have forgotten how to connect with them.'

He then gets back on to his pet subject, the issue of weight. 'We found out the hard way that what you carry on here'—he taps on his shoulders—'can cause all sorts of problems here and here.' He points to his hips and knees. 'Before I set out I weighed all my vitamins in weekly doses and sent them to different post boxes in towns along the trail so I wouldn't have to carry that extra weight.'

I nod gravely, but inside my head I'm thinking, you, my friend, are ker-azy.

'And for this trip,' he says, warming to his theme, 'we've measured the exact amount of porridge oats we'll need in half-cups. Not a single oat more than we need. As for the book, well, more than one is a luxury you can't afford here in the backwoods.' He gives me a lopsided smile. 'You'll feel that extra weight every step you take.'

Fantastic. I rub my hip bones and lament how sore they are after just one day.

Later, back at the campsite, I'm unpacking my bag when Rich wanders past. He spies the jar of peanut butter I have inside.

'Oh Lord,' he exclaims, recoiling at the sight of it. 'You have that as well? Heh heh heh!' He shakes his head. 'You Aussies, you're downright wack jobs!'

What does he know that I don't? I put it away. Am I going to make it through this trek or am I carrying too much stuff? I feel like an inexperienced airhead, as if *The Simple Life* has come to Chile and I am playing the part of Paris Hilton.

In the morning, after sleeping soundly from the unfamiliar exertion of the trek the day before, my pack doesn't feel quite as cumbersome. Perhaps I'm getting used to it. Today's trek is a mere eighteen kilometres—one of the shorter days—and we are in high spirits as we set off.

After an hour or so, we climb up to a pass that has a 'wind warning' marked on our map. We chuckle at that, saying, 'It's windy everywhere here.' The gravel path climbs up and up, past the scene of a recent landslide. At the top we get our first look at the ice-blue waters of Lago Paine. It's one of the bigger glacier-fed lakes in these parts and is cupped on all sides by snow-capped peaks. We round the corner to traverse the skinny goat trail that crosses the exposed pass.

Suddenly ... smack! We walk straight into an invisible wall. I stumble and flail my arms. Tom grabs me and I see the shock in his eyes. The wind is so strong it's practically cyclonic.

Edging forward and planting our trekking poles firmly into the dirt, we clutch our caps to our heads. But then a second stronger gust hits us. It throws me off balance completely. I look up at Tom to see that his sunglasses have been ripped off his head. I watch powerless as a ghostly hand tosses them high up into the air like a flimsy piece of tissue. Then the wind bounces them off a rock about twenty metres above us.

I can barely believe what's just happened. Thoughts of future snow blindness flash through my mind and we dump our packs and go searching through the shrubs to retrieve the glasses. We find them a few minutes later and continue shuffling forward, hats and sunglasses safely tucked away this time. Tears stream down our cheeks as the wind continues to blast our eyes and make our noses run.

The elements are certainly brutal out here. Every time we stop, we slather ourselves with sunscreen but the sun has still managed to lick us in the most peculiar spots. The spot between my thumb and index finger, exposed from holding the trekking pole, is badly burned. It's weird how much sunlight there is. The sun rises at four in the morning and doesn't go down until after eleven at night. It is great in one respect—you can read in your tent at night without wasting the batteries on your torch—but it also tricks your body into staying awake. We had to drape our socks across our eyes last night as makeshift masks to block out the light.

We walk down into a valley where there is a cluster of trees around a trickling stream. It's sheltered here, a perfect spot for lunch. Rich and Candy thought so too. They are just finishing up as we arrive. 'According to *Lonely Planet* we have just two and a half hours to go,' Rich tells us.

'Great,' I say panting, and tie back my wind-knotted hair. 'I thought it was much further than that.'

Four hours after lunch and we are still walking. Bloody Rich. My feet are so tender I feel like I have stood on scorched sand. I lift up my T-shirt to see two purple patches where my waist belt has been biting into my hips. Where is this frigging campsite? We climb up a steep hill. The ground is covered in small pebbles, which my boots are having difficulty getting purchase on so I skid every second step. The sun has disappeared behind a cloud too, making the wind feel colder than is comfortable. But at the top, we are rewarded for our efforts.

Stretched out before us are the milky blue waters of Lago Peron and I can see our campsite on its grassy banks. The lake is fed by a glacier less than a kilometre away that is carving a deep valley between two mountains. The real prize, though, is the two icebergs floating in the centre of the lake. They're not that big, but they're the first I've seen. The one on the left glows Listerine blue. It's spectacular.

I am not the only one hurting. A Spanish woman next to us in the camp has blisters on her heels which are bleeding. All the dozen or so trekkers here tonight are hobbling delicately around like patients in a wartime hospital—except for Rich, who comes strolling over like he's been here for hours. He inspects my pack, which is lying next to me.

'If you were with me that would have to go,' he says, pointing at the small padlock attached to my zip. 'Every gram counts when you're on the uphill, you know.'

I muster up the last of my energy to give him a look that suggests where I may insert that padlock if he doesn't mind his own business.

Later, as we settle down for the night I look at our map, trying to figure out if there is any way of cutting the trek short. 'I don't know if I can do this,' I whisper in the half-light to Tom, who's zipped up in his sleeping bag. 'This is harder than anything I've done in my life and right now I feel as though I've been hit by a truck.' But Tom doesn't hear me. He is already fast asleep.

In the morning, I roll open the tent flaps and am confronted by the sight of a creepy German guy who's strutting to the toilets wearing nothing but his navy blue undies. Gross. I stand up tentatively and test my muscles. I feel fine. Tom joins me, stretching out and remarking on how rested he feels too. Miraculously our bodies have healed themselves during the night. We feel strong again, something that seemed impossible just eight hours ago. I'm ready to get back on the trail.

If I had an inkling that morning what was to happen to me the following day, I doubt I would have gone any further. But for the moment I am full of optimism about the rest of the trek, and downright chipper to be among such beautiful scenery.

During the morning we walk beside a roaring watercourse called The River of the Drowned Dogs. Apparently a pack of dogs 'came to grief' here. It seems there's a lot of 'coming to grief' in these parts. Lunch is at a clearing with a million mosquitoes. We try to open a tin of tuna with a Swiss army knife but end up breaking the tin-opener attachment. Terrific. Luckily, we have the peanut butter and make sandwiches instead. Ha, take that, Rich. We Aussies might be wack jobs, but at least we're not going to starve.

After a shorter and easier afternoon, we make it to just below the top of the tree line for our camp that night. We decide to bed down early in preparation for the next day, the longest walk on the trek.

Tom ducks outside for a final toilet stop before sleep. A short while later he returns, laughing softly. 'You'll never believe what I just saw,' he whispers as he wriggles into his sleeping bag. 'It's bloody freezing out there, but I saw this guy stark naked, bathing in the creek.'

'What?'

'Yeah! He had his back to me but I could see him pouring water over himself slowly, like it was some kind of weird ritual.'

'Which one is he?' I ask, propping myself up on an elbow. 'Is he the gross German guy with the blue undies?'

'No,' Tom says. 'I'm pretty sure it was someone new. Maybe he came from the other direction?'

We put the mystery of the bather's identity out of our minds and try to get some sleep. I lie looking at the tent's roof. Tomorrow looms like an ugly cloud. Day four, when we climb Paso del John Garner, the hardest, highest part of the trek. At 1241 metres, it's not high compared with the places we've gone in Nepal. But apparently it is the descent that is crippling. A thousand metres of sheer scramble down a muddy trail, which is torture for the knees. I sleep restlessly, with vivid dreams that make no sense.

The alarm goes off at six. We hear rain on the roof of our tent. Shit. We reset the alarm for an hour later, hoping the weather will clear, but at 7 am the fat drops continue to patter down. Tom goes to see how the clouds are looking up at the pass. I scramble into my waterproof gear and throw my bag into the cooking shelter. A few minutes later, Tom's back, declaring it looks pretty clear up there, so we make a mad dash to pack up. We are on the trail twenty minutes later, breakfasting on muesli bars as we walk.

The trail begins with a steep climb up a long slimy slope. It is truly disgusting. I go to put my foot in a place that seems solid only to sink into knee-deep mud. This is accompanied by a loud sucking sound, as if the mud is alive and genuinely thirsting to consume me.

Before too long my boots and legs are covered with diarrhoea-coloured goo the texture of pudding batter. The rain is still falling and plague proportions of mosquitoes keep going for our eyes. The mud continues for about an hour. Eventually we clear the tree line, arriving in a rocky, almost lunar landscape where thorny alien-looking shrubs grow. I squint up above where I can make out the pass. It's a long way up.

Still sticky with mud, we begin the climb. Just put one foot in front of the other, I chant to myself. I think I can, I think I can. We have intermittent periods of rain and then intense sunshine that sends the humidity soaring and makes me sweat so much the insides of my clothes are soon just as wet as the outsides. We stop for nuts and dried fruit, not even talking now, just chewing our food like robots and focusing on what's ahead. Big patches of snow come into view. Sheets of ice form frozen tunnels under which icy waterfalls tumble down the mountain side. It is so steep that I am practically bent double.

I cry out to Tom that I need a rest and collapse against a rock with my pack still on. My eyes close involuntarily. All I want to do is go to sleep. Just go to sleep. And when I wake up I'll be in a nice hotel with soft sheets and room service and a hot bath. No mud or hills to climb. Mmmmm.

'Honey. Honey!'

My shoulders are being shaken. My eyes flutter open a crack.

'Honey, can you hear me? Look at me. Open your eyes.' It's Tom. He looks panicked.

I wake up completely. 'What?' I say blinking. 'What happened?'

'You fell asleep for a few seconds. Your body wants to shut down but you can't give in to it.'

'Arghaghhhh,' I reply.

'Stand up. You need to get the blood circulating. Your blood sugar levels must be really low.'

I am force-fed a few biscuits and after a few minutes I am okay again. I hear someone behind us and turn around. It's a man, perhaps in his late thirties, wearing a pair of old sneakers, a T-shirt with a Nepalese motif and brown suit trousers like the kind you get from charity stores. He nods at us in acknowledgement as he strides past. He is vaguely handsome, in a Don Johnson during his *Miami Vice* period kind of way, with sandy hair and a fit muscled frame. But there's something weird about the leather thonging he has wrapped around his neck and wrists. And his outfit couldn't be more at odds with the outdoorsy gear all the other trekkers wear.

'That's Creek Man!' Tom whispers to me.

We both stifle sniggers as we watch him bound up the rocks ahead.

After a lot more climbing we finally hit the lip of the pass. We stop to don more warm clothing, bracing ourselves for the icy blast that's said to lash off the park's biggest glacier, which is just over the other side. There is a part in the clouds so we

decide to make a dash for it. Pausing for a hug, we then crest
the top to find it's perfectly peaceful. There's just a gentle
breeze. The other side is clear and dry and there are incredible
views over the valley.

Directly below us is the enormous Glacier Grey, a crinkled icy
quilt that stretches off into the distance. It's furrowed with bright
blue and white canyons, some of them several hundred metres
deep. At its cliff-like edge is a vast frigid lake which the glacier
regularly feeds with chunky icebergs. I look behind to the valley
below and marvel at how far we've come. I can't see any sign of
human existence. It feels as if we are the only living souls on earth.

We take a few photos, but quickly now as we're worried about
the approaching snow cloud shifting from the mountains next
to us. It is a sad privilege to be looking at this icefield. The rate
of melt from the Patagonian glaciers, which are the largest non-
Antarctic ice masses in the Southern Hemisphere, has doubled
in recent years thanks to global warming. Their thinning now
accounts for nearly ten per cent of the world's sea-level change
from melting glaciers. It's devastating to think that by the time
my grandchildren are my age, this formidable force of nature
that is thousands of years old will have all but disappeared.

It has begun raining lightly, so using ropes that have been
hammered helter-skelter to posts beside the trail, we climb
down. It takes several hours and is incredibly steep. Legs
trembling, we spot a ramshackle shelter and decide to rest. I
sniff the air. What is that delicious savoury smell? Easing off
our packs, we duck through the doorway.

In the gloom, I can make out Creek Man standing beside a
portable gas burner. He's chopping a clove of garlic with the
speed of a professional chef and pauses every so often to shake
a skillet where he's sautéing an onion.

'You take your food very seriously,' I say by way of starting
a conversation.

'Yes,' he replies coolly, looking us up and down as we sit on a
log, sharing cordial and a few squares of chocolate.

'Just because you are trekking,' he adds pointedly, 'doesn't mean you have to sacrifice taste. I also carry fresh ginger and herbs.'

He speaks with an accent I can't place, that sounds like a hybrid of American and Scandinavian. As he chops and stirs some more he asks me if I've tried a particular berry that grows wild in the national park.

I tell him, no, that knowing my luck, I would eat the only poisonous thing in the whole of Patagonia. I laugh as I say this, but again he doesn't share my joke.

'No, I don't think so,' he says quietly. He ceases his stirring then to study me more carefully. 'I see this now. You are far too cautious.' He picks up his spoon and serves his food into a bowl. Then he goes and sits in the farthest corner and doesn't say another word. Tom and I look at each other and shrug. It is difficult to know how to respond to this strange man.

The sound of voices heralds the arrival of more people. It's a young French couple who we've seen at campsites the last two nights. Damien and Celine set themselves down on the log next to us. A few minutes later in come Rich and Candy, who look miserable and sodden. They were about twenty minutes behind us on the trail and, in that time, bad weather has set in over the pass. They were caught in a snap storm and couldn't see anything more than a few metres in front of them.

We pore over our maps, debating whether to camp here on the dirt, or push on to Refugio Grey, which is the end point of the W circuit and caters for less adventurous types. Damien and Celine say they have heard that the *refugio* has hot showers and a dining hall serving three-course meals and cold beer. We are sold. Even though we'll need to trek for at least another four hours, it is only just past one o'clock so we have plenty of time. Rich decides he and Candy are staying put. Damien and Celine set off ahead of us and Rich shakes his head dubiously as we get up to follow them.

'We met some German trekkers last night,' I tell him, as I tighten my shoulder straps on my pack. 'And they told us it wasn't so hard.'

'Eh?' Rich looks at me questioningly.

'Yep, they said it was a bit up and a bit down, but easy.'

He scoffs. 'If you guys make it to Grey, I'll write a book about you. It'll be an exposé about Aussies on the trail and steroid abuse.'

As we leave I wonder whether Candy will ever get her own copy of this book to read.

◆ ◆ ◆ ◆ ◆

I can hear the river thundering in the distance long before I first see it. By the time we get there, Damien and Celine are already picking their way along its bank across boulders that look like they've fallen in a recent landslide. We follow their lead. It's half rock-climbing, half rock-jumping to get up to the spot where we think we should cross. My trekking pole keeps skidding on the smooth surface and the weight of my pack makes me sway dangerously.

Tom looks around frantically. 'Over here!' he yells over the roaring water. 'I'll cross first and help you.'

The force of the torrent is so strong my pole won't hold in some spots. The rocks I try to get a footing on teeter as well. I feel my anxiety rising. Tom waits patiently, holding out his pole for me to grab on to. Heart pounding, I finally reach the other side.

Further downstream, I can see Damien and Celine trying unsuccessfully to reach a rope ladder that someone has built up a high ravine wall. They are forced back towards us and, with great difficulty, scramble up a cliff face. I watch as they embrace with relief after making it to the top. Then they shout down that it is too dangerous to follow them up because of the risk of rock slide.

'Go back down the river,' they yell through cupped hands. 'Turn around—and then you can climb the ladder.'

We try to go down, but the only path is through the most turbulent part of the water and over the top of a fierce waterfall. We would never make it. We climb back to where we were.

'I think we're going to have to go back across the river again and cross further down near the ladder,' Tom bellows. I look at the torrent of whitewater. I just can't face doing it again. I dissolve into tears. Then I lose my footing again, almost falling into the water, and cry even harder.

'Okay,' Tom relents. 'Let's try and climb up the ravine wall then, like they did. You stay behind me. And, please, be careful.' So, we try and find hand- and foot-holds among the fine dust-like soil—me crying, Tom yelling at me to pull it together.

He dislodges some rocks and shouts at me to move. I shift as far to the left as I can, but can't get a grip. I try and explain this but it won't come out right. I'm sobbing somewhat hysterically now. I claw at the dirt, desperate for something to grab on to. Finally, my fingertips connect with a big rock. But just as I hoist myself up it starts to move. If I fall now, I realise, I'll plummet about five metres. Straight on to the jagged rocks below me. And this big hunk of rock is going to flatten me.

My feet slip into nothingness. A chilling realisation sweeps over me. I feel my muscles go slack.

This is it. I'm not going to get out of this alive.

But then, as if by magic, a figure appears out of nowhere. It runs confidently up the ravine towards us like a commando. It is Creek Man.

He gets to me just in time. Catching my legs as I start to slide down the face, he scoops me up and lifts me across to a solid platform. All I can do is stand there stunned. He yells up to Tom, 'Stay where you are.' Creek Man then takes off my backpack and orders me to climb. I go ahead while he shadows me, carrying my pack and barking out instructions as to which rocks are safe and where to put my hands and feet.

In no time at all, I'm up the top. Damien and Celine lie over the edge and grab hold of my hands to hoist me up. Creek Man goes back down to help Tom, scuttling over the ravine wall like a spider on a web, oblivious to the weight of my pack. When Tom reaches the top, I hug him tightly, my legs still like jelly.

Creek Man checks I am okay and I thank him tearfully for saving me. He gives a dismissive wave of a hand and disappears back down the ravine wall. I watch him go in wonder.

Creek Man is not of this world.

The remainder of the afternoon passes painfully slowly, but thankfully not as dramatically. We stop at the closest lookout to Glacier Grey. I can hear the ice creaking and moaning as it melts and inches forward.

Finally Tom stops ahead of me at the top of another steep hill and I know he's seen it. As I crane my neck over the rise, I see it too. It's the *refugio*, in all its twenty-first century glory. Equipped with all the mod cons that we haven't seen for days: flushing toilets, shower cubicles, a small general store and that dining hall.

Tom throws down his trekking pole, holds up his arms and cries, 'Behold Jerusalem!' It is now 7.30 pm and we have been on the trail for eleven hours.

After a quick shower, we sit in the big heated dining room clutching beers we're too tired to drink. The wind picks up and I see someone's tent go sailing past the window with its owner following, like a Benny Hill chase scene. I try to smile, but even that hurts. What a day.

◆ ◆ ◆ ◆ ◆

Now that we're on the back end of the Circuit Grande, the bit that makes up the W trail, the going is much busier. The thick shrubs lining the path have been brushed by so many thousands of trekking poles and bodies that over time they have grown like rows of perfectly manicured hedges. The weather stays kind and we walk in sunshine by clumps of rare bright purple ground orchids. Tiny finches hop along the track ahead of us. We pass fields of buttercups, a big whorl of rock that resembles the inside of a tree and a turquoise lake that is so vivid it looks like an old-fashioned postcard that's been coloured by hand.

We both feel so much fitter and stronger now than we did on the first day and we've lost a lot of weight despite eating half a block of chocolate each night.

This part of the trail is frequented by day trippers from the national park's seriously luxurious resorts. They get ferried in by speed boats and totter past clad in Burberry and designer trainers. We move to the side to let them through and they sweep snootily by, not even saying thank you or acknowledging us. I guess we don't smell that great.

The next morning we leave our bags in our tent and do a side-trip up a valley where there are supposed to be incredible views. The guidebooks don't lie. An hour and a half later we are sitting with our backs to the sun-warmed rocks, spoiled for choice with spectacular things to look at every way we turn. In front is the aqua lake we passed yesterday, dotted with small islands. Behind it are snow-capped mountains. To our right a glacier spills over the top of a mountain with more than a dozen waterfalls cascading down its face. Sporadically, chunks of ice break off, making a thundering sound as they explode on the rocks. Behind us, the valley is all lush, curved like a wine glass.

Another chunk of ice crashes down, fracturing into powder. I lean my head against Tom's chest and he brushes a strand of hair off my forehead. I'm so glad I finally got on board. Here, in Tom's arms, is the only place in the world I want to be. I can't believe that just a few weeks ago I was even contemplating putting our relationship on the line for the sake of trying to score a few more runs on the career board. My heart bursts just thinking about how patient he's been to stand by me as I've waxed and waned about being on this trip. I'm never going to take him for granted again.

On our final day, we get up early. We have a short climb up the mountain to see the *torres* up close before we head down the valley to the finish point. I am so sore now from the days of relentless slog that it even hurts to roll over in bed. We set off into a biting wind. There is a big crowd descending, the eager beavers who got up at 4 am to see the sunrise. I feel a twinge of regret that we didn't do the same, until an English guy tells us it was a waste of time—cloudy, raining and you couldn't see anything.

When we do get there it is a bit of a let-down. The three towers appear like stubby fingers. They sit on a high rocky platform and look much more majestic from a distance than they do up close. As mildly disappointed as I feel, it still seems a fitting end to our trek, visiting the first place we saw when we got off the bus all those days ago.

We pack up and trek down, down, down, past the hordes of day trippers, and eventually arrive at the entrance of the park. What a feeling to finish. We hug, leaning against each other in utter exhaustion.

As we sit and wait for the bus to Puerto Natales I can't figure out whether this trek has been a great or a horrible experience. On the plus side, there was the physical achievement, the weight loss (I reckon I've lost about three or four kilos), the feeling of being in a 'bubble' in which only you and the people you are trekking with exist in the world, and the mind-blowing scenery.

But this trail really does live up to its name. It was sheer unadulterated pain. I've pushed myself over these last few days to limits greater than I thought I could. But I wonder if it's always the case that the things in life that I'm afraid of doing are the things I'll get the most from? Like going on this trip.

I can't wait to email our photos to people back home. We've got some spectacular shots and I am so bloody proud I did this I want to share it with everyone.

Three hours later, we stand on the kerb outside our *hostal* watching our bus pull away. With it, never to be seen again, goes our new digital camera containing every single photo we've taken. In my bone-weary daze, I had failed to notice I'd left it on the seat.

CHAPTER 12

A secret experience

'ARE THEY ALL BLIND?' TOM ASKS.

'Maybe,' I shrug. 'Can't be sure though. Where would they find so many blind people to do the job?' I pause. 'Maybe some of them aren't. I guess we'll find out this afternoon.'

The rickety Star ferry rocks up and down as it hits the wash of another boat. We are hemmed in among commuters and other sightseers travelling across Victoria Harbour to the Wan Chai pier.

Across this body of water—which is foghorn-honking with all manner of junk boats, fishing dinghies and luxury cruisers—stretches Hong Kong's commercial sierra, Central. It's a concrete and neon range where financiers and lawyers line their nests. Among the smoggy haze, big eagles soar around the tallest buildings, the tips of which seemingly scrape the upper atmosphere. Off the sides of the skyscrapers giant TV screens and speakers howl with Canto-pop, M-pop (Malaysian-pop), J-pop (Japanese-pop) or whatever else is hot this minute. At ground level, the city streets are lined with high-end shopping malls. In some places the streets are shopping malls and you have to walk through them, shaking off the touts. 'Cheap watch, copy watch, sir, madam. Copy handbag, custom tailor, madam.'

In the row next to me, the sharp sound of a woman jabbering into her mobile phone draws my attention. I do a double-take. She is decorated like a Christmas tree of labels: Dior shoes, fur-trimmed D&G jeans, Gucci belt, Moschino top, black Chanel sunglasses, Louis Vuitton bag. This whole place is an offering to capitalism.

We are still in a fog of jetlag after making it through nearly fifty hours of travel from South America to get here last night. The humidity doesn't help our woozy feeling. Thankfully, we acclimatised to summer heat after our trek, spending the last two weeks admiring the quirky architecture of Santiago, swanking about the stylish bars of Buenos Aires and stepping around really fat tourists at the spectacular Iguaçu Falls. I have never seen so many obese folk or all-you-can-eat buffets in the one place. They even hire out wheelchairs to make it easier for the largest to get around the walkways.

Today we are treating our addled selves to lunch and a massage. I have been researching my smaller post-trek butt off and have discovered there are things called 'secret kitchens' here. These small restaurants are known only by word of mouth. They are run not by chefs but by families cooking in their homes. If you are after authentic food that the locals eat, these places are supposed to be the ticket. The phone numbers and addresses of secret kitchens were closely guarded, but for better or worse the internet has blown the lid off much of that mystery.

We get off the ferry and weave through the streets, tracing our route on the map with our fingers. We are trying to find the apartment that's our destination for lunch. It feels like the entire population of almost seven million is here with us. Everyone's blissfully untouched by the idea of personal space. Hong Kong locals will walk in front of us, barge ahead in queues, nudge our backs and kick us in the swimming pool—all without shame or apology.

A stench wafts from the grate on the side of the road. It's a bit like cooked elephant dung. Mostly though, the street is full of cooking aromas, of soy and oyster sauce and frying spring onions or the sweet tang of joss sticks smoking in tiny shrines outside the shops. All of it makes me hungry, unlike the bizarre interpretation of western food displayed in the shops we pass: bacon and chive doughnuts, pork floss danishes, mung-bean ice cream and Kentucky fried tofu.

'Careful!' Tom grabs my arm, pulling me out of the path of an oncoming double-decker tram. It rumbles deafeningly down the street. I rub my ears which are throbbing from all the racket. In the newspaper this morning I read how the government is cutting the tram timetables in a bid to improve noise pollution. The sound is literally driving people crazy. Just yesterday a tram driver was attacked with a knife. A mental patient, who was putting up posters protesting against the noise snapped when the tram came past. Not surprisingly, lifestyle-related stress seems to be a big problem. Already today I've seen many advertisements for free stress workshops. 'The first step is recognition,' they read. 'The second is acknowledgement. The third is doing something about it.'

After a few more minutes of walking I see a nondescript white building up a dead-end street. It has letters on the outside spelling the word 'Winner'. 'This is it,' I say, relieved. 'It's in the Winner Building.' We get into a jolting lift and climb a few floors to a pokey corridor. There is nothing to indicate we're in the vicinity of any clandestine gourmet haven. I guess that's the whole point. A TV blares through an open door down the end. I look at my piece of paper to check the apartment number. This door here, to the left, the one with the 'members only' sign on front, has got to be Mum Chau's Sichuan Kitchen.

I knock and the door is opened by a teddy bear of a woman with a pink apron tied over an embroidered Chinese jacket. Her face creases into a smile as she ushers us to a table in what looks like a converted lounge and dining room. It has speckled lino floors, old tourism posters on the walls and air-conditioning units hanging from the ceiling. Crowded into the space in a hodge-podge fashion are ten small tables covered with plastic cloths. Down the far end is an open kitchen where another mature-aged woman stands at a portable gas cooktop with a younger man. They stir bubbling liquid in big stockpots and taste things that sizzle in pans.

We have come at midday to beat the business lunch crowd. Only two other tables are taken. A group of Chinese businesswomen are at one, a couple at another. The woman who seated us plays with her toddler granddaughter on the floor. We are handed menus in characters we don't understand and point, hoping for the best. Out come slippery wontons in a chilli sauce, wet noodles with minced pork, crispy ham in crunchy Sichuan pepper and iceberg lettuce leaves steamed in soy sauce. We dive in as our fellow diners watch us.

The first mouthful's delicious. As is the second. On the third I get the strangest sensation in my sinuses. Sweat prickles my scalp. My nostrils feel like I've snorted paintstripper.

'Jesus!' I exclaim, looking at Tom in shock. His face is purple and his eyes stream tears. The diners at the other tables titter behind their hands. Clearly this is sport for the Sichuan trained—watching how long it takes for westerners to go into meltdown.

Afterwards, we decide to cool off in the shady botanic gardens, a short walk away. We pass signs saying 'Watch out for Dengue Fever and Japanese Encephalitis', 'Do not feed feral pigeons' and 'If you come into contact with birds or their excrement wash yourself immediately and contact a health care professional'. The regular bird aviary is closed, with more signs warning of the risk of avian flu. Further in we see a memorial to the doctors who died during the SARS outbreak. If you weren't a paranoid person before you came here, it wouldn't take long to become one.

Our massage appointment is at 2.30 pm. I read about this place in an article about the top ten value-for-money things to do in Hong Kong. The masseuses have been taught their craft in a tradition dating back two thousand years. And if that's not attraction enough, there's something even more impressive about this experience. The fellows who will be pummelling our backs this afternoon are blind.

We sit in the bright pint-sized waiting area. After a while, two men come out wearing white coats. One of them is clearly sightless. He keeps his head stiff, just tilting his ears towards sounds, and he also wears dark sunglasses. I am not so sure about the other man. Maybe he's one of the sighted trainers? And then he walks smack into a wall. Ah. There would be my answer.

We are told to lie down fully clothed.

'Hello, I'm Johnny,' my masseuse says in halting English. 'What's your name?' I tell him and he gets to work, somehow knowing exactly where all my limbs are without having to grope around. After a bit of chitty chat—where are you from, where are you tight, is this pressure okay—he gets deeper into the points up and down my spine. It is extraordinary. Even when he has to move around the table, he'll still touch me in exactly the same spot he left off. The only sound in the room now is that of the robotic talking clock: 'Thirty. Five. Minutes. To. Go.' Of course. How else would he know how long to carry on for?

I leave feeling as loose as a goose and walk hand-in-hand with Tom back to the ferry terminal. What a crazy town. In one day I have had my eardrums blasted, my sinuses scorched and been kneaded by a blind man. Odd but somehow wonderful experiences.

At four o'clock the next morning we are both sitting up in bed, wide awake. The whine of sirens drifts from somewhere in the city. Our body clocks are still on South American time and we've stirred several hours before sunrise with a pressing matter on our minds.

'I'm just not sure,' Tom says. 'It's been niggling at me for a while now.' He draws his legs up, fidgeting. 'Something about it feels weird.'

I breathe in slowly, wanting to handle this situation carefully, the way you'd hold a baby bird. We're talking about London.

Ever since our visit, the thought of relocating there permanently has left me feeling, well, cold. I'm not trying to be cute. The weather is really just a small part. We picked London because it seemed an easy option to try the whole 'living overseas' thing. But to be honest, the greater motivation for me has been the chance to start afresh and be a different person in a different town. It seems easier to embark upon that exercise in a place devoid of old hang-ups.

'Well then,' I say slowly. 'I think we've got to sort through this rationally.' I get out my notebook. 'Let's make a list.'

On one page we write 'London Pros'. On the other, 'London Cons'. We chock pillows behind our backs and think.

'Look. The main reason we came up with the London plan in the first place was to keep travelling,' Tom says. 'So let's work out how much travel we would actually do.' We speculate that maybe it would be one weekend a month and the four weeks of annual leave we'd get each year. Not too bad. We put a big tick beside it on the Pros page.

'I'd get to spend a lot more time with Jess,' Tom continues.

'And I'd get to see my brother a lot more too if he stays living in Newcastle,' I add. Down goes another tick for London.

'But who else do we know?' I ask.

'Yeah. There is a loneliness risk,' Tom replies. 'I miss our friends already.' Down goes a con.

'On the other hand, it is an exciting thing to do, going to live overseas,' Tom says ruefully. 'We'd be injecting some more excitement into our lives. It's not a staid or dull option.'

'Mmmm,' I agree. 'I would love to live overseas somewhere at some point. But is London the right place for us?' I click the pen a few times. 'What about Italy, France, South America?' I hesitate. 'I have to be upfront here,' I say looking down at my hands. 'I wasn't that taken with London. Did you like it? In the way you could see a life for yourself there?'

'I don't know,' he says after a time. 'Not for certain. I mean, I am having doubts.' There's another pause. 'It's just not sitting right,' he says, repeating his sentiments from earlier.

He takes the notebook. 'Let's start on a Sydney list,' he says. Over the next few minutes we write down: getting a dog, buying a house, better career prospects for both of us, proximity to friends and family, the opportunity to have babies with family and friends around and a good health-care system. Then we put big ticks next to all of them.

'We should do the negatives now,' I say. We both look out the window, searching our minds.

'I guess there are the complications from changing our decision if we were to go back,' Tom says, sounding embarrassed. 'I'd feel a bit weird about that. We have gone and told a lot of people.'

'Yeah,' I agree. 'That's a bit awkward. We could say we were drunk maybe?' We laugh.

'Well that's not too far from the truth,' Tom says. 'We'd polished off a bottle of wine as I remember.'

I kick off the blanket. 'I don't know, baby,' I say. 'London is an attractive option because of the European travel. But think about it this way—ninety per cent of the time we'd be living in a place that, in my opinion, is not nearly as nice as Sydney for the opportunity to travel just ten per cent of the time.' I sigh. 'Then again, now that I'm really enjoying myself, I hate the thought of this travel we're doing coming to an end.'

Tom bows his head thoughtfully.

Then he takes the pen and scribbles down another line in the 'cons' list for Sydney.

I peer over his shoulder as he writes. It says: Anti-climactic. The risk of returning to rut.

'This isn't just about you. It's about me too,' he says. I tilt my head in surprise.

'I've gone through my own changes on this trip, you know,' he continues. 'This time away has given me the chance to reflect on the differences I'd like to make to my own life. We were both in a rut. I don't want to get stuck in one again.' He puts down the pen. 'Let's go to Cambodia, take a few weeks, maybe talk to Will and Bridget about how they've found being expats. And,' he takes my hand, 'just think about it.'

CHAPTER 13

Beggars and friends

TOM'S IDEA OF CAMBODIA BEING A PLACE TO DO SOME thinking is a good one, in theory. After all, we are just about to spend the next week chilling out with our friends, Will and Bridget, who are now Phnom Penh locals. It is just that as soon as we get off the plane my brain won't function beyond two thoughts: iced water and air conditioning. I peel my T-shirt off my back and inspect my feet, which have swollen up like a pregnant woman's. I don't know how anyone gets anything meaningful done here when all you want to do is float in a cool pool of water. This place is seriously scorching. Turning my face to the open window of the taxi, I'm hit with an olfactory shock that is amplified by the heat. A witch's brew of diesel fumes, chargrilled meat, garbage, piss and methane. The air sears the insides of my nostrils like steam from a kettle.

As the streetscape passes by, I'm surprised at Phnom Penh's tropical beauty. I was expecting a bit of a dust bowl. There are hibiscus trees, eucalypts and bougainvillea as we get closer to the river front, where the roads widen into French colonial-style boulevards. Adding to the charm are great stands of frangipanis which scatter carpets of sunshine-centred flowers on to the footpaths. Another thing that surprises me is the contrast between the fat cats and the flat broke. On the same streets where hard-up families gather to work and play there are razor-wire fences belting in mansions that look like wedding cakes. Small children beg on the footpaths. Behind them glittering chandeliers swing from the porches.

We check into our hotel, the Foreign Correspondents Club, which is on the banks of the Tonle Sap. This river is the landmark around which everything happens. All the tourist restaurants, big hotels, street vendors and even the royal palace are along these shores. The FCC has pole position. It is, as its name suggests, a popular hangout among the international press corps. It received 'institution' status following the bloody coup of 1997 when the leader of the Cambodian People's Party overthrew the prime minister. Reporting to Washington on the social and political climate, the then American ambassador wrote in his report, 'The FCC is open; things must be returning to normal'.

It is all resort-style elegance, lazy ceiling fans and the chill-out beats of Café del Mar. By far the swankiest place we've stayed, it costs a relative pittance thanks to our weighty Australian dollars. We are just packing our bags away in our room when I hear the knock of our friends on the door.

'G'day!' Tom cries, stretching his arms wide as Will and Bridget come inside.

After hugs and kisses all round we laughingly comment on how casually they are dressed, even though they've come straight from work. Bridget ruffles a hand through her short dark hair which has been flattened by her bike helmet. They ride their bikes everywhere now, she tells us, and I see their lanky frames are lean and muscly from the exercise. The sandals and shorts Will have on are what all his colleagues wear, he says. It's too hot for suits.

We've known them both for ages and have been promising to visit them since they moved here four years ago, but one thing or another always got in the way. I marvel at how tanned and relaxed they look. Back in Sydney they had demanding jobs as managers of a government authority, working the long hours that went hand in hand with their career success. Then they heard about an opportunity to come to Phnom Penh as part of the Volunteers Abroad program. Ready for a change of pace, they adjusted their lives to local wages and downsized to a traditional Cambodian house.

These are the kind of friends you feel proud to know. They live with such integrity you feel positively shallow by comparison. For example, Tom and I felt pretty good about including donations to a few charities on our wedding gift list. But they got all their wedding guests to donate money in lieu of presents. The proceeds went towards providing crops and running water for an entire Cambodian village. Humbling stuff.

Thankfully, these modern-day saints also like to let their hair down. They tell us about a party they'll be taking us to tonight. It's the opening of the Pontoon Bar, the city's first nightclub on a barge. Never having been on a barge before, I'm intrigued.

In the evening, our tuk-tuk driver drops us off in a dirt car park about a kilometre up the road from our hotel. The warm night air carries fragments of babbling voices and the dull whump of a bass line from the river below. It's dry season and the tourist longboats tizzied up with exotic pot plants lie languid on water that resembles a shallow puddle. Business is quiet so early in the year and the longboat operators spend their days dozing on hammocks. Believe me, though, they go from coma to salesman in point two of a second if they think they can woo your trade.

By an entrance ramp near the edge of the dirt, a tangle of lights has been arranged in a tree to mark tonight's auspicious occasion. Instead of imparting glamour though, the misshapen neon tentacles look like a bloated orange and yellow octopus. A couple of drunken American girls add a touch of class. They stagger around the tree in short skirts, whispering and giggling.

Nearby is a bloke in his thirties wearing a tight white T-shirt and doing his best to discreetly perve on them. I suppose he must be the doorman by the way he has his chest puffed up like a canary. He could pass as professional were it not for the beer he's clutching in one hand.

'You on the guest list?' he asks, full of sass and Heineken. I notice he's Australian.

'Um, no,' says Will, surprised. 'But we were around this way last night and the owner said to pop by.'

He looks Will and Bridget up and down. His eyes then move over Tom and me. Several uncomfortable moments pass. I hear one of the girls retch.

'Ordinarily, I'd have to turn you away,' he slurs in a broad ocker accent. 'We're almost full. But,' he pauses to make a show of his perceived generosity, 'I like ya, so I'll squeeze you in.'

He moves aside to let us on to the rickety gangway made from overlapping sheets of chipboard. Will turns around to raise his eyebrows at us as we make our way on board. The barge is a covered floating rectangle about the size of a small apartment. The base is so thin it is nearly flush with the water. In the far left corner, a disc jockey stands behind turntables spinning bad 1990s hits to an almost-empty dance floor. I see that he's wearing a T-shirt with a slogan that says 'Fuck the DJ'. I also see that, so far, there are no takers.

'Welcome to The Expat Hangout,' Will whispers in a mock David Attenborough voice as he shepherds us to a table. 'An intriguing habitat that emerges after dark in Phnom Penh. It's a place so removed from local customs and rituals that most tourists would never see anything quite like it.'

I look around giggling. He might be joking, but what he's saying is true. You don't see pictures of any place like this in your guide book. There are none of the usual signs of being in Southeast Asia—no tropical décor, Buddha statues, temple relics or camera-wielding holidaymakers. It's been decorated to evoke a different world, one with pristine white leather booths, big bubble lamps, Parisian-style trellises and the strong smell of perfume and bourbon.

Tonight's opening has attracted a few hundred people who stand in tight groups around the big open bar in the centre. Elbowing my way to the counter to get drinks for everyone, I see that the bartenders are having more fun than their customers. They seem to be operating on the one-for-you, two-for-me rule. The guy who's standing up my end has a long sweaty fringe which he tosses around to the music as he pours from a bottle high above his head. Without asking, he plonks a shot of spirits in front of me.

'On the house,' he winks.

'Uh, thanks', I say, tentatively taking baby sips. The rough liquor hits the back of my throat and I stifle a cough. Pushing it aside, I ask for a Malibu and pineapple juice instead.

'Is that what you want?' His eyes widen. 'I mean, are you really going to drink that?'

I nod self-consciously. 'Yes, I like it.'

'What are you? Thirteen years old?' he asks, then tilts his head back and whoops a few times. 'You're nasty,' he cries. I look down, thinking, if I just ignore you then maybe you'll go away.

I grab my drinks without thanking him and turn back. Through a gap in the crowd, I notice a man in his fifties rushing towards me. He is wearing tight pink jeans and dragging a gangly twenty-something man by the hand. Next to his friend he looks like a garden gnome going to Mardi Gras. I stop, confused.

'Thank god you've arrived,' he shrills, making large flapping motions with his free wrist. I look at him in surprise. Should I know who he is? I've never seen him before in my life.

'I was beginning to despair about the fashion stakes,' he continues. He gestures toward his companion who is looking at the floor mortified. 'We rank you the best dressed of the night.'

He then leans in conspiratorially and lowers his tone. 'Love the strapless darling, very Kylie.'

'Well, I'm flattered,' I stammer. I'd thrown on the only halfway-decent item of clothing I had in my backpack: a navy blue sundress. But as they stand there grinning at me, I can see my choice of attire is red carpet compared with the curious mixture of clothes on display in the room. These are outfits that must spend most of their days mothballed in expat wardrobes, because they'd be far too offensive to wear on the streets. Over there tittering is a red lycra dress with a navel-deep neckline, at the bar behind me is a cluster of backless tops and in the corner stand a gaggle of skirts so short they could double as belts.

I smile and balance the drinks I'm holding. 'Nice party, isn't it?' I say and try to edge away.

'Oh, it's all well and good now,' my new friend remarks, pursing his lips. 'But wait till wet season when everything's soaking, darling. The whole kit and caboodle will absolutely reek of fish. It'll be like the time Curtis here swiped the salmon canapés from the hotel buffet and left them in my handbag.'

I see Will and Bridget's heads over the crowd and excuse myself. They introduce me to a guy they work with, a lawyer originally from Sydney. He shakes my hand then retreats to the dance floor and starts flailing about on his own. I watch mesmerised as he spins and leaps in a stripy tight sailor's top and jeans with one leg rolled to mid calf. He's a good lawyer, Bridget tells me, and is about to start work on the Khmer Rouge trials. I try and hide my surprise. He seems seriously weird and not at all like someone you would trust to give you legal advice, let alone prosecute the leaders of a murderous regime.

The gyrating mob is now getting more intoxicated by the minute. I have never seen any place quite like this before and it's not what I expected to find in Cambodia. Expat hangouts like these cater for homesick foreigners who need to pretend, just for a couple of hours, they are someplace else. There are no Khmer faces here at all. Will, who notices me watching the lawyer, tells me that after you stay here for a while, you tend to adopt a live-for-the-moment approach. Many foreign workers let their hair down when they go out in a way they wouldn't at home, he says. Most of the expats here tonight work for not-for-profit groups or aid agencies. Parties like this are an opportunity to scrub away what they are forced to see every day. The turnover for new ventures like this one is ridiculously high. They're cheap to set up and even cheaper to run when you factor in the cost of local wages. But they are always closing down because after a month or so the expat crowd moves on to the next one.

We leave at about 1 am when the party is really hitting its strides and the dance floor is crammed with sweaty bodies. As our tuk-tuk takes us back to our hotel, we pass other bars that sound lively too. Outside one of them, two middle-aged overweight men with shiny European faces hold hands with local girls half their age. Bridget sees us stare at them. 'We have a term for blokes like them. Sexpats,' she says. I make a face. 'Apart from those girls, it's rare to find Cambodians about at this hour. There's a culture of not going out much after dark among the Khmers,' she explains. 'It's a bit of a hangover from the days of the war when it was really dangerous.'

We continue to rumble along the road lit by yellow streetlamps, swerving every now and again to dodge a pothole. As we pass the darkened houses, I think about the effect of the events of that time.

Actual estimates of how many people were killed between 1975 and 1979 vary, but it is thought to be somewhere in the order of two to three million. That's about a quarter of the current population. After seizing Phnom Penh, the Khmer Rouge, led by Pol Pot, emptied the cities, marching their occupants to the countryside and forcing them to work in the fields. Social structures in communities were broken down. Books were burned and intellectuals killed. Businesses and universities were destroyed and even wearing glasses was considered 'elitist' and punishable by death. Those with tertiary educations who managed to evade capture fled the country and many have never come back.

At face value, it is not difficult to see the long-lasting impact those years had. After the Vietnamese forced the Khmer Rouge leaders into exile, the country was plunged into a state of economic crisis from which it still hasn't recovered. But now, as we pass by entire families sleeping rough on the banks of the river, I can't help thinking about the stuff that has been swept under the social shag pile. A country needs strong intellectual capital. Spending power helps, but the human wealth factor— the skills, social structures and ideas—are a much more powerful engine for change. What has been the result of the extermination of nearly an entire generation of the country's brain's trust? Where are the great thinkers and strategists who can generate ideas for the future?

We get out at our hotel and pay the driver. As we make our way to the door and bid Bridget and Will goodnight, we pass a girl about sixteen years old begging with a baby attached to her breast. Tucked away in the luxury of our room, I wonder whether the government is encouraging young Cambodians to embrace education again as a tool to fight poverty? I've heard that a third of the population lives below a poverty line of a dollar a day. And in an environment like that, the pursuit of ideas has to be sacrificed for subsistence's sake. Unless you can eat an idea then it is probably not worth having.

◆ ◆ ◆ ◆ ◆

We set off early in the morning to try and beat the heat and make our way past a group of kids screaming excitedly in a park on the river bank. The commotion is being caused by a bearded European man who is taking his pet monkey for a walk on a long leash. We watch dumbstruck as it chases an excitedly barking dog around in circles on the grass. Crossing the road, we duck under electricity wires where a whole family of

monkeys, wild this time, is doing the high-wire act. The baby
swings by its tail as its thick-headed father squats on hind legs,
chattering admonitions. On the other side is the place we're
looking for. Flanked by shady tropical gardens with a giant
clock that has digits carved from shrubs is Wat Phnom. Legend
goes that seven or so centuries ago, an old woman called
Madame Penh found four Buddha statues in a trunk washed up
on the banks of the nearby Mekong. She built a temple for the
statues on this hill and worshippers loved the place so much
they set up camp around the base. These makeshift dwellings
eventually morphed into a village called Phnom (meaning hill
of) Penh. The temple still stands today and on weekends, days
like today, is the place to be.

At the entrance we make our way past dozens of beggars,
grubby children carrying their baby siblings and sellers
peddling offerings to Buddha. We see other tourists taking
rides around the temple's perimeter on a geriatric elephant with
a chocolatey-bristled hide. The elephant's owner walks him up
the road past our hotel each morning and night. The sight of
such an imposing beast plodding along the asphalt as
motorbikes whiz past is crazy but somehow fits with this city's
eccentric air. Over by a wall is a group of Khmer teenagers
hanging out and trying to look cool, sending text messages and
comparing mobile phone rings. The uniform for the young men
seems to be jeans with fake Diesel logo T-shirts and, for the
girls, pyjamas with Disney characters on them.

Ahead of us is a steep set of stairs. We climb up, pick past
dozens of pairs of flip-flops kicked off at the entrance and
inhale spicy incense which curls through the temple doors.
Inside, at the feet of several dozen Buddha statues, are brass
trays full of oranges, paper money and chubby sugar bananas.
Despite the hustle outside, it is hushed and sanctified in here.
This temple is the spiritual heart of the city. It's been so ever
since Phnom Penh was chosen as the capital when Angkor was
mysteriously abandoned in the mid 1400s.

It is too hot to walk around when we leave, so we catch a tuk-tuk to the southern end of the river. We get out in front of a row of international flags which lie limp in the flabby air. Behind them stands a high wall guarded by machine-gun toting lads in fatigues. The wall curves around an area that takes up about five city blocks. Over the top, we can see the tips of opulent gold spires and curved ornamental roof edges. This is where the king lives.

When it comes to unusual royal families, Cambodia definitely takes the rice cake. Hollywood couldn't have invented a more peculiar cast. The current king took the throne somewhat reluctantly, when his dad abdicated for the umpteenth time in 2004 ('This time, I really mean it'). Before then, King Norodom Sihamoni, a fifty-one-year-old ex-ballet dancer, had led a low-key existence in Paris, caught public transport and had a day job as the Cambodian ambassador to UNESCO. He now lives in the palace where the Khmer Rouge held him and his family under house arrest during the 1970s. The billboard-sized photographs of the king around Phnom Penh don't give much clue to his character. They show a gaunt, startled-looking man with a pursed red mouth wearing traditional costume and smart European dress shoes.

Ballet dancing aside, it is the old king who is the real kooky character. Crowned at the age of nineteen, Sihanouk was a presence throughout every major historical event of the last century. He is named as the 'politician who has held the world's most political offices' in *The Guinness Book of Records*. He has been king, sovereign prince and prime minister twice each, as well as president, the country's non-titled head of state and leader of various governments-in-exile.

In between all that Sihanouk somehow managed to find time to be a legendary pants man and a Cambodian Spielberg, directing numerous films and forcing journalists to watch and praise them. Now, at the age of eighty-two, he has gathered a cult following for two blogs. The first is his official one, www.norodomsihanouk.info, which averages about two thousand visitors a day. This features his rants, many on progressive stances he supports, such as equal rights for gays, lesbians and transvestites and a push for same-sex marriages. He cheers on the French football team, praises the beauty of Cambodia's women, posts reports on his health and links to 'royal songs' he has composed.

But it is the blog Sihanouk hasn't put his name to which has the Cambodian community talking. This one is written by his longstanding 'pen pal'. The blog has diatribes against the Cambodian government and rallies opposition to its policies. Many find it more than a little coincidental that this pen pal has become the mouthpiece for the very same things that get the old king's goat.

We laugh about it with Will later. 'Everyone knows this "pen pal"—he makes inverted comma gestures with his fingers when he says this—is really the retired king,' Will tells us. 'But he probably thinks he's got one over everyone. I think the government looks at it and just goes "yeah, yeah, he's mouthing off again" and ignores it.'

Sightseeing done for the day, we relax at the upstairs bar at the Foreign Correspondents Club. This is where all the expats and tourists converge for insanely cheap sunset drinks on the breezy wooden balcony. From up here, with a happy-hour cocktail in your hand, you can gaze imperiously down at the street below and see the industry that your presence has created. The clusters of tuk-tuk drivers badger you on arrival and departure with cries of, 'You remember me? If you need tuk-tuk tomorrow you remember me.'

There are also the moto owners and the young boys with dirty hands trying to flog photocopied books which they carry in boxes tied around their necks. On the edges stand the hammock sellers who yell out, 'Hammock, okay?'

Worst of all, it's from up here sipping mojitos, which probably cost more than a week's local wage, that you can look directly into the eyes of the beggars you've just said no to. They attach themselves to hotel doorways, holding on to small children with one hand while cupping their other palm up towards their mouths. Occasionally you'll see among them the melted face and hands of an acid-attack victim. This vicious practice has become disturbingly popular in Cambodia and is usually carried out by jealous women.

Just this morning I read a story in the local paper about a woman who caught her husband canoodling with a prostitute in a hammock. She threw acid in the woman's face before stabbing her in the head and chest. The most high-profile acid attack involves Cambodia's version of Madonna, Tat Somarina. A glamorous model and karaoke video star, she was doused with nitric acid about six years ago by the wife of a government official with whom she was having an affair. The rumour is she is now in hiding having plastic surgery and planning a comeback.

This evening, as we have drinks with some friends of Will and Bridget's, conversation turns to how they cope with the fact they have so much wealth compared to the locals. I've noticed that every conversation with expats somehow seems to end up here.

'I never know whether to give when I see beggars on the street,' says an American woman who works for the World Bank. 'I don't know who I should give to, who legitimately needs the money and who is going to use it to go out and buy glue to sniff. I don't want to be contributing to a habit that might kill them.'

The rest of the group makes noises of agreement.

'Why would they feel like they need to do anything different to change their lives if they're making a perfectly good living begging?' someone says. 'How is Cambodia ever going to move beyond being a developing nation if that mentality continues?'

'Well, the government would have to crack down on corruption for a start,' says Bridget angrily. 'The pilfering of foreign aid that goes on among senior officials—it's disgusting.' She puts her drink on the bench and fiddles with her straw. 'All the Khmer officials do is sit and nod, promising not to put their arms too deep into the cookie jar. Then they hope they don't get caught with too big a handful.'

I think about this and try and imagine what I would do if I lived here. It's a tough one.

There's at least one place that's tackling the problem head on. We make plans to visit it the following night. Down a back lane in a building with brightly coloured murals on the wall is the very popular Friends restaurant. The candlelit tables are full of well-heeled foreigners and it even has its own cookbook. It's a slick modern operation. But it is a whole lot more than just a good place to eat. All the staff are homeless teenagers who are being taught hospitality skills. Many have already graduated to work as professional chefs or run their own businesses.

One of the co-founders is Sebastien Marot who, like the king, is a former Parisian. He started the restaurant with two friends twelve years ago. The conversation in the bar last night still plays on my mind and I'm torn between wanting to give to every heart-breakingly destitute child I see and wondering just how much good it will do. I ask Sebastien what he thinks.

'It is difficult for the foreigners to come here and see this poverty and not give,' he says. 'But this only maintains Cambodia as a begging country.' He tells me there is no incentive for kids to change their lot when they can make over a hundred US dollars a month from sympathetic foreigners. More than half the population of around thirteen million are under nineteen and there's been an explosion of kids living on the streets. One estimate has it at twenty thousand. Increased tourism in recent years has worsened the situation. Some kids have come up with elaborate scams, including renting a small baby and begging tourists for milk. Then they return the milk can to the shop where they get fifty per cent of the price refunded to them.

'Any handouts given by foreigners just keeps them on the streets. It makes our job to reintegrate them through education and training much more difficult,' he continues. 'We have parents forcing children to beg and refusing to send them to school because they provide income. That means the parents don't have to work.'

'What about if I just gave them food then?' I ask.

'Well, food is an alternative to money, but in the end it has the same consequence,' he replies. 'When children don't have to pay for food, they can use the money other tourists give them for drugs or gambling at gaming parlours.'

Afterwards, Tom and I decide to take advantage of the crisp night air and walk the rest of the way back to our hotel. We turn down a street with French-style patissieries and lush day spas where all the expats get pedicures. We hear a noise and turn to look. Under the lamplight I can see a couple of children digging in piles of rubbish. They're collecting plastic bottles, which they can resell for a few cents. I am still reflecting on all of the stuff Sebastien and the others said to me, when one of the kids stops foraging and wanders over. I tense up, expecting him to pull on my sleeve and ask for money. But instead his eyes lock into mine and he breaks into a smile. He lifts his hand and gives me a high five, then bursts into spontaneous playful laughter. I smile back as he runs to rejoin his friend.

I think about the family we saw earlier today who, despite appearing destitute, hooted with joy as they splashed each other with a hose left to water the grass by the river bank. Being here is reminding me of the importance of finding happiness in simple things. I want to hold on to that when I return to the material world. My palm tingles from where the kid made contact with me. I touch it gently and feel a rush of warmth. As we continue down the street, I can't wipe the earsplitting grin off my face.

◆ ◆ ◆ ◆ ◆

I'm told there is a woman in Phnom Penh who can reduce grown men (and women) to quivering rabbits. And she does it without saying a thing. It's the mere thought of her steely gaze that gets them. Yet every morning, these same people suck up their courage and make the short journey to the Boeng Keng Kang Markets. Because what this woman offers is irresistible and addictive. And it'll keep you going for the rest of the day. Bridget and Will have told us about this local legend and say they visit her most weekends. I am intrigued by what all the fuss is about and decide I have to see her too. They agree to take us there the following morning.

We pull up out the front just after eight o'clock. Tom and I are squeezed into a cyclo, with Will and Bridget riding their bikes alongside. Bridget told us we would need to arrive early because the thing we are coming for often runs out by nine. I stretch out the kinks in my legs on the dusty footpath as Tom pays our driver. It's sunny but the air is still cool, a welcome respite before the searing midday heat. There are swarms of locals everywhere, chattering in the middle of the road, unloading vans full of vegetables and puttering in on motorbikes.

We follow Bridget and Will inside. The markets are made up of four squares which fit inside each other. We pass by the outer square where the 'valet parking' is—big chicken-wire cages filled with scooters and bikes. You pay a couple of cents and get a ticket ensuring your vehicle is watched over while you shop. Very civilised. Also out here are the flower sellers holding armfuls of musk lotus buds with petals folded back like origami and bright orange blossoms shaped like crabs' claws and parrots. When you buy a bunch, the seller wraps them for you in giant tropical leaves instead of paper.

All the clothing shops are located in the next layer, selling plastic hair clips and batik sarongs. In the very centre is the

produce section. Down one end are the meat stalls. We hold
our noses as cleavers are taken to carcasses left hanging in the
open air and unidentifiable offal is given to customers in plastic
bags. The fruit vendors are at the other end. I pause in front of
one stall and am handed a slice of custardy jackfruit to sample.
At another, a grinning shopkeeper cuts me off a piece of
strong-smelling mango. Women wearing white face cream to
lighten their skin gossip as they squat on their haunches,
shredding green papaya to order. The final layer, surrounding
the produce section, is the food stalls with their hot dishes and
sweet treats. I see banana in sticky rice wrapped in banana leaf,
sago balls glistening like pearls and green and pink jelly in
wobbly slabs.

Then Bridget grabs my arm and points to the corner. 'There,'
she whispers. I crane my neck. Tucked off to the side I can see
a large crowd. Their heads part every few moments and I notice
a petite woman in the centre with long dark hair scraped into a
bun. I look at Bridget and she nods. 'That's her,' she says.

Remember the Soup Nazi from *Seinfeld*? He was the
pedantic chef whose soups were so coveted, queues would form
out the door. Elaine became so unhealthily obsessive about his
delicious wares that the Soup Nazi banned her from buying it
for a year. 'No soup for you,' he cried. There's a female version
right here in Phnom Penh. But she doesn't sell soup. The
woman at the stall next to her does that. This modern-day
despot peddles caffeine.

We elbow our way through the crowd and find some spare
plastic stools along a low bench covered with shiny white tiles.
The bench wraps around in a square and there are customers
jammed along every inch. In the middle stands the Coffee
Nazi. Assisting is her ten-year-old daughter who, by her
solemn unsmiling stare, looks to be in training to take over
Mum's mantle. Dad hovers on the outside, refilling big
aluminium kettles with tea and fetching fresh water in plastic
containers for the coffee. The Coffee Nazi is dressed in a clingy

black lace top with a black apron tied firmly around her middle. She has a round face with lines etched into her forehead from frowning so much.

We sit for a while and watch her serve with blurred quick gestures. It's a bit like a circus performance. First she juggles a dozen glass jars then flings metal coffee filters on top like she's dealing cards. The thick syrupy liquid drips into the base in fat dollops. She also does a roaring trade in takeaway. Faster than any barista, she tips the old coffee grinds in the bin, flips the fresh brew into a plastic sandwich bag, drizzles in condensed milk and ties the opening around a straw. All this for just a few cents. She also makes a batch of soy milk from scratch every morning. I watch some of the regular customers help themselves from a stockpot that's kept simmering on a hotplate, adding generous spoonfuls of sugar.

She looks in our direction and, with a curt nod, indicates she's ready for our order. Bridget is a repeat customer but loyalty doesn't win you any currency here. She talks to her in Khmer, asking for coffee the way the locals have it: in tall glasses filled high with ice, about an inch of sweetened condensed milk in the bottom and a long-handled spoon to stir it all up. Seconds later, we have it in front of us. The thick coffee mixed with the milk tastes like rich caramel and coats my tongue like melting chocolate. I catch the woman's eye to gesture that I think her coffee is delicious but she gives me a look that would wilt a pot plant.

Bridget cracks up. 'I've been coming here for four years and have brought so many people. It took until last week for that little girl of hers to even acknowledge me,' she says.

A milky-leathery odour wafts over from the stall next door. It's from the *trei ngeat*, the dried salted white fish which is used to make the Cambodian breakfast of champions, *bor-bo*. This is a Khmer version of *congee* and they've got a production line going on over there. Bridget explains that the coffee and the *bor-bo* stall have a reciprocal deal. You can sit at either place and order from both, and they help each other pass things across.

I pay about fifty cents and get a bowlful that looks like gruel. I try a spoonful tentatively and widen my eyes at the different textures. The dried fish has been mixed with short fat rice noodles, deep fried shallots, bean sprouts and a wedge of lime. It has a very fishy taste but is also starchy and zingy. And it doesn't seem out of place for breakfast at all. I watch as the women next to us stir in several spoonfuls of chilli paste, staining the porridge lipstick red. They must have guts of steel. They notice me looking at them and smile.

We sit for a while longer, finishing our *bor-bo* and order a second coffee. The locals around us crowd in curiously, fascinated with Tom and me. Bridget has to translate how old I am, what we are eating, how long we are in Cambodia and whether we like the food. I sit and breathe in all the different smells. The vivid colours and the easy sunny mood of this place are so enchanting. Wouldn't it be great to live somewhere like this? It is certainly gritty, but there is also something really beautiful about the place and the people that gets under your skin.

I glance at Will and Bridget who appear so relaxed and carefree. Maybe I too could do something here that could make a real difference? My daydream continues for a few moments longer and I imagine myself coming to these markets on weekends to do my shopping and conversing in Khmer with the stallholders. Then I catch myself. Hang on a second. I'm supposed to be thinking about London.

◆ ◆ ◆ ◆ ◆

It's assumed that if you are visiting Phnom Penh and have a foreign face you have come to see just two things, the Killing Fields and the Tuol Sleng Genocide Museum. We decide that going to look at a dirt pit where thousands of bodies were piled on top of each other would be too much. So, feeling like we should see at least one of these famous landmarks, we choose to visit the museum instead.

'You want to go to Killing Fields after this?' asks our tuk-tuk driver eagerly. 'I'll give you two for the price of one for six American dollar.' I shake my head, no thank you, only to have him ask us again about three times during the next hour.

It doesn't sit well in my stomach that these sites of terrible deeds are tourist attractions. I suppose some of the tourist operators, like our teenage mobile-toting tuk-tuk driver, are too young to have been affected by the events. Inside the museum, we see a young guide laughingly demonstrate how prisoners' legs were shackled to the wall as she swigs from her can of Coke. The history of a place, even if it is based on unthinkable acts of genocide and torture, becomes just another way to make money. Through necessity, I guess. Life has to go on.

The old school that became one of the worst wartime prisons in Cambodia is buried in suburban Phnom Penh, around family homes where children play in the street. The Khmer Rouge converted the breezy classrooms into interrogation rooms and the play equipment into torture devices. The monkey bars became gallows where prisoners were hung upside down before their heads were dunked in excrement to bring them back to consciousness. It is all still behind razor wire and has an unsettling stench of rotting garbage and decay, which is stirred up further by the oppressive heat. Everything about this place makes your heart ache. In the quadrangle, frangipani petals scatter over the tombs of fourteen prisoners whose remains were found in one of the now crumbling buildings. Inside is a simple glass vault filled with layers of dirt-encrusted clothing found in the Killing Fields.

By far the most confronting part of the museum is the room filled with the hundreds of black and white photographs of those who were imprisoned and killed here. There is a wall of children's faces, one just a sweet-looking toddler. There is terror in the eyes of some of the prisoners as they pose for their headshots. Many are visibly malnourished with ribcages pressing against skin. But some of the younger boys are smiling shyly as if posing for happy holiday snaps. On another wall, a woman with some kind of torture device strapped to her head clutches her baby to her breast, a single tear streaming down her cheek. The single most shocking detail of the prison's history was the recruitment of children aged between ten and fifteen who were used as prison guards by the Khmer Rouge. Innocent children made to perform truly evil acts.

That night, our last in Phnom Penh before we catch the slow boat to Siem Riep—and the temples of Angkor Wat—we sit and drink wine on Will and Bridget's front porch.

The boys huddle over the new digital camera we had to buy, trying to work out the gadgets. Meanwhile, Bridget and I chat in the corner. Smoke from the mosquito coil spirals lazily around our legs.

'What's it been like for you, leaving your job and travelling for this long?' she asks after a while.

My laugh sounds more wry than I intend. 'You know what? I thought this trip would just be about seeing places I'd never been to before. But it's become so much more than that, in the strangest and most unexpected way.' I tell her everything.

When I finish, she reaches over and grips my hand. 'God, that's a lot of stuff to sort out.' she says quietly. 'I think it's something loads of people struggle with. I know I did.' She shakes her head. 'Sometimes I still do.'

'Really?'

'Yeah, we were stressing ourselves out so much in Sydney. Killing ourselves for work. It got to a stage where I just thought, enough. There's got to be more to it than this.'

I nod.

'This probably sounds a bit new age and everything, but when you are defined by what you do and you leave it, you have to learn what you're about all over again,' she continues.

'So how did you get over that?' I ask.

'Well.' She thinks for a second. 'I've had to find other things, like charity work or concentrating on my relationships, and even,' she pauses and bites her lip, 'I dunno, baking the best bloody batch of brownies in the office. Whatever.' We both laugh. 'There's no use pretending the need to achieve is not a part of who I am. But I can change how it affects me,' she says.

We sit in silence for a little while. I start telling Bridget about the London plan—how I'm not sure about it but don't really know how to make the decision.

'Believe me, I am not into reading self-help books,' she says. 'But a friend lent me one that compared life with building a house. It said that, say, if you want a house but you don't plan for the kind of house you want in a year, ten years, you'll probably buy one you need right now.' She leans forward and tops up my glass. 'But then you might have kids, so you'll tack on an extension, renovate the bathroom, whatever, modifying as you go,' she continues. 'And, yeah, you might end up with a perfectly nice house. But will it be your dream home? Wouldn't it have been better to draw up a blueprint about the kind of home you really wanted and make your decisions based around that?'

I wait for her to tell me what the hell she's going on about.

She leans back in her chair. 'So, anyway, this book said that just like getting the perfect house, in order to get the life you want you have to draw up a plan.'

'What, like goals for your career, where you see yourself in ten years, that kind of thing?'

'The career stuff is part of it. But only a small part. It sounds so wanky, but it's really just about figuring out the kind of person you want to be—on all levels. I wrote down stuff like wanting to spend more time with my mum and getting to know her better and finding a hobby to do in my spare time.'

'Hobbies,' I snort. 'Who even has time for hobbies anymore?'

'Well, I do now. This is kind of the whole point of doing a plan like this. Finding things that make you happy apart from competing or career goals.' She takes a deep breath. 'And then, no matter what life throws at you, you can keep returning to the core of it.'

I sit and think about that. A life blueprint. The door swings open and the boys come back out. Tom presses a chilled bottle of beer against the back of my neck where I've tied my hair up to try and keep cool. I murmur appreciatively and smile up at him. A life blueprint, eh? I guess it's worth a shot.

CHAPTER 14

That holiday feeling

A COUPLE OF LONGTAIL BOATS SPUTTER NOISILY ACROSS Koh Tao's turquoise bay below me. As their curved wooden noses crest the small waves that lap the island, I can make out the brightly coloured ribbons and garlands of flowers the fishermen have tied around their bows as offerings to the gods. I swing languidly in the hammock, which is tied to the large wooden balcony of our villa, grateful for the slight breeze whispering through the meshy holes and tickling the backs of my knees. Over to my left is the small white sand beach where Tom has gone, snorkel and flippers in hand.

'*Sawadee ka.*' The voice of a woman surprises me. I turn my head away from the view and see a petite woman wearing a batik dress. She is one of the resort staff and has a bowl laden with the tropical fruits that grow in abundance here in southern Thailand. She puts it down on the table next to me, replacing the one she left there yesterday. Tonight she'll be back again to scatter rose petals on our bed. I smile and thank her and in reply she makes a bowing gesture with her hands pressed together in prayer.

Lazily, I reach over to cup a mango in my hand and bring its cool smooth skin to my cheek. I look back at the ocean. This is fantastic. No sightseeing to do, no bookings to make, no planes or trains to get on. Nothing to organise. Not even where we're going to live after this trip. We have decided to wait until we get home to work out whether we move to London. All the clothes we need are swimmers and sarongs. Our only movements are between our bed, the beach, the bar and this hammock. Bliss. A perfect way to end the trip.

We have already been here for nearly a week, following exactly that routine. Well, except for the day we went diving. When Tom and I came to Thailand for a holiday five years ago, we promised ourselves that one day we would return and visit this place. Last time we only got as far as Koh Samui, a bigger island a couple of hours away by boat. Back then, Koh Tao was considered fairly remote and unspoilt. It's a shame we didn't see it earlier. In the intervening years it has been discovered by the masses. It is still beautiful but now has dozens of resorts and even a 7–11 supermarket. The dense tropical forest is being chainsawed to make way for yet more development. The island's reputation as one of the best diving spots in South-east Asia has been a blessing economically but a curse for the local environment. Plastic bottles clutter the streets, generators belch fumes and some of the underwater sites are littered with rubbish and cigarette butts.

Among those making hay while the sun shines are the resident dive instructors. Many of them are British or South African and they all seem to get more sex than Shane Warne. Just yesterday we were sitting at the beach when we saw a young instructor take some giggling floozy to the bamboo pontoon a short distance offshore. There, in full view of all the families playing on the sand, he tossed her bikini top in the air and humped her as she spread out like a starfish.

I doubt if any of the other beachgoers cared too much, though. Most of them are older German women who wear nothing but leopard-print G-strings. As they sashay between the water and their deckchairs, they make the place look like a retirement home for geriatric porn stars.

Okay, time to stop daydreaming and get to it. I bring my attention back to the open notebook in my lap. It feels a bit weird to be writing this. I've been putting it off ever since we left Cambodia. But I've set aside this morning to work on it because there are only a few days before we fly home. I want my thoughts straight before I get there.

Home. The place I couldn't let go of for so long. I didn't appreciate this before I left, but the world is only as big as your mind allows it to be. I think we all imagine our holiday selves strolling along a beach without a care in the world. But of course all your hopes, fears and neuroses get packed up along with the suncream and the Dan Brown novel. You can escape your everyday surroundings, but you can't escape yourself. So, as my feet were exploring all these extraordinary faraway places, my head has been catching up. Now that home is finally just a few days' away I find myself feeling strange about it, as though it will be yet another foreign place.

A fat gecko scurries up the post at my feet. He and his family kept us awake last night with their excitable chirruping. Another creature that has also found its way up the stilts and through the cracks of our wooden floor is a little frog. Every so often he lets out a squeaky croak. It makes me laugh because it sounds like Daffy Duck farting.

I watch as the gecko flicks his tongue at an insect. Will I regret that I didn't embrace this trip sooner? I don't know that I will. The mental journey has ended up being just as significant as the physical one. It's inconvenient that it had to happen while I was supposed to be enjoying my 'trip of a lifetime'. But then again, I don't think I could have worked so many things out if I stayed at home. I feel like a completely different person to the one who sat on the plane last September, anxious and in mourning for the life I was leaving behind.

I don't want to be her again.

I pick up my pen and look at the top of the page where I have written 'Life Plan'.

Stop defining myself by what I do, I put first. Stop comparing myself with others—they will never be me, I will never be them. Be more assertive. Try harder to care less about what other people think. Be braver, live with less anxiety.

All right, what next? Well, there are the non-career fulfilment things Bridget said I should think about. This is more difficult. My free time has mainly been taken up with socialising or vegging out in front of the television. I pick up my pen again and start with an easy one: watch less television and read more. Then I'm inspired by my friend Wil, so write down, learn to bake bread. After that it gets easier. Track down my grandmother's recipes and type them into a book. Learn Italian. Take piano lessons again. Make more quality time for Tom. Read fewer trashy magazines and stop filling my mind with useless gossip. Write about this trip. Call my family more. See more art exhibitions and live music.

Half an hour later, I have four pages covered. Only one of them is work-related. I'm surprised I've come up with this much. I read through all of it with a sense of wonder. If I even did half the things on this list my life would be amazing. I want to live my life differently but I have been struggling to figure out how. I suppose that this is the how.

I push off the railing to make the hammock swing gently. My mind drifts back again to that first flight six months ago, when I couldn't get that demon voice out of my head. *You're making the biggest mistake of your career.* It's funny, but when I think about those words now, I don't feel any panic at all. And I certainly don't think I've made a mistake. How sad to be blind to anything outside of the four walls of your own office. There's a whole world out there that doesn't involve work. I understand this now, because I've seen some of it.

Tom trudges back up the stairs still salty from his swim. 'Fancy a cocktail?' he asks, flinging his wet towel over the rail. I look at my watch. It's just gone midday. Well, we are still on holiday.

I flip my notebook shut. 'You bet!'

◆ ◆ ◆ ◆ ◆

The arrivals gate, Sydney airport. It's six-thirty in the morning. My head is whirling as I attempt to catalogue my feelings—tired, excited, sad and nervous. I shift the weight of my backpack from one shoulder to the other and clutch a plastic bag containing pictures we bought in Hong Kong and Buenos Aires. Will Australia feel strange to me now? Will the 'new me' fit in?

There's already quite a crowd gathered to greet relatives and friends and we scan faces looking for Tom's mum. She stretches her arms wide, enveloping us both. 'Welcome home.'

Outside the morning is bright and blue. The air is deliciously cool. It will be a few hours yet before the real heat of Sydney's summer sunshine kicks in. Tom's mum guides us to where she has parked our car. We promise her we'll have lots of stories to tell tonight, but now she has to catch a train to work. We rummage around in our packs and eventually find a few Australian coins and a keycard to pay for parking and buy breakfast. Then, as we get in the car, we have to remind ourselves again which is the driver's side. It all feels so odd.

We head towards the carpark exit. A thick-set man with a blond goatee beard is leaning a heavily tattooed arm out the booth window. Tom reaches out to pass him the money.

'Mate,' the guy says. His broad Australian accent seems even more pronounced than it normally would. 'Watch your shirt, mate,' he continues, looking worried. 'You've got a piece of bird poo on your car.'

We laugh. His tell-it-like-it-is approach makes us feel like we are really home.

We drive to Newtown only a few suburbs away, where we're sure there'll be a café open along the main strip. I surf the radio stations. The stories that headline the news bulletins are about Sydney train timetables, State government spats, local celebrities. Nothing about Europe, South America, Africa or Asia. Just a bunch of names and places I haven't heard for ages—and so many Australian accents all at once. It's overwhelming. I have the sense of being somewhere small and isolated. But at the same time, it is comforting to be back among people who sound the same as I do. I'm really looking forward to being able to have conversations without struggling to make out broken English or having to look up words in a phrasebook.

We park the car in a back lane and walk towards King Street. 'Were there this many trees here before?' I ask Tom. He shrugs and grins at my childlike wonder. 'They're all so big.' I stop and sniff the air, breathing in eucalyptus, jasmine and the rich scent of wet soil. 'God. It smells so good.'

Above the faint hum of the morning traffic I can even hear magpies carolling. 'I used to think Sydney was such a big city,' I say. 'So crowded and stressful. But this feels so relaxed.' Everything seems worth remarking upon. The light is so bright, there's so much sun. There's so much sky here. The streets are so wide and so clean. It's familiar yet different, somehow so much nicer than before.

We eventually find a good-looking café and grab a table. We should be exhausted, but being back has charged us with adrenaline. I look around me. There is a constant bustle of people in suits getting coffees on their way to work. At the table next to us sit a couple of off-duty policemen comparing war stories. At another a woman reads a newspaper while her dog lies at her feet. Just another ordinary morning. Up on the blackboard menu are the breakfast items: Vegemite toast, poached eggs and raspberry muffins. A far cry from some of the fare of the last six months.

Tom gets up to pay. I wander outside to stand in a patch of sun. It's funny, but all that time when I was on the trip thinking about what I'd do next and which direction my life would take afterwards, I always thought there would be a 'moment' when I came home. One that would show me the right path with blinding clarity. Armed with that revelation, I'd tie up the loose ends in a pretty bow. That's what happens in movies and books.

The sharp sound of a woman's laughter carries through the open café window. Tom is joking with our waitress at the cash register. I turn my head back towards the sunshine and shut my eyes, feeling it warm my eyelids. There haven't been any fireworks or sweeping orchestral music to signal 'The End'. I doubt we are about to ride off into any sunsets. Real life's just not like that. Things often reveal themselves to us in small ways, nag at us in quiet voices. I've noticed them these past six months because I've made time to listen.

Tom joins me on the footpath and wraps an arm around my shoulders. I tilt my head up towards his.

'You look happy,' he says with a faint note of surprise.

'Yes,' I reply, drawing him closer. 'I am.'

We walk back to the car, talking about going to the beach this afternoon after we've unpacked.

'A swim,' I say, 'on an afternoon when everyone else we know is at work.'

I smile. For now, that holiday feeling is continuing. I want to hang on to it. I can't say whether I'll be able to. I don't know whether I'll get things right from here. I can't tell you whether I'll live happily ever after. I have no idea where I'll be even one year from now.

But I am sure of one thing. I'm ready to try a new way of living. Mistakes and all.

ACKNOWLEDGMENTS

All the home-made banana cake, fruit loaf and gourmet lunch boxes in the world can't express the gratitude I feel towards Tom 'Catch of the Century' Sansom. Thank you for living, then re-living, this trip and helping me summon the confidence to write it down.

My immense appreciation also goes to the group of people without whom this book would have remained mere ramblings in my tatty journal: Juliet Rogers and Kay Scarlett who gave my proposal the thumbs up so quickly and with such enthusiasm, Sean Anderson, Mary Trewby, Jacqueline Blanchard, Diana Hill, Lauren Camilleri and Ellie Exarchos.

Huge thank you's to my family for their support. Mum for bestowing and encouraging my itchy-travel feet, Dad for your wonderful pep-up conversations and my little bro Ben for your intel on all things Chav, Jordy and Parisian.

And last, but certainly not least, I am very grateful to the friends who either played a starring role in this book or have been sounding boards throughout the process: Kellie and Simon Crouch, Greg Wilcock, Wilhelmina Van Beers, Jessica Sansom (and Di, Graham and Claudia), Paul Murray, Katie Ingwersen, Josh Murray, Andrew Williamson, Bridget McIntosh, Liz Ennis, Dean Hyland, Fiona Boyce, Lisa Hayes, Emily Smith, Nic Mackay-Sim, Rod Yates, Jenny Watson and my furry friends, Kaiser and Bello, who lay at my feet as I typed and typed and typed. Thank you for helping me tune back in.